Beyond the Malachite Hills

JONATHAN LAWLEY is consultant to the Business Council for Africa (BCA) where he continues to make use of his unique experience of Africa as a whole. He was born in the North-West Frontier Province of pre-independence India where his father was in the Indian Service of Engineers. After school in Kashmir, the UK, Southern Rhodesia and South Africa he went to Rhodes University in South Africa and Cambridge before joining the British Colonial Service in Northern Rhodesia. He worked there for 9 years including 5 in independent Zambia. Almost his entire career has involved Africa, particularly southern Africa including the Congo where he worked for 5 years on a mining project. He has had a life-long interest in and involvement with Zimbabwe. More recently his work has taken him to West Africa and to Portuguese- and French-speaking countries including Madagascar. In 1996 he was awarded a doctorate from the City University, London, for his Ph.D. thesis 'Transcending Culture: Developing Africa's Technical Managers'.

Beyond the Malachite Hills

A LIFE OF COLONIAL SERVICE AND BUSINESS IN THE NEW AFRICA

Jonathan Lawley

I.B. TAURIS
LONDON · NEW YORK

Published in 2010 by I.B.Tauris & Co Ltd
6 Salem Road, London W2 4BU
175 Fifth Avenue, New York NY 10010
www.ibtauris.com

Distributed in the United States and Canada Exclusively by Palgrave Macmillan
175 Fifth Avenue, New York NY 10010

ISBN: 978 1 84885 049 1

A full CIP record for this book is available from the British Library
A full CIP record is available from the Library of Congress

Library of Congress Catalog Card Number: available

Typeset in Perpetua by Macmillan Publishing Solutions
Printed and bound in Great Britain by CPI Antony Rowe, Chippenham

Table of Contents

Foreword

This fascinating book is an account of a varied and adventurous life, more commonly experienced in the days of the British Empire. Born in India and brought up there at the time of independence, Jonathan Lawley writes of that country with great affection. Later he spent many years in Africa, and it is that long association with the Central African states and the Congo with which the main part of the book is concerned.

The love and understanding he has for Africa, and perhaps particularly for Africans, is a dominant feature in this book. Afterwards, as a successful businessman, he spent much of his time working in that continent.

The enormous area which district officers covered in Africa, with little help, much responsibility and poor communications, was a feature in the life of the colonial civil servant, and Jonathan Lawley reminds us of this when, aged 27, he became a district commissioner a few months before independence in Zambia, shouldering all those responsibilities which public servants in the colonial office were required to do at that time. There is no doubt that during this period he became aware of the inexorable move by many countries in Africa to independence and the need not only to understand but also to be able to speak to Africans in their own language and appreciate their point of view. He had, at that time, the opportunity to meet Presidents Kaunda and Nyerere and many others in high places, and it was no doubt his wide knowledge that made him such a suitable person to be appointed as an election supervisor at the Zimbabwe election in 1980. Unlike many others, he realised that Mr Mugabe and the Patriotic Front were inevitably going to win that election, and the belief that so many white Rhodesians and South Africans had held — that Bishop Muzorewa would be able to form a coalition with Mr Nkomo — was unrealistic. He understood too the difficulties that a Patriotic Front victory might cause Mr Smith and his allies.

He rightly congratulates Mr Mugabe on his emollient speech on becoming prime minister and praises General Walls and Lord Soames for the most vital part they played in ensuring that the result of the election was recognised. He was in an ideal position to observe all these events and comments on them with knowledge and conviction.

As to what has happened since, he writes with sadness and regret that Zimbabwe, a prosperous and happy country, has been reduced to its present state. Reduced by its president, Mr Mugabe, who started well but who has in these last years led his country to disaster.

In Dr Lawley's final chapter, he reflects on the past 50 years or so. He is understandably nostalgic about the handover of power in Zambia and the immediate aftermath. It must have been a very depressing period for him, though the present situation in that country is most encouraging. There will no doubt be continuing arguments about the timescale of British decolonisation, but timing is never very easy and there is no doubt that in some territories it would have been foolish to delay independence and endanger the good relations between our two countries.

The last two paragraphs sum up sensibly and accurately what our attitude towards Africa should be.

All this and much more, Jonathan Lawley has seen or of which he has been a part. To those of us who have lived through these times, it is a useful reminder of those days. To those new to the problems that Jonathan Lawley faced, it is an entertaining and instructive read.

The Rt Hon the Lord Carrington KG, GCMG, CH, MC

Acknowledgements

I have been incredibly lucky with the friends and colleagues to whom I have been able to turn for understanding, encouragement and help with this book. Principally it is my old boss and mentor at Rio Tinto, Sir Donald Tebbit, whom I thank many times over for his help and advice and for always being available as a sounding board and bastion of good sense and a motivator par excellence. Thanks are due too to the publishers and particularly to Dr Lester Crook who had the idea of a concluding chapter on the new Africans. Crucial early encouragement came from Tony Kirk-Greene and Chris Paterson, who understood what I was trying to say and led me to believe that I might be producing something worthwhile. Others who gave me encouragement and advice over publication or after seeing drafts were Sam Wilson, David Le Breton, John Hudson, Shirley Cammack, Chris Cunliffe, Jane Nicholson, Susan Connolly, Professor Elizabeth Colson, Sally Dean, Chris Stone, Terry Barringer, David Bell and Judith Todd. Professor Kenneth Ingham, John Smith, Wilf Mbanga, Michael Holman, Sir John Margetson and Lord Luce as well as Sir Donald wrote helpful critiques and Ken Severs produced the photo of the malachite hills. I am deeply grateful to them all. I am particularly grateful too to Lord Carrington for his marvellous foreword. I have always admired him for his courageous intervention in Rhodesia/Zimbabwe through the Lancaster House Agreement, which brought a longed-for peace to that country in 1980. I thank my children for their encouragement and support. Lastly and most importantly, I thank Sarah, who typed the whole book, parts of it several times over, Karen for her help with the technical intricacies of my computer and with putting the manuscripts together and Hamish for putting up with it all.

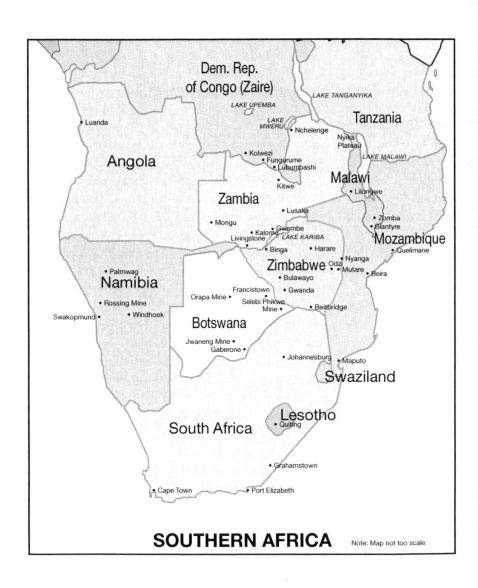

SOUTHERN AFRICA   Note: Map not too scale

Note: Map not too scale

ZAMBIA, ZIMBABWE, MALAWI AND SOUTHERN DRC

1

Raj Child to Rhodesian Boy

Over the years Africa has become a special love, but as a child I loved India and still have the strongest memories. After the separation, as a bereft schoolboy at a ghastly boarding school in England, these memories sustained me and subsequently the way my family saw people in India came to have a profound influence on the rest of my life and particularly on the way I saw Africa.

In the winters we were in the town of Bannu on the North-West Frontier (now in Pakistan) with tribal territory right next door, and from April in the summer capital, Nathia Gali, at 9000 feet in the Himalayas, amidst stunningly beautiful scenery with firs and pine trees. We were allowed total freedom to go wherever we wanted all day, but we never came to any harm. We used to collect basketfuls of most delicious wild strawberries. My sister Veronica and I became totally fluent in the lower-class version of the local Hindustani or Urdu language. My father was a civil engineer in the Indian Service of Engineers, working principally on building roads and bridges in the frontier area facing Russia. He was awarded an OBE in 1944. My mother, who was born in the Andaman Islands, came from a family of administrators and soldiers in India since the days of the East India Company.

When my father arrived in India in the 1920s, his first boss was an Indian and race was never an issue for him and our family. A coolie was a coolie, but we were brought up to respect everybody. At eight I was sent away to a boarding school called Sheikh Bagh that was set up in Kashmir during the Second World War to cater for the sons of people who but for the war would have sent them home to boarding schools in England. At Sheikh Bagh we had as much freedom as we could possibly be given in a school and were trusted with it too. However, the regime was physically tough and our motto was 'In all things be men'. By the age of nine I had swum the three-mile length of the Dal Lake and had climbed 13,000 feet to the top of Mahadeo Mountain, which overlooks the vale of Kashmir. The school had several Indian boys and before I left the school in 1946, I had made particular friends with Mardan Mehta the head boy. Under the headmastership of Eric Tyndale-Biscoe (known as TB), the ethos was muscular Christianity. Accordingly, race was not an issue. I became aware that it just might have been an issue in Peshawar where aged ten I was with my parents in the months before our final departure from India at independence in 1947. I had made friends with two Anglo-Indian boys Roger and David Ahmed, whose mother was English and whose father was an Indian vet. There was cluck clucking from some of my mother's friends, but for me, Roger and David were quite simply my best friends. We continued to correspond for several years.

The part of my life I spent in India is important because of the way I came to view race. This was crucially important in view of the new life to which I would soon move in southern Africa. The other impact was that I left India with the most positive view possible of the exercise of British power and influence. It came as a shock when we left India and my father told me that Britain was no longer the most powerful country in the world. 'Who is?' I asked. 'America', he replied. 'Who will be after them?' China' was his answer. Before Africa I had to face the horrors of prep school for a year in the north of England. At Sheikh Bagh, most of the time we had not even worn shoes. Now, we had house shoes, were not allowed to play outside, went for walks in crocodiles and had our temperatures taken every day. Looking back I feel I was deeply unhappy then. Certainly I was very naughty. I longed for India, Kashmir, Sheikh Bagh, Mehta and the Ahmeds.

In the summer of 1948, carrying a cricket bat and a copy of the *Daily Graphic*, I set off from Heathrow or whatever it was called then, by York airliner to join my parents in Southern Rhodesia for the holidays. I was scheduled to go by flying boat via the Nile at Cairo and Khartoum, Lake Victoria, the Zambezi at Victoria Falls, the Vaal Dam and then up to Salisbury, but the service was cancelled. Thus, I had to spend the night in the equivalent of an Indian rest house or *dak bungalow* at Tripoli in Libya. Then, flying via Cairo I spent another night in a hotel on the Nile at Khartoum. I can remember the old gents, some wearing panama hats, sitting under fans and reading local newspapers that, to my amazement, had up-to-date details of the county cricket scores. The next day was another ordeal of being sick as we flew over the seemingly endless Sudanese swamps. In Nairobi I stayed at the old Stanley Hotel where I ate my way right through an extensive menu before going off to buy a bottle of linseed oil for my cricket bat. The next day a Viking aircraft took me via Tabora, Ndola and Lusaka to Salisbury, the capital of Southern Rhodesia and to the arms of my parents. I remember the suburbs spread out with their large houses and extensive gardens and in the middle of town were modern shops. There was no teeming mass of humanity like India and to my surprise there were more whites than blacks. As I walked with my parents, I saw a burly white man elbow a black man off the pavement. Some whites I was told, did not believe that blacks should be allowed on the pavements. After a night with friends, we set off along the 200 miles of strip road towards Fort Victoria in the country's midlands, where my father was the head of the government's irrigation department catering for a third of the country. The strips were a brilliant Rhodesian idea to save money, with two parallel strips of tar along which you drove until you met another car and you moved left leaving your right wheels on the left-hand strip as you passed. We stopped at the Enkeldoorn hotel and had a Mazoe orange and water on the veranda. I was told that the area was one of the main strongholds of Afrikaner farmers in Southern Rhodesia. Further along the road we saw a large herd of impala and once a kudu bull with massive horns flattened against his back leapt right across the road.

Fort Victoria was a small town with a single street of shops which included a small café selling wonderful doughnuts, a hotel, a butchery, three general stores and a couple of filling stations. The few blacks around were served through hatches at the back of the shops. The Europeans were friendly towards us and my parents had obviously settled down well. When I was taken around the town to be introduced, I remember my mother being taken to task for referring to England as 'home'. 'But this is your home Betty', said the bank manager. And that was the essential difference from India. Southern Rhodesia was their country and they ruled the roost with their white man's constitution, their law and their democracy. You went there to make it your home. Our house was four and a half miles out of town, down the strip road towards The Great Zimbabwe ruins, Beitbridge and South Africa. It was a mile off the main road down a lesser dirt road serving smallholders' plots and a few farms. Our house was a bungalow with a wide veranda and a 25-acre *mealie* field whence the cat would bring in endless quail, of which she was sometimes dispossessed for father's breakfast. My parents had established a beautiful emerald green lawn, which contrasted sharply with the winter brown of the *mealie* field and the surrounding bush and hills. My father had blasted a swimming pool out of the *kopje* at the back and had planted lots of trees including an apple orchard. He was in the process of drilling a borehole using a flexible gum pole from which was suspended a drill bit. A gang of Africans repeatedly pounding down the drill bit provided the drilling power. My father said this was an Australian method which he was testing for possible use in the native reserves. We had three servants, Simon the houseboy and two garden boys Dick and Sam. I immediately made friends with Simon, who was a serious, sensitive man. Having spoken Urdu in India like a native, I wanted him to teach me his own language Chikaranga, one of the Shona dialects. He was unhappy about this because he feared I might learn to insult and swear at Africans like the white plumber who came to put in a second bathroom at the end of the veranda. The latter kept up a constant stream of invective at his small gang of African workers in a way that could not have been imagined in India. He used a mixture of English swear words and a language full of imperatives which at the time was called kitchen kaffir. I soon learned that very few whites spoke a real African language. I remember Dick digging a new fish pond and wearing a tattered shirt. Being winter when I arrived, the weather could be cold and feeling sorry for him; my mother knitted him a short sleeved jersey. He loved it so much that even in September when the weather was hot, to my mother's consternation, he continued to wear it. Sam, the other garden boy, used all his monthly wage of 15 shillings to buy a grand Stetson hat.

As the summer holidays came to an end, I was asked if I really wanted to go back to school in England. I gave a definite no and so was sent to a prep school called Whitestone near Bulawayo. Before that my father said he thought I should start learning Afrikaans. I agreed and so I was sent to the wife of one of the other smallholders down the bush road to the Mtilikwe River. I had thought the language would be useful because at first I was under the impression that it was a native language. I never used it and in Rhodesia in those days it would only have been spoken amongst Afrikaners themselves. So I made little progress. Learning Greek to communicate with all the Greek boys or young men who came to Whitestone all the way from Beira in Mozambique, would have been more useful. Some of the latter seemed to be about 17 years old. One of them even made a proposition to the not-so-young matron, who politely turned him down. I spent two years at Whitestone during which a new management including two top masters from Michaelhouse School in South Africa turned it around. All of a sudden lessons started to be interesting, a chapel was built and the school managed to get boys into the top public schools in South Africa as well as Rhodesian schools like St Georges and Plumtree. I remember the cricket, boxing and athletics matches against other local schools like REPS and Baines. I was the fastest runner in school in my last year at Whitestone and would have been *victor ludorum* but chicken pox intervened. Other activities included acting and for two years I played the lead in the school play. I also sang solos in chapel or at concerts. In Bulawayo there were two boys' secondary schools – one academic, Milton, and the Bulawayo Technical School – and several all girls' schools. There were big sporting occasions like when Rhodesia played the visiting MCC or Australian cricketers or when we beat the All Blacks rugby team in Bulawayo in 1949. We schoolchildren were there in thousands – all white, not a single black. Apart from school servants we never had any contact at all with blacks. I don't think there was a single black boy at any white school in Rhodesia. We certainly did not think of this as an issue though sometimes I would think about Mardan Mehta or the Ahmeds. There was a boy at Whitestone called Pizey who was my best friend. His parents had been tea planters in Assam and he thought like me. Otherwise you might as well have been talking about men from another planet. Mention of non-white friends in India would be likely to attract the comment 'sus' roughly the equivalent of 'yuk' or 'how disgusting'.

At just over 14, I passed the entrance exam to the top public school in South Africa, St Andrews College in Grahamstown. We used to travel to school in the Eastern Cape by train via Bulawayo. It was a three-day journey and we drank a lot of castle beer and smoked a lot of Rhodesian Gold Leaf cigarettes on the way. At one stop at Mahalape in Bechuanaland there was a band and an outdoor dance floor so we all danced, sometimes with the girls from other South African boarding schools and sometimes with each other. On one of my holidays, my projected week's stay with a friend at Ndola was cancelled. So my parents were not expecting me and were not there to meet me when I arrived back at Fort Victoria railway station. I was 14 and my suitcase was too heavy to carry by myself all the way home. I had a shilling in my pocket which I offered to a young African if he would carry it the four miles. He readily agreed and we started walking through the bush. Within a couple of hours we were home and my delighted parents handed over another couple of shillings to my kind helper.

In those days if I thought about black people it was in the same way as I thought of Indians. I did not know many, but I supposed that there must be some who were anybody's equal. This was not the attitude of whites in southern Africa at that time. Conversations about blacks tended to centre on whether you would want your sister to marry one or on how stupid they all were. They were considered inferior in every way. Any question of them being allowed into cafes or cinemas was laughable. As for being allowed to share toilet facilities with whites, that was unthinkable. Yet in 1953 came a very significant step, which looked as if it was going to change everything. The all-white Southern Rhodesia electorate voted in favour of entering into a federation with Northern Rhodesia and Nyasaland. The latter were genuine British colonies and protectorates, whereas Southern Rhodesia, though technically a colony since the days of the Chartered British South Africa Company rule in the 1920s, was in practice virtually a dominion like Australia, New Zealand, Canada or South Africa. There was much talk of the economic benefits that the federation would bring to the whole region. Thanks to early confidence in a multiracial future, business boomed and the Rhodes Centenary Exhibition in Bulawayo in 1953 attracted exhibitors from all over Africa and around the world. There were Mozambique and South African restaurants and a new concert hall was built to accommodate the Royal Opera Company which performed Gloriana, Aida and La Boheme. George Formby did a show and there were lots of visiting businessmen and potential investors. Salisbury, the capital of the new federation, boomed and became known as *Bamba Zonke* (grab everything) in jealous Bulawayo. Associated with federation was the concept of 'partnership' between the races. Many whites thought this would merely give blacks ideas above their station. For us as a family, it seemed a very good idea as it would surely mean the end of racial discrimination and make for more opportunities for African advancement through new job possibilities and special training programmes. It would also mean the end of petty discrimination and so-called 'pin pricks' which hurt the dignity of Africans and made a shared and peaceful future seem less likely. Though under all the circumstances race relations were surprisingly good, it did not take much imagination to guess what many blacks thought about regularly being called 'boy' and told to 'take off your hat' or routinely shouted at, denigrated or abused. With the beginning of popular support for African nationalism, I could see that these were the things Africans in Southern Rhodesia thought about. I did not think that they could have any confidence in white leadership. However, surprisingly there was little hate then – though if I had been a black man bicycling in my best suit and then deliberately splashed by a passing white motorist going out of his way to drive through a puddle, I would have started to hate. Mostly there was the cumulative effect of failure to take any account of human dignity. In those early days of the federation we waited for change but little came. Granted, Messrs Savanhu and Hove now sat in the federal parliament, but the post offices remained segregated and with the exception of the Jameson Hotel in Salisbury, blacks were not allowed into hotels or restaurants. Most important and most damaging perhaps was the fact that genuine black advancement was being blocked by the trade unions protecting the power and privileged access to work of white artisans. Reinforced by the arrival of thousands of British artisans after the war, they formed a block to the entry of Africans into trades such as plumbing, electrical work and motor engineering. They also formed a block on political change. As a family we were affected by this when my father was supervising the building of our new house in Bulawayo and hired a black plumber to do some work. After that no white artisan would touch any work on the house. So where he could not find a black contractor to do work, he had to do it himself. It was clear to us that if vital black support for the federation was to be gained and maintained, then rapid progress towards bringing about genuine partnership was essential. This principally meant getting rid of discrimination and providing genuine opportunities for black advancement. All this was a separate issue from the difficulty of convincing blacks in the Northern territories that federation was good for them. As I was to learn later, they wanted to continue their progress towards independence, and the last thing they wanted was to have anything to do with Southern Rhodesian whites.

Despite the failure to put partnership into practice, many white Rhodesians continued to support federation and were proud of the ongoing progress such as it was. Virtually all white South Africans were sceptical. I remember the parents of a school friend with whom I went to stay in Johannesburg. They were moderate, successful and English-speaking people. When I told them that in Southern Rhodesia black policemen directed traffic, they said that they must be different from South African blacks who would not have the mental capacity to cope. At school the only black people I ever talked to were the motherly and matronly old women who worked as a team in the house to darn our socks and mend our clothes.

I left St Andrews at the end of 1954 with a third-class matric after an undistinguished four years. I had been secretary of The Debating Society, taken the lead in several school plays and played countless games of rugby and cricket. Actually, the school seemed to be mainly about sport at which I was only moderately successful. The only master with whom I really communicated was the senior chaplain Hugh (Horse) Harker who somehow managed to get to know every boy in the school. I do, however, have the Headmaster

Ronald Currey to thank for indirectly getting me through my matric. My parents had been visiting for the first time all the way from Rhodesia during my second-last term, and Currey told them that there was a serious danger that I would fail. When they told me I was shocked, but I did start working seriously from then on. Though my life-long friend Richard Valentine, a Rhodesian farmer's son, was in my house, I had never been really happy at St Andrews and I was pleased to leave. I did not much like South Africa. I still hankered after Sheikh Bagh, Kashmir and TB and India. I had had enough of exams and did not want to go on to university.

After I left school I wanted to earn money, be independent and have fun. My father dropped me in Salisbury at the Central Hotel in January 1955. I was due to become one of the clerks of the Water Court of Southern Rhodesia, which determined on the use of so-called public water from rivers around the country. Both the accommodation and the job itself were shocks to the system. I found myself sharing a room with a middle-aged man who snored loudly and had a very loudly ticking alarm clock. I did not meet him straight away as he was asleep when I came to bed and he got up very early. To help me sleep, I used to cover the alarm clock with my towel. When eventually we met, he was incandescent.

At work, despite enjoying driving the judges' official Humber Super Snipe to hear cases on farms around the country, I soon came to realise what a lowly position was that of a mere clerk. Besides, my £29 per month wage left me with £11 to spend after accommodation. It was certainly not enough to take out all the girls of my schoolboy imagination. Soon I was the paying guest of my young English immigrant boss and his wife, a potentially intolerable situation after a day with him at the office. However, it suited me as it was cheap and I had started studying for government law exams so I could be a trainee magistrate and escape to a better life. I spent evenings and most of the night at weekends studying. My father noticed all this and asked me whether I would like to go to Oxford. Would I! It would be paradise after being an impoverished 18-year-old nobody. I studied hard with the help of a local teacher for the St Edmunds Hall entrance paper in Latin. I had taken no interest in the subject at school and could not relearn enough to pass. So I went to Rhodes University in the Eastern Cape instead. Rhodes had been founded from the sixth form of my old school, St Andrews. It was wonderful to have friends, sport and other interests catered for and not to have to worry about money. Now I had a girl friend and even went by ship to Mauritius during the long Christmas holiday to improve my spoken French. Since

I had not studied the subject at St Andrews, I did an intensive introductory course in the language. If I got a first class in the exam held at the start of the second academic year, I could go straight to second-year French. On board the Dutch *MV Tjichilenka* on the voyage to Mauritius, the only other European in the second class was a Belgian from the Congo who spoke no English. For ten days I spoke nothing but French. He told me the Belgian philosophy was to give no political rights whatsoever to the native population. In that way, the issue of majority African rule would be avoided, he said. With all the talk and some study, my wonderful hosts in Mauritius helped me to get my first class and eventually I majored in the language. It was a vital factor many years later in helping me get jobs in Morocco, the Congo and later one which took me back to magical Mauritius for two years.

Now my political awareness really started focusing on the federation and on South Africa. I continued to support the idea of federation particularly while Garfield Todd, a genuine liberal, remained prime minister of Southern Rhodesia. Yet it became ever more apparent that there had been little progress of the sort that was so clearly needed. Instead there were ridiculous issues raised as to whether or when Africans merited being referred to as 'Mr' or whether they should be called 'Africans' rather than 'natives'. Contact between the races remained non-existent except on a master and servant basis. I remember a debate being generated in the correspondence of a national newspaper on 'whether natives had a sense of humour'. I remember taxing our local MP in Bulawayo with the lack of progress. She talked about the overriding need to maintain standards. In 1956 when I set off hitchhiking from Bulawayo to stay with my farmer friend Richard Valentine near Umtali, I was picked up by a man who I knew to be a leading member of the pro-federation United Federal Party, Ian Smith. We talked politics for the whole six-hour journey to Salisbury. I gave him my view that unless the federal and Southern Rhodesia governments took drastic action soon, partnership and with it the federation were bound to fail. All he did was to repeat endlessly that the issue was standards and that the white man was best placed to decide what was good for blacks. This was deeply depressing. Yet I continued to think of Southern Rhodesia as being special and surely with a special future if only whites could see the light. If they could be far-sighted and generous, blacks would surely respond to their lead. At university I soon saw what the federation had, compared to South Africa. In Southern Rhodesia, despite everything, relations between the races were amazingly relaxed. On the whole, in Southern Rhodesia people talked to each other man to man.

Being at university gave one more opportunity for contacts of all sorts and a chance to understand what South Africa was really about. At Rhodes nearly a quarter of the 700 students were Rhodesians, obviously of the more educated and enlightened sort. We were proud of our country's move towards change and support for the federation, and the concept of partnership was pretty well unanimous. We were aware, if we thought about it, that there was racism in Rhodesia, but it was nothing compared to South Africa. Contact for us students with blacks was nil. I remember in Grahamstown a local curiosity was a rare Asian who was working in a greengrocer's, who was said to be educated. There were no black students or lecturers and though technically the nearby University College of Fort Hare was part of Rhodes, there was no contact for ordinary students. We once marched to show disapproval of government moves to separate us from Fort Hare. There was a hoo ha when it was discovered that one of our Students Representative Council members was spying for the nationalist government. Clearly the government regarded us as being dangerously radical. The only political activity I remember though was when I went to a packed nationalist election meeting during the 1957 election campaign. The nationalist candidate during his speech said in Afrikaans that 'the kaffir is an animal from the veld'. About that time my Swiss colleague, the secretary of the French Society (I was the treasurer) who came from Basutoland, must have had black contacts in Grahamstown. One day he crossed the street and was talking to a black man when he was pulled up by a policeman and told that that sort of behaviour could not be tolerated.

Some of us at the university had cars; otherwise travel from Rhodesia to the Eastern Cape was by train or we hitchhiked. South African whites were and are friendly and hospitable. As one travelled around the country, talk was nearly always about politics, though not necessarily about race. While South African concerns centred mainly on points of contention between Afrikaners and English speakers, I became ever more interested in race as an issue. People one met did not hesitate to tell you how they saw things whether it was in a car or a bar or on a train. I would give my view that it was an unsustainable position to discriminate against all blacks and not allow for the possibility that at least a few of them might be educated, civilised, talented or in some way worthy of being given a vote or at least be allowed into a cinema or a café in their own country. Almost countless were the times when the response to such postulation was 'let me put you straight'. Out came all the boringly familiar reasons why blacks were inferior. The Tomlinson report on how the philosophy of apartheid or separate development should be applied came out in 1956. It recommended separate but equal facilities for the races. This idea was never taken up. However, in the Cape Province which had historically been more tolerant than the other provinces in the Union, it was still possible in 1957 to travel in a mixed race bus. I was with a few Rhodesian friends, including Chris Andersen and Barry Walker, en route back to Rhodes when we boarded a bus in East London. We were the only passengers, apart from a young black man and a white girl of about 12 sitting a couple of seats away from each other at the back. We saw the child lean over and strike the man with a roll of paper. He did not react, so she did it again, and again no reaction. She did it a third time, and this time he reacted with a sideways flick of his hand in her direction. Immediately she was on her feet, complaining to the white conductor that the kaffir had hit her. The conductor immediately stormed to the back, grabbed the black man by the collar, dragged him to the front and literally threw him off the bus. My friends and I who had witnessed the whole incident, protested to the conductor that the man had done nothing and that the fault lay entirely with the girl. His reaction was 'If you love these people so much why don't you go to live with them in the location?' We all got up and left the bus. Such incidents would have been everyday occurrences. More sinister and dangerous were manifestations of the odious nature of pure racism like when a black ambulance in Port Elizabeth stopped at the scene of a bad accident involving whites and started attending to the injured. White passers-by were not prepared to witness such inter-racial contact and drove off the ambulance men. As a result, at least one of the accident victims died. Of a comical nature was the case of the European woman in Durban who had a heart attack when she discovered that her hero hitherto, the singer Nat King Cole, was black. There was simply no place at all in the society for mutual sympathy or understanding. The pathetically few white liberals, who had no political voice at all, argued that getting rid of discrimination was essential if South Africa was to have a real future. Nationalists argued that give them an inch and they would take a mile.

Back in Rhodesia, by 1958 it was becoming ever more desperately important that action should be taken to make partnership a reality. However, definitions of partnership like the one given by the first federal prime minister, Sir Godfrey Huggins, comparing partnership with the relationship 'between a rider and a horse' was hardly likely to inspire confidence amongst blacks (when Northern Rhodesia became independent in 1964, one of the first acts of the new Zambian government was to tear down the statue of a horse and rider in Lusaka).

An all round consideration of the federation should have been the effect on South Africa. Surely even the apartheid government would take note of a multiracial success story and amend its own policies. The potential for change was there. South African black nationalist leaders such as Chief Lithuli were moderates and there were many thousands of Afrikaners who had fought for Britain and its allies in the Second World War. Like the English-speaking South Africans, they would surely respond to a British lead in Africa. I saw very clearly that many South Africans of all races longed for a British lead. Britain had been part of the South African equation for centuries, and most recently South Africa had been a staunch ally in two world wars. At St Andrews the war memorials in the chapel showed that at least as many old boys had been killed as from equivalent British schools. There were many on the sub-continent who knew that a British lead was the only hope for a multiracial future. Having put their faith in Britain, in the end they were left disappointed. Part of the reason for this of course was a general failure among South Africans to understand how the Second World War had sapped British power and changed the way the mother country saw its role in the world.

Though I had not yet been to Northern Rhodesia or Nyasaland and seen British colonialism in practice, I had been to Mauritius in 1957 and to Basutoland several times in 1957 and 1958. This was part of my efforts to get really fluent in French, which following Afrikaans at school, I took up at Rhodes in 1956. Mauritius was democratic and multiracial and clearly valued the British connection. Whites or Franco-Mauritians who had had the primacy of their Catholic religion, language and law maintained following the British conquest in 1812 were proud to be British rather than French. During the short university vacations, I went to stay in Basutoland with gentle, educated and highly civilised French protestant missionaries. The atmosphere in this tiny country was totally different from that in South Africa, and it gave me a great thrill to see the Union Jack flying over the DC's office in the little outstations like Quiting.

In the colony of Southern Rhodesia, by 1958 partnership was still not going well. The Prime Minister Garfield Todd seemed to be the only politician prepared to put genuine partnership into practice. Unlike his colleagues in the Southern Rhodesia cabinet or indeed federal politicians, he was genuinely colour blind. I remember wondering how he could still be prime minister after several years in the job. I suppose it must have reflected the strength of his considerable personality. Also he was no softie. He had called up the army when the miners went on strike at the Wankie Colliery on which the country depended for its coal-fired power stations. No doubt he got a good mark for that from right-wing colleagues, but it was inevitable that he was going to fall out with them if partnership was not going to be a total sham. Opponents started racist smear stories about him supposedly beating black girls on bare bottoms. I remember it caused a rumpus in Salisbury when Todd was seen crossing the main Jameson Avenue to his office in Chaplin Building holding a small black child by the hand. Finally, he was replaced by Edgar Whitehead who though he was fairly liberal was much more acceptable to the white electorate. Todd's departure killed any chance of a multiracial future for the federation. Later, in a further move to the right, Whitehead was replaced by Winston Field.

After leaving University at the end of 1958, I still believed in the federation but had come to the conclusion that only positive British policies could save it. It seemed to me that it was high time for the British to tell the federal government that it would no longer tolerate the sort of discrimination and racism which prevailed in Southern Rhodesia. It was very clear to me that Britain still had a vital role to play in leading the sub-continent away from extremism on both sides, though it was the effects of short sighted and damaging white racism which I saw as posing the biggest threat to future peace and stability. I decided I could best do my bit by joining the Colonial Administrative Service, part of Her Majesty's Overseas Civil Service (HMOCS). I knew that if I was accepted I was most likely to be sent to either Northern Rhodesia or Nyasaland, which, though part of the federation, were both conventional British colonies and protectorates. A special interview panel consisting of people like retired colonial governors was convened for me in Salisbury in early 1959. During the interview I said that I supported the federation and that I felt that I could have more influence as a civil servant than as a politician. I was accepted and was told that I would be required to attend the Overseas Services 'A' course at Cambridge for the 1959–60 academic year.

2

Bush and Boma

In January 1959 I taught for a term at the all-white co-educational Hillcrest High School in Livingstone, capital of Northern Rhodesia's Southern Province. I had charge of French for the whole school. Otherwise I took some classes for English and mainly just read good books to the children. Life was wonderful and free and fun and I loved Northern Rhodesia immediately. I occupied myself by playing first cricket and later in the term, rugby for the Barbarians club. Livingstone was a delightful small town with an African population of mainly Lozi people from nearby Barotseland, a protectorate within a protectorate or 'Lozi in urba' as one rather pompous provincial commissioner once called it. There was a sizeable Asian population of mainly traders and about the same number of Europeans, mainly Rhodesia Railways workers. The races all got on well together. There were very few educated blacks apart from a few school teachers and government clerks, but then the country had only been a colony since 1924 and the end of British South Africa Company rule. One thing I noticed immediately at places like Chandamali, the government hostel where I stayed, was that the African staff all called you 'bwana' instead of the 'boss' or 'master' as in Southern Rhodesia or South Africa. There was still no black–white socialising and the mainly white working class railway workers were hardly likely to be pioneers in building partnership. The children at Hillcrest High School, however, were polite and disciplined under the excellent headmaster Fergus Dwyer. It was depressing though to find when I asked a class to write an essay on 'What can we do to improve our town' to find that the majority mentioned getting blacks off the streets. On the social side I met several younger colonial service administrative officers from both the Livingstone urban district commissioner's as well as the provincial commissioner's office. Apart from one, all lacked racial hang-ups and were learning or were fluent in local languages like Tonga or Lozi. The exception whom I remember well, told me he hated blacks. I ventured that I thought he was in the wrong job. He was not happy with my remark, but I became aware a year later that he had left the service.

There then followed a wonderful year at Cambridge. Before going up to the university, I was mostly in London doing supply teaching at a secondary modern school. One weekend I was asked to go and stay with the retired Governor of Southern Rhodesia Sir John Kennedy and his wife who knew my parents. The Kennedys lived in a National Trust house on the edge of the Lake District. We discussed the Federation and British policy in Africa. I gave my view that Britain should be a lot more positive and give the lead that I felt was called for. The Kennedys disagreed strongly with my views on a continuing British role in southern Africa and suggested I should go and live in Natal. At Cambridge I spent most of the time playing rugby and cricket for my college, St Johns. As part of the course, those of us who were destined to go to Northern Rhodesia were given lessons in one of the main vernacular languages, Bemba. Our teacher, the Reverend Quick, a retired missionary who came all the way once a week from Swansea, inevitably was known as Bwana. He obviously knew rural Bembaland very well, but he kept saying things like 'so don't lets regard black people as backward in any way', which I took from the other things he said as meaning that that was exactly how he did see them. Bwana sometimes took us in a group down to the river below Kings College for lessons. There, puzzled passers-by would stop in amazement as we rendered some Bemba song about a bird 'with a shell on its head' (one of the hornbills).

The more I thought about it at this time, the more I realised that I knew nothing about Africans as people. I had never met an African on totally equal terms. Now at last there was the chance to get to know the few Tanzanians and Kenyans on our course. I was also fascinated and impressed by a talk given by Tom Mboya who seemed to embody good sense and reconciliation. It was interesting, however, that the average undergraduate at Cambridge in 1959 cared little for the Commonwealth or the remains of empire. I remember a young New Zealander in the pub pleading with friends to take an interest in the Commonwealth. I supported him, but we were quickly pooh-poohed. There was certainly no question of anybody feeling that we still had an important job to do in preparing countries for independence. Macmillan's 'Winds of Change' speech delivered in Cape Town came at the beginning of 1960 and seemed to indicate a new British willingness to play a new positive role in Africa. In the event, it came to signal a total withdrawal. In contrast, about that time the colonial office sanctioned a campaign with posters going up all over Cambridge advertising 'A Career for you in the Colonial Service?' Most of us going to Kenya or Northern Rhodesia would have guessed we had about 15 years before independence. In the event it was less than five.

The boat trip to Cape Town in June 1960 was the perfect opportunity to recover after the hectic round of exams and social and sporting events culminating for me in the wonderful St John's College, May Ball. I took Jane, the daughter of a Kenyan DC who had been on the 'B' course for senior colonial service officers at Cambridge. Memories of the evening were a major solace during the sometimes lonely times out in the African bush. We continued a low-key correspondence over the next three years and I could not help harbouring hopes of a future with her.

On arrival in Cape Town, I arranged a lift up to Salisbury and my parents with a very attractive single and obviously successful first secretary designate at the British High Commission there. Margaret Archer had a wonderfully stylish Sunbeam Alpine car and was interested in everything; we talked non-stop for the three or four day journey to Salisbury. When we arrived, every second car in the city seemed to be from the Belgian Congo. They were part of the great panic and white exodus following independence at the end of June. It was depressing, but I told myself that the Belgians had done little or nothing to prepare the Congo for independence. In response to world and particularly to American pressure, they had gambled that a precipitate withdrawal would leave the Congo so dependent that they would be able to continue to play the dominant role in the country.

A week in Salisbury showed me that little had changed in Southern Rhodesia in the year I had been away, except that African nationalism was very much on the march and now seriously threatened the old order. I had some old friends in the country but I no longer identified with it. The ideal of Federation was virtually dead through, as I saw it, lack of white foresight in the south and black nationalism in the north. The British government having backed the idea was now backtracking and was being seen by southern whites as being both weak and perfidious. It seemed to me that had it cracked the whip with them, there might have been some hope. As it was, it gave the impression of just wanting to get shot of the whole thing and was thus giving a growing right wing the incentive to move further and further to the right. There was even talk of breaking with Britain. Luckily the Federal Prime Minister Sir Roy Welensky, a big man in every way, did not try and do anything so rash. He could not have taken the northern territories with him.

In Southern Rhodesia though, there was Ian Smith who promised the white electorate that there would be no giving way to black nationalism.

The dry savannah gets thicker and lusher as the train climbs from the Victoria Falls and Livingstone up to Kalomo on the plateau. Kalomo was and still is farming country and farms occupied by whites stretched almost to Livingstone and 40 miles up to Choma on both sides of the railway line and the Great North Road. Beyond the farms are the chief's areas from Mukuni and Sekute each side of Livingstone up and down the Zambezi to Simwatachela in the lower Zambezi Valley and the adjacent plateau. North of the Great North Road are Musokotwane going up to Mulobezi and the Zambezi sawmills, and nearer Kalomo, Sipatunyana, and Siachitema and Chikanta bordering the giant Kafue National Park. It is, as I was soon to discover, a magnificent district with huge variety. The most interesting in the country I think. I was met at Kalomo station by Ian Holland who was acting district commissioner. He had been in charge for only a few weeks and was about to go on leave. He drove me into the little town with its hotel where there were usually a few farmers in the bar and their wives sitting on the veranda, two general stores, a chemist, a garage, a butchery and a cafe in those days patronised only by whites. It was run by Johanna, a lady of Greek origin who was rumoured to have killed a German with her bare hands during the war. All the businesses were white owned apart from one of the stores called Elvinas (L V Nayee) which was run by Asians. They served a clientele of mainly white farmers and a few civil servants including four European policemen. At the hotel, mainly farmers or travellers patronised the bar, while wives sat in groups on the veranda. To the west of town was the African township and to the north a gravel road led to the boma. The boma (government offices) was on the boma farm which was the site of the original capital of North-Western Rhodesia up to 1907. The offices were modern with lawn and flagpole and a road led to the DC's house, built about 1903, and a national monument. Along the way on one side were houses for African civil servants and on the other side well spaced out modern bungalows occupied by the two district officers and an agricultural officer. One of these, occupied until recently by the Hollands, was going to be mine. No farming took place on the boma farm, but there was an airstrip and the European cemetery, again the oldest in the country. It contained the graves of tax collectors, administrators and traders, nearly all of whom seemed to have died of black water fever. Mainly, however, the boma farm was hundreds of acres of open rolling grassland kept short in those days by a herd of small prancing oribi antelope which were relatively tame and must have felt safe as they never moved away. Through the farm ran a tributary of the Kalomo River which in July was reduced to pools beside which grazed larger reedbuck that when disturbed ran off with white fluffy tails in the air like a rabbit. The pools, I was to discover, contained abundant yellow-bellied Kafue bream, delicious to eat and caught with a spinner.

I did not see much of the Hollands. They were off on leave within a day or two of my arrival. However, I was allocated an office at the boma and met the district messengers for the first time. It was impressed on me from the start that there was something special about the messengers. There were 30 or so of them and they wore smartly starched and ironed uniforms of blue bush jackets with red collars and blue shorts, stockings and bush hats. On the morning of my first day, they were lined up outside the boma for inspection by the DC. I was introduced to them and was greeted with a smart salute by the head messenger, Silas Nyambaulo. The messengers gave immediate priority to finding me a manservant or houseboy as they were known in those days. As I sat at my desk that first day, a couple of messengers brought in a wrinkledlooking little man only just five feet tall. I was told that he was really good and reliable and a very hard worker. His name was Stephen Mbwainga and he was married with two small children. Though he was hardly an imposing figure physically, I liked his level look, and having agreed terms as advised by the messengers, I took him on.

Though following my days in Southern Rhodesia I could speak the lingua franca of communication between blacks and whites throughout most of southern Africa known as Kitchen Kaffir or more politely as *Funagalo* or *Chilapalapa*, I did not let on. I was certainly not happy to be associated with knowledge of this so-called language with its heavy emphasis on Zulu-based imperatives. Stephen, educated to Standard Two, could make himself understood in English. I made it clear to him and to the messengers that from the word go I wanted to communicate in Tonga, the local language and only resort to English as a last resort. This was not as fanciful as it might appear, as much of the Bemba that I had learned at Cambridge was similar to Tonga. In the house, Stephen set to work with enormous energy and staying power. When all was clean, I bought African dress material made in Manchester for curtains in the sitting room. The government-issue armchairs did not have to have covers. I did not bother too much about privacy. I stuck newspaper to the windows in my bedroom. I bought a teapot, a kettle and pots and pans at Elvinas or at Behrens. There was no fresh bread or milk in Kalomo in those

days. I made do with Ryvita and with powdered milk. One day shortly after
my arrival, I told Stephen that I had a very important man coming to tea. In
fact it was Brian Fagan the archaeologist, ex Cambridge, who was attached
to the Rhodes Livingstone Museum in Livingstone and was currently digging
for ancient Tonga bones on a neighbouring farm. When we sat down for tea
on the veranda, Stephen brought us ryvita with butter and jam on both sides.
Brian became a very good friend and we had a lot of fun together when I
could get down to Livingstone.

When Ian Holland left to go on leave, my colleague the district officer Jeff Stone was not considered senior enough to act as DC, so the DC
from the neighbouring district of Choma was appointed to be in charge of
both districts. His name was John Durant. He was in his late 30s, and I was
impressed by his charm and by the relaxed authority he exercised over the
messengers and other African civil servants on the boma staff. These were
an executive officer, a Mr Munalula, and accountants and clerks. I started
to become aware of a relationship between white and black that I had not
come across before. John spoke to the messengers in Lozi, a language they
all knew. He was interested in them and their work, and you could sense
the mutual respect. They were all on the same side. I was soon to learn
that the effectiveness of the administration as a whole depended completely
on the messengers and their relationship with the DC and DOs. The messengers, recruited almost exclusively within the district, were the eyes and ears
of the provincial administration or PA as it was known. To carry out this role
effectively, they had to know the district and its personalities and problems
intimately. They had to earn the genuine respect of local people through their
intelligence, integrity and leadership qualities. It was not a one-way process.
They represented the views and feelings of local people to the administration. If they carried out this role properly they had the trust of both sides
and were indispensable to good, fair and effective district administration. I,
with my ignorance, lack of contact with Africans and attitudes influenced by
Southern Rhodesia and South Africa, was slow at first to pick up this point.
'Trust your Messengers', I kept being told. It took a few months before I
really did.

Meanwhile John Durant decided he was going to take me on my first
tour. He announced that this was going to be in Chief Sekute's area along the
Zambezi upstream from Livingstone and inland. He would take the opportunity to do some fishing. The boma lorry and a Land Rover would take six
messengers, camping equipment, our food, bicycles and us and drop us at

a campsite prepared by local people near Chief Sekute's village. One messenger had gone ahead to recruit our entitlement of 16 carriers to move the camping equipment as we moved from campsite to campsite. The afternoon of our arrival, Stephen supervised the erection of the tent and saw to details such as hanging a wet sack in a tree to keep our food and beer cool, and installing a canvas bath in the bathroom enclosure. John and I walked over to the chief's village past lines of women giving their traditional gesture of welcome and greeting with a sort of courtesy combined with hand clapping with cupped hands. It was difficult not to feel terribly important. The chief turned out to be a crusty old man whose preoccupations centred on the fact that a previous DC had reduced the sentencing powers of his court. He also had grazing disputes along the river with the government forestry department and with a Southern Rhodesian rancher who was continually bringing his cattle across the Zambezi to graze the chief's land. That evening as the sun set spectacularly with the winter dust in the air, we drank our beers cool from the wet sack, before supper and a walk over the sandy soil through the trees to where the chief had laid on a traditional dance. We sat with the chief in a circle entranced, while men and women separately danced to the music of drums, cow horns and *mbiras*, their faces shining in the light of the bonfire. I knew I was in the real Africa and the right job for me.

The next day we were up with the sun and after breakfast inspected the small parade of messengers lined up under the Union Jack fluttering on its makeshift flagpole. Then we set off on a long bicycle convoy including messengers, the chief, his court clerk, assessors and *kapasus* or tribal police and with John and me bringing up the rear, heading for the first village. Village to village touring was one of the mainstays of our work as administrative officers. It took us into direct touch with ordinary village people through meetings with all the adults in all the villages. The drill was that the cadet DO or DC would sit on chairs with the chief and his clerk facing the village headman beside his people all sitting on the ground. The names of male residents contained in a large leather-bound register would then be read out and ticked if present. If a man was away working, say in Bulawayo or the copper mines, or on a social visit, a note would be made. The names of young men considered to be adult were added to the register. The number of women was also noted. The messengers particularly enjoyed their traditional role of deciding which of the young women yet to be considered adults were now 'matured'. John conducted the whole business in tandem with the chief and next on the agenda was a general discussion on matters such as the tidiness of the village, the construction of pit latrines (often a forlorn hope), the state of the crops, illness or plans to dig a well. After that we would ask if there were any complaints. It was then that we were most likely to get the best idea of the real feelings of the people. In 1960 there was a general contentment and little or no politics. Common complaints concerned elephants raiding crops or government campaigns to inoculate cattle against deadly trypanomiasis or sleeping sickness. In the case of the latter, the problem often arose because villagers sometimes took their cattle for inoculation to the veterinary department only when they were already ill and then blamed the department for the animals' deaths. All this with someone like John Durant in the chair was conducted in the local language. Otherwise one had to speak English as I had to on subsequent tours in the early days. Clearly the whole thing was going to be much more worthwhile and enjoyable if one could speak to the people in their own language. I became determined from the beginning to become fluent in Tonga as soon as possible. I imagined myself going for walks in the evening and chatting to the old women about the way they saw the world, whilst they pounded the corn or prepared the evening meal.

That first day on tour, by the time we had visited five or six villages, it was past two in the afternoon and we got to our new camp under some big trees, but with a beautiful view down towards the Zambezi. After lunch the local headman wanted to show John and me what he thought was a good potential site for a small dam which he hoped the government would build for the village. As we crossed a large dambo known in the south as a vlei, we came across a pair of giant kori bustards. The dam site was a good one with a large catchment area. One could only hope that mention of it in one's tour report would result in it being acted upon by the government. Carrying on down to the great Zambezi River, the countryside becomes much lusher and there are huge trees including great vegetable ivory palms growing in the deep riverine soil. John and I stayed at a forestry department rest house near the river with a great grove of lime trees. Lime juice mixed with cool water and some sugar makes the most wonderfully refreshing drink on a hot day. In the afternoon we met the two elderly murderers who worked at the nearby Katombora Reformatory for boys. The old men, delightful characters, had both killed their wives. After many years spent technically as prisoners, they were no threat to anyone and could be relied on not to escape. The head of the reformatory, which came under federal government control, was a Yorkshireman called Saunders. After John had fished in the afternoon and caught a couple of magnificent fighting tiger fish, we went for supper

with Mr Saunders. Nearly all his boys were from the Copperbelt where they
had become involved in petty crime due, I was told, to the breakdown in
traditional African customs and moralities in the new urban environment.
Saunders' recipe was hard useful work such as carpentry or growing vegetables, which gave the boys a skill and a sense of achievement. The better
they behaved and the more they achieved, the more freedom and privileges
they were given. Saunders told us proudly that when occasionally a new in-
mate escaped, he would send out all his 'trusties' to go after him. Invariably
they found the escapee and brought him back. I have often thought that a
similar approach would be appropriate in the United Kingdom in many circumstances. After another day's touring, John left me to continue on my own
and the Land Rover came to take him back to Kalomo and Choma. I visited
more villages along the river and one night camped close to Kazangula pontoon, opposite the point where Southern Rhodesia and Bechuanaland met
on the southern bank of the river (a few years later this would be the famous
freedom ally between white and black Africa). Eleven years before, aged 13,
I had been to a little country hotel just into Southern Rhodesia with my parents for a few days' fishing and shooting. I decided this evening to cross the
river in search of a beer and some company at the hotel. The pontoon operator was happy enough to take me across for a few shillings and within a
few minutes I walked through the front door into what had been the hotel
lounge. There were two white men sitting at a table drinking beer. One got
up and asked me, 'What can we do for you?' 'I'll have one of those please',
said I pointing to his beer. 'I'm afraid this is a private house', he said, 'but
anyway have a beer; the hotel closed five years ago'. I was mortified but
grateful.

By the time I got back to Kalomo, the new DC Philip Farwell had arrived. He was nice enough and a kind man, but I did not feel at first that we
would get on. Pretty soon I would discover I had much to learn from him.
Meanwhile I was settling down with Stephen, and having acquired a Tonga
grammar book, practised on him constantly. I started going out on day trips
in the Land Rover accompanied by a couple of messengers to visit the other
eight chiefs in the district. I particularly remember trips with second messenger Joshua Kanana and another called Shamboko. Both were men old enough
to be my father and with little education. Both were as wise as any men I have
ever known. As we drove, they would tell me in Tonga about the district, the
chiefs and the farmers. I could tell from the way they related to everyone they
spoke to in the villages that their principal care was for the people. In return

they were deeply respected. In those days, crime of any sort was rare in the villages and theft virtually unknown. The Kalomo chiefs had an average of about 6000 or 7000 people in their areas. The day-to-day maintenance of law and order was in the hands of chiefs and headmen and about five *kapasus* (tribal police) per chief's area. It would be difficult to imagine a more peaceful and law-abiding society. There were no national police stationed in the chief's areas in those days and no need for them. Only in the event of a murder did they become involved there. Back at the boma I would leave my house unlocked even when I went away for a few days. There was an understandable exception to all this honesty in the case of chief's court clerks. These men, who were paid not more than six or seven pounds a month, dealt daily with what for them were large sums of money collected for various Native Authority-imposed taxes, permits and licences. They might be holding up to a hundred or more pounds at a time and the temptation to avail themselves of these funds was sadly and often overwhelming. There was a very simple system of checking, basically involving comparing the money with the totals as shown by the receipts. Many was the time when a quick spot check on a chief's court ended with a drive back to the boma with the unfortunate clerk in handcuffs.

Of course there was petty crime and a little violence, mostly it seemed to me at the time, involving women beating up their husbands. I do remember one case of serious theft by a young man from Chief Sipatunyana's area. He was in our local Kalomo prison near the airstrip waiting for his sentence to be carried out. This happened to coincide with my first inspection of the prison one early morning. The sentence imposed by the chief's court was six strokes of the cane. I as a cadet and a Magistrate Class IV had to witness the punishment. There was procedure and ceremony involved, including a sort of drill with messengers on prison duty marching and saluting and along the way the youth was relieved of his trousers and made to lie face down on the ground. Then came the careful placing of a damp cloth on his rounded buttocks. At this point my surprise and shock at this whole carry on took over. I regarded myself as an expert on caning after literally dozens of such punishments at all my boarding schools. I ordered the messengers to stop, to restore the young man to his feet and his trousers and to bend him over in the conventional way. What happened of course was that every time the messenger wielded the cane, the victim merely straightened up and the power of the blow was dissipated. He did not actually laugh out loud, but the messengers were furious and I learned not to be so judgemental.

Kalomo was unusual for Northern Rhodesia as there were about 50 white farmers occupying so-called crown land along the line of rail. I soon got to meet most of them at the club where we played tennis, cricket and rugby at weekends. We had strong teams and the gentle giant Andy Mac-Donald was in our rugby team. Five years later in 1965, he was picked to tour New Zealand in the Springbok front row. This was after Zambian independence and therefore not well viewed by the new government. He was forgiven because of the kudos he earned among the local people by managing to fight off a wounded lion which attacked him. He lost an eye and a few fingers in the process. The farmers were a mixed bag. About half were Afrikaners who tended to be pragmatic. For the English speakers, we in the PA were regarded as being on the other side and against them. They were mainly pro-Federation, while we were seen as wanting to hand the country over to the African nationalists. They did not know the extent of opposition by the Southern Province chiefs to any political activity in their areas. They saw any concessions as being the beginning of the end of the white man's authority in Northern Rhodesia. They knew little about the bulk of the district which was tribal land. There, local government and the administration of justice were in the hands of the chiefs who, sitting together with African officials under the chairmanship of the DC, formed the Native Authority. Every rural district in Northern Rhodesia had a Native Authority, which operated according to the system of indirect rule, developed by Lord Lugard in Nigeria and Uganda. I well remember at the Native Authority headquarters the council in session and the DC trying to persuade the chiefs to give a hearing to a Mr Sikota Wina and a Mr Mainza Chona, two very senior officials of the United National Independence Party (UNIP) destined to become Zambian cabinet ministers, but they refused point blank.

By 1961, political activity in the urban areas, especially the Copperbelt towns, was gaining momentum with politicians being encouraged by the likes of John Stonehouse and other British Labour Party politicians. It seemed to many of us on the spot (unofficially of course because we were civil servants) that there were a number of UK politicians with little knowledge of local circumstances, who were applying values and principles to a situation where they did not apply, whilst furthering their careers through adopting specious moral postures. Though there remained virtually no overt political activity in Kalomo district, I think generally the chiefs sensed that the nationalists were pushing at an open door as far as the British government was concerned and feared for the future. Three of ours, whose areas bordered on Barotseland,

Chiefs Sekute, Musokotwane and Mukuni, asked to be allowed to join Barotseland with its status of protectorate within a protectorate, which they then assumed would stay British.

Meanwhile whilst change might have been in the air, we were not really affected in Kalomo. Johanna kept blacks out of the cafe and none ventured into the hotel. There were rural rumblings in the Northern and Luapula provinces in 1961 and we sent the senior District Officer Jeff Stone with some of our messengers to be attached to bomas up there for a month or two. The troubles, involving some burning of cattle dips and schools, but with very little real violence, were soon over. The nationalist cause had not been advanced and therefore there was a feeling afterwards that the good work done by the PA in dealing with the troubles was negated by official apologies for doing what was clearly the right thing. This, not unnaturally, encouraged the nationalists to redouble their efforts. In sleepy Kalomo there was some political agitation in the township and one day a delegation of people arrived at the boma dressed in what looked like voluminous maternity dresses. They were supposed to be togas, but since no one had ever seen them worn in Northern Rhodesia, they only looked comical. They were a sign though, of the search for an identity.

Meanwhile I was making good progress with my Tonga and within nine months had passed both the lower and higher level exams in the language. Now it really was possible while I was on tour, to go off into villages and chat to people and make the old ladies laugh. Most evenings on tour I would take my dog Bounder (embarrassingly pronounced Banda by the locals), and the tough little .410 and look for *kwale*, the local francolin (partridge), in the maize fields. Sometimes I would come back with a guinea fowl or two. They were quite easy to shoot if flushed out of the long grass. Duck, knobnose or whistling duck from the rivers or wet *dambos* were best as they could be eaten straight away. The only time I tried to eat a *kwale* the evening I shot it, it was impossible to chew. I loved the evenings. After a day of hard work and exercise in the heat, Stephen would prepare my bath in the grass shelter with a bucket of cold water beside it which I would pour over my head when I was finished. Then I would put on long trousers and a clean shirt and even a jacket before settling down to a cold beer outside my tent as the sun went down and the *kwale* called from the fields. Sometimes before dinner, the chief would come over for a beer, though the likes of Simwatachela would have preferred *bukokobukali* (fierce beer) like whisky. Unless there was game, like at home, supper was steak, sausages or chicken curry in rotation. I slept on a comfortable camp bed with the tent flap open. Sometimes I had a net if the mosquitoes were bad. Otherwise I remember the fearsome-looking hunting spiders – large, fast and hairy, but totally harmless. There were of course assorted bugs and beetles which one became used to, even the odd snake. At night I adored the sound of nightjars and frogs calling, both wonderfully sleep inducing. Of course malaria was likely. It was easily dealt with, however, by taking four nivaquine tablets at the first sign. Bilharzia was another problem and virtually inevitable when perforce one washed in water taken from pools along rivers flowing through populated areas.

One night at a village in Simwatachela's area, the messengers came after I had gone to bed and said that a toddler was missing, having wandered away from the village in the afternoon. The parents were distraught. I organised the four messengers in searching a nearby pool in the river while the villagers all fanned out into the surrounding bush. It was not long before joyous shouting told us that the child had been found curled up asleep under a tree.

In camp, the day started with early breakfast followed by an inspection of the messengers lined up under the Union Jack flying from a newly cut pole. Then off we would set on our bicycles with Bounder bounding along beside me. Though superficially the villages were similar, the standard of housing varied as did the general tidiness. Chief Mukuni was a real stickler for tidiness and the whole area of the village had to have been swept. I remember him upbraiding one headman because there was human hair outside one hut following a haircut. Some villages had no pit latrines and with flies everywhere, health – particularly of the children – was affected. Flies collected around the eyes of children who had not been kept clean. I remember several cases of young women sitting apart from the rest of the village. These unfortunate people had suffered ruptures during childbirth, which made them sometimes doubly incontinent and caused them to become tragic outcasts. Normally villages were led by headmen. I do remember, however, being impressed in Musokotwane's area to find that the headman was a headwoman. She was doing a good job.

Actually in rural Northern Rhodesia, it was the women who seemed to do most of the work in tilling the fields, in constructing the houses and in making the beer. Men drank the most, though it was not uncommon to see women, particularly older ones, in a drunken heap outside villages. It was always sad to come across handicapped children, particularly those that were blind and/or deaf. The handicap of their affliction meant that they were

treated as if they were mentally deficient. This did not mean that the handicapped or the orphaned or the elderly were neglected or badly treated. On
the contrary, the culture and close family relationships and interdependency
ensured that the weak or dependent were always cared for.

The annual or biannual visit to a village by the DO was an occasion which
called for celebration. The singing, dancing and drumming in which the messengers were willing participants went on well into the night. If a child was
born on the day of a visit, he or she would often be named after the visiting
officer. This custom gave rise amongst the uninitiated to speculation about
the nature of the officer's relationships. This reminds me of one village in
an area bordering on farms near Zimba. During the meeting with the men
and women and children in separate groups, I noticed a little girl about three
years old. She was fat and healthy and very light skinned. When she saw me,
surely the first white man she had ever seen, her face lit up and encouraged
by her mother, she came and held my hand. It was quite moving. I asked the
messengers about her origins. 'One of the farms', they replied.

Looking back and reflecting on how I thought and was motivated in those
days, I remember how I knew that there was so much to be achieved. There
were the principal problems of sanitation and health, and of a shifting system of agriculture whereby when the land was exhausted, the village simply
moved on. With health, it was always a battle between modern medicine
and the witch doctor. Measles with the attendant pneumonia was the biggest
killer of children. Sadly, parents would take their children to the clinic or
hospital only when they had given up hope of the witch doctor being able to
cure them. It was often too late for modern medicine to effect a cure and
then if one child died, the parents would fail to bring in their other children
or take them out of the hospital, so they all died.

Clearly, shifting agriculture was not sustainable and we in the PA would
try and back up the Agricultural Department by trying to get villagers to
maintain the fertility of their land by rotating their maize with groundnuts or
beans for instance. They could also make use of the often abundant manure
produced by their cattle. The cattle themselves were a problem, because
they were regarded as money on the hoof. This was fine, except that no
regard was taken of the quality of the animal. This was despite the fact that at
government sales, a good-quality beast would fetch five or six times one of
low quality. They also wanted to keep the best animals as oxen for ploughing
and not breeding from them. Then there was the question of cassava, which
though not a traditional part of villagers' diet, grew easily and was hardy and

could be held in reserve to stave off hunger and starvation in drought years. To an enthusiastic cadet or DO, it seemed like a not too daunting challenge to be able to persuade villagers to start changing their ways. One talked no doubt very sincerely with eyes shining. One sees now that it is similar to the talk of politicians and other people of the greatest goodwill and with the welfare of Africa and Africans very close to their hearts (Blair and Brown come to mind). Such talk was always listened to in rapt attention and with the utmost politeness. 'The Bwana is so wise and speaks such truth' was the basic reaction. If, however, one was impatient or discourteous enough to press the issue, the basic relation could be summed up as 'You have your way of doing things and we have ours'.

Actually there were African agricultural and medical assistants who were totally on our side. It was a question of education. We reckoned the vital messages would best come from them. There were also the so-called improved farmers living in houses away from the villages, *bazidina* (people who live in brick houses). They received all sorts of agricultural extension advice and services and were expected to show an example. It really had little effect. All this went to show that like all human beings, the Tonga were basically conservative and that culture change certainly does not come easily.

Back again at the boma, Philip Farwell had settled in quickly as DC. He was not really my cup of tea, but he did me a great favour. It followed the funeral of old Mr Mitchell who ran the butchery. A death of someone in the European community was a big event and the DC told me to oversee the clearing of the road to the little pioneer European cemetery on the boma farm dating from 1903 when Kalomo was the first capital of North Western Rhodesia. Prisoners supervised by a couple of messengers were to carry out the work. Broadly, I failed to see to it that the work was done properly and the boma came in for a lot of criticism as a result. The DC was justifiably furious and gave me the biggest telling off of my life. I am sure it was much needed and I never forgot it.

It was Philip Farwell who asked me to take Mr Munalula on his first tour. He was an executive officer rather than a district officer but he was destined for promotion and the move demonstrated both our policy of bringing on high-potential blacks and the importance to us of village to village touring. We took only one largish tent for Munalula and me to share. Stephen produced a good dinner and we had a pleasant evening. The only problem came later when we had settled into our camp beds and Munalula almost immediately started to snore incredibly loudly. I thought of moving my bed outside but desisted as I feared the move would be interpreted as racial. The snoring continued at the same decibel level. If I wanted any sleep at all I had to act. I carried my bed outside. Happily no offence was given or taken.

At the boma there was a magistrate's court and an office dispensing licences and permits of various sorts. As a cadet I was a Magistrate Class IV and as a DO from mid-1962, a Magistrate Class III. One was legally empowered to preside in court but one's main function was to review the cases recorded on a special form that came in from the different chiefs' courts. The record was always in Tonga. One I can remember told at length in Tonga of some dispute which ended with the word 'fokofi' followed in brackets by the only English words ('go away'). One case was regarded as so serious and unusual by the chief that he could not deal with it himself, so he referred it to the DC. It concerned a man who had had sexual relations with his neighbour's cow. The new DC Ian Mackichan was a bit taken aback but decided that it would be inappropriate to deal with the case himself, so he referred it to the tribal court with all the chiefs sitting together. The offender was found guilty and sentenced to the considerable punishment of giving three cows in compensation to the owner of the cow that had been violated.

Another major activity in the office was to act as labour officer. Many were the occasions when a man would come in with a sorry tale of how his employer, usually a white farmer, had allegedly refused to pay him, had beaten him and taken away his 'chitupa' or registration book. The drill was to phone up the farmer and try to mediate. Sometimes it was necessary to call the farmer in to the boma. Commonly he would regard this as a waste of his time and was irate. It clearly irritated farmers that one was able to communicate with their employees in the vernacular, which few farmers could speak. On occasions the employee could not resist embroidering his story in ways that could rebound on him. On average, fault was pretty evenly distributed on the two sides. One farmer whose workers never came to the boma was Peter 'Mutonga' Peers. Peter spoke very fluent Tonga and this minimised misunderstandings. I remember one such on a day when a worker was sitting on the floor of my office in the presence of a messenger, giving me his side of the story. Suddenly the farmer who had, no doubt, just heard that the man had gone to the boma burst in. The man remained sitting. 'Why doesn't he show some respect and get up when I come in?' asked the farmer. I can't remember whether I pointed out that local custom, of which the farmer was no doubt ignorant, is to show respect by sitting down. After Stephen and I had had one of our occasional blazing rows, usually after I got back perhaps from a weekend away, tired and hungry, to find him the worse for drink, we would always sort things out the next day with me standing and him sitting on the floor.

I got to know some of the younger farmers pretty well, particularly those who played rugby. They were hardly liberal in their attitudes, and we were likely to differ on issues of politics or race. However, we had some good games at Choma, Livingstone and even at the Wankie Mine across the border beyond the Victoria Falls. On one trip to Choma, we were looking for the hospital where one of our number was having treatment for some injury. We stopped the car to ask a group of Africans the way; I shouted to them, 'Excuse me could you tell us how to find the hospital.' The Africans came over and politely told us the way and we said thank you. One of my passengers was moved to observe 'Hell it pays to be polite hey'.

The arrival of Ian Mackichan the new DC and his wife Pam in late 1961 coincided with that of two agricultural officers, John Alder and Martin Whittemore with their wives Helen and Pippa. About the same time, a new Cadet Richard Pelly and his wife Ruth arrived. All of a sudden we had a new fun community on the boma farm with hilarious evenings as we entertained each other. I liked everybody and I could not help thinking how nice it would be to be able to share my wonderful lifestyle with the right girl. Of those, unfortunately there were none in Kalomo.

There was, however, the young Irish teacher whom I took to the police ball in Choma. She was delightful but fairly soon was transferred to Mazabuka. Later on I heard the dreadful story of how when the man she was with in a car tried to pass another on a dirt road in thick dust, they collided with an oncoming car and were both killed. Meanwhile I was still writing to the girl whom I had taken to the May Ball at St Johns, Jane. I felt she could understand what I was talking about as she had been born in Kenya and her father was a DC there. We both kept the correspondence from getting passionate or eager through concern, on my part at any rate, that the relationship such as it was would quickly burn itself out that way. It was not that one was not tempted by the thought of local girls. Jeff Stone's cook offered me his charming daughter, a girl of about 17 whom I used to chat to as she sat outside her father's kia when I walked home from the boma for lunch. I was dissuaded from accepting by the thought that because of the huge cultural and economic gap, such relationships would inevitably be exploitative and be likely to be seen as a sign of weakness.

No such inhibiting factors applied to the girl, let's call her Audrey, from Croydon I think, who arrived to sort out the telephone exchange in Kalomo.

She was large, wore thick glasses and clearly appreciated a situation where she was the only available, single European woman. In her enthusiasm she used to go into the bar of the hotel where women seldom ventured, put her hand under men's shirts and tickle their backs exclaiming 'lovely flesh'. The intensity of clucking of the wives on the veranda can only be imagined. When I asked her to dinner, Stephen thoughtfully and perhaps optimistically made up two beds. The girl eventually and inevitably got pregnant by a farm assistant and had an abortion. The story ends happily because Audrey went on to marry a handicapped man on the Copperbelt and produced several healthy normal children.

At about this time I met Mike Priestley, then DC at Sesheke in Barotseland, who called in at the boma. Later on all bachelors, cadets and DOs throughout the country had heard the story of how two beautiful young North American girls travelling around in Africa had found their way to Sesheke. Mike had proceeded to snap one up and marry her. We bachelors on bush stations dreamt that such things would happen to us.

Looking back, Kalomo helped me to acquire a real love of Africa and its people and to begin to understand. I was rather stuck though and at first never got up to Lusaka. I got away occasionally to stay with my parents who were still living in Salisbury. In mid-1961 I was sent with about 20 other DOs and cadets as well as police officers, some of them black, to the civil service training school at Chalimbana outside Lusaka. A senior DO, Paul Bourne was in charge, and he and his wonderfully attractive and vivacious wife, Ruth, who was in charge of the catering, ensured we had an enjoyable and stimulating time. We were taken to ministries, for instance, and senior civil servants came to talk to us. The whole thing helped give us a perspective on where the country was going after, for some of us, years spent on an outstation. At that stage I still believed in the Federation though I could see that ordinary people did not want it and nor did many civil servants, particularly senior officers. Nationalist politicians like Kenneth Kaunda were becoming increasingly vocal in their opposition to Federation and were increasingly pressing for independence. The latter issue worried us on the course though few of us thought that it would come in less than ten years. It seemed to me that not enough imaginative thought was being given to how the country could best be prepared for independence and how the nationalists could be persuaded that it was not a matter merely of the whites clinging on to power. When the Secretary for Native Affairs F M Thomas came to talk to us, I suggested that we should involve the Commonwealth more and perhaps take on some

Nigerian or Jamaican judges and perhaps some Indian DCs. His reaction was to turn to one of the African police officers. 'Bwalya, would you be happy to see Indian DCs in this country?' he asked. 'Oh no Sir' was the inevitable reply, and that was that. It had to be a worry though that there were at the time only a handful of African cadets and no DOs at all. A senior DO in Livingstone, John Hannah, whom I knew quite well, gave me his opinion about that time that every one of us should be shadowed by an African trainee. He was way ahead of the game. Most of us did not see the training priority as being that urgent. The signs might have been there that a rapid move towards independence was coming, but we chose not to see them and there was no real lead from the top and certainly not from the British government. It could not possibly let the country down was my feeling.

Through 1961 and 1962, life carried on very much as ever in the Southern Province. I was on tour about a third of the time. Memorable journeys included a walk to the remote Kalomo River Falls in the Zambezi escarpment country. Only two Europeans had ever been there. My erstwhile colleague and friend Jeff Stone and many years before somebody called McCabe. Access was on foot from an outlying Mukuni village and we were up before dawn and walking by 5.00 am. By mid-morning it was stinking hot and heavy going up and down steep, heavily wooded slopes. The messengers and I were in the hands of a guide from the village, and we arrived at the falls a little after 11.00 am. They were a wonderful sight: an unbroken drop of about 100 feet with a heavy volume of water falling into a deep clear pool. I could see crocodile footprints, and so I did not let Bounder swim and only took a quick plunge in and out myself. Then, feeling much refreshed, I opened a tin of Portuguese oysters from Elvinas and after discarding the more unpromising looking bits of them, put them on the ryvita biscuit I had brought, and ate them. Then I lay down under a tree for a brief rest before we needed to start back on the six-hour walk to camp. It was not long before I started to feel very queasy indeed and in a few minutes I was being violently sick. It was obviously the oysters. I drank some water and decided that, however, I felt, we had to get moving as we were in just about the remotest spot it was possible to find. As we climbed, the messengers and guide noticed I was being sick and persuaded me to drink more water. Within half an hour I was fine. Clearly I had had severe food poisoning but could thank my lucky stars that I have the sort of constitution that rapidly makes me throw up anything that is seriously not good for it. When we got into camp at sundown at about 6.30, Stephen had anticipated my very greatest want and need. It was a large glass of fresh lemon juice from trees in the village, mixed with water and plenty of sugar.

Another time I took a party of chiefs to a camp in the southern part of the Kafue National Park. There we met an experienced game warden called Mitchell. The aim of the exercise was to introduce the chiefs to an area where game of all sorts was plentiful and thus to encourage them towards conserving the environment. Mr Mitchell, his game guards and I camped out in the open under a big fig tree. I wondered whether we would be safe from lions, which could be heard roaring all round. I was reassured by being told that even were lions to wander through our camp in the night, we were in no danger as they were healthy and well fed. The chiefs were not reassured so easily, and they were relieved to be allowed to spend the night in a sort of stockade nearby. Overall their reaction to the trip was to be deeply impressed by the quantity of game and to wish that somebody could come and shoot some of it for them.

I probably toured in Simwatachela's area more than any other. The old chief was a bit of a rogue and almost totally uneducated. I liked him and he liked me calling me 'mwanawangu' (my son). His village was right at the top of the escarpment before you start to drop down nearly 3000 feet through the hills to the valley bottom and the top end of Lake Kariba at just over 1600 feet.

There were a few villages such as Pukuma in the rough escarpment country which stretches up to and past the Kalomo River to the west. The Kalomo flows into the Zambezi some 60 miles below the Victoria Falls and its awesome gorges. Between the Kalomo and the gorges is some of the roughest country in Africa. I had always wanted to get into this country which I had not really seen, apart from the quick dash to the Kalomo Falls. There was only one Simwatachela village on the valley bottom. It was called Madiongo on the Mulola River, which forms the border with the Gwembe district. I was determined to visit Madiongo and the escarpment villages in between and then go on to where the Mulola joins the Zambezi at the very top end of Lake Kariba. There was no question of going with the chief as the journey was too far and too rough for an elderly man. There was no road down the escarpment for him or for us to go by Land Rover. There had, however, been a track via somewhere called Walkers Drift, which had been used by missionaries at the turn of the century. As we set off through the woods from Simwatachela's village, we started to get views of the far distant hills and mountains of Southern Rhodesia on the other side of the lake. On that side too the people were Batonga, speaking the same language as their brothers on the plateau and in the valley on the northern side. As we bicycled along towards the first village, suddenly there were shouts ahead of me and the convoy stopped and there crossing the path was an enormous python, the biggest I have ever seen, over 20-feet long. Everyone was terrified of the animal but thankfully left it alone and it was able to continue on its way. Past Pukuma village we saw a flock of the rare and distinctive race of Zambezi escarpment guinea fowl. Soon the path became very steep and I was advised to hand my bicycle to one of the carriers. It was October and as I walked ever downwards into the valley, it got hotter and hotter. At Pukuma it must have been well into the 90s, but at Madiongo, where we arrived in mid-afternoon, it must have been 110. Stephen and the carriers had arrived and camp had been set up by the sandy Mulola River under some massive *acacia albada* trees.

The next day the villagers and Headman Madiongo were delighted to see the DO for the first time in two or three years. I took the census and discussed local issues including the damage being done to crops by elephants. Breaking camp and leaving the village, we carried on basically following the dry river bed. We stopped at the hot sulphur springs on the Mulola and carried on past hills of massive red rocks where I saw my first klipspringer. This little antelope specialises in rocky hills and can cope with virtually any slope. Meanwhile the carriers, a truly hardy bunch of men, coped wonderfully with the rough terrain and led us to a superb campsite. There beside the Mulola, just where it joins the very top end of the mighty Lake Kariba, was a magical place grazed almost lawn-like by the hippo and with large shady trees. There were numerous Egyptian geese on the grass and in the water the tail fins of fish appeared and reappeared. I suddenly realised that between us, Stephen and I had forgotten to bring my fishing rod. There were hippos, a plenty doing their honk honking as well as more crocodiles than I had ever seen before. I was used to them being very shy, but in this very remote place they were un-shy and swam with heads clearly visible. One of the messengers managed to catch a particularly large tiger fish of nearly 20 pounds and Stephen gave me a chunk for dinner cut from near the head. That night we went to sleep lulled by the roar of lions and the barking alarm calls of impala and baboons.

The next day our plan was to walk westwards and inland and then descend again to the river and walk down it and back to camp. I was looking forward to an exciting day. Though we were in Simwatachela's country, technically native reserve, the area was totally unpopulated. It was about as wild as Africa gets. We set off at dawn – two messengers, a guide and me and the dog. I had gathered beforehand that this was not tsetse fly country, so Bounder would be okay. Not far from camp we were passing along a game path through an area of very thick riverine bush when all of a sudden from almost on top of us to the right came a very loud scream or squeal followed by crashing vegetation. We had walked right onto an elephant. I caught a glimpse of it about 20 yards away and as I ran I saw the three men running down the path in front of me followed by the dog. We kept going for about 400 yards then stopped. All was quiet so off we set again. We had brought plenty of water, so as the day wore on and it became infernally hot, there were no worries there. For some reason I had not tanked up in the African way before we started, so I soon started to feel thirsty. The trouble in those circumstances is that once you start drinking, you sweat all the more and you soon get thirsty again. It becomes a vicious circle and I was right in it all day. The Africans drank virtually nothing. Soon the path broke out into open grassland and there in front of us was a wonderful herd of fat zebra. There were lots of impala too and small groups of kudu. There were not many baboons, suggesting the presence of plenty of leopards. After about three hours' walking, we arrived at a flat area of about 40 acres, bare of trees and bushes, indeed of virtually all vegetation. The ground was covered by a discoloured crust. This was indeed a rare salt pan to which, before the arrival of the white men at the turn of the century, people would travel for days to collect supplies. At about midday we turned left and soon arrived at the river. It was vast and clean and fast flowing through a series of rapids. If the crocodiles at the Mulola mouth were un-shy, here in the deep pools and bays they were positively tame and they swam around the open stretches of water showing no fear. Now the difficult part began. Though the terrain with the changing backdrop of the mighty river was beautiful, it was hard going trying to keep to the bank. There were gullies and patches of thick vegetation. It took us about six hours to get back to camp, by which time I was totally exhausted. I remember sitting in my camp chair a few yards from the water bag feeling very sore. Instead of getting up to help myself, I yelled for Stephen whose kitchen was at least 50 yards away.

The next day we returned to Madiongo and started to climb the escarpment. I must have been quite fit in those days because I was feeling strong enough to feel I wanted to carry my bicycle up the first steep 1000 feet of the escarpment. I remember thinking that if the carriers would do it so could I. It would be good for my prestige and I was young enough and fit enough, or was I? I started to suffer after about half an hour and it got worse and worse. My shoulders and arms ached and I was pouring with sweat. By mid-afternoon when we got into camp I was just about done in. Relief came in the form of a fast-flowing mountain stream which, considering the time of year, must have come from a spring in the hills. I half sat and half lay in a pool with the water gently flowing over and round me and stayed there for the rest of the afternoon.

Back at the boma, a strong report came in from the Game and Tsetse Control Officer responsible for the Zambezi Valley and escarpment area, Joe Brooks. Joe, a tough Scot and an ex-serviceman, was known as a bit of an eccentric. He had already made a name for himself in the valley rescuing game as the Kariba Lake rose. He was an expert on bush-craft and spoke excellent Tonga. His report which the DC found hilarious, told of a village of 'Amazon' women which he had heard had settled in a very remote area of Simwatachela somewhere further upstream of the Zambezi and inland from where I had toured a few months before. The village was led by a woman, who it was said could fell an ox with her bare hands. Perhaps most intriguing was the part of the report which spoke of the women ensuring that they had their way, by force if necessary, with any passing male. 'You'll have to check this one out Jonathan', said the DC with a grin on his face. Certainly I was fascinated and consulted Joe who was based 40 miles up the road at Choma. Clearly he felt the whole story was authentic and suggested that the best way to reach the area where the village was supposed to be was by following the Kalomo River down through some of the most rugged country in Africa to its confluence with the Zambezi. Meanwhile, of course, I consulted Chief Simwatachela about these renegade women. His response was brief and dismissive. He knew of them, but they were merely a bunch of whores. Joe and I were not to be put off, but as the rainy season approached, we would have to postpone any expedition until at least April. Nevertheless, I asked my farmer friend Bruce Rodwell who had his own aeroplane, if he could fly me over the escarpment country and we could try to spot the village from the air. So I asked Bruce and his wife, the local doctor, to lunch on the afternoon of our planned flight and we had various exotics such as foie gras in addition to cold meat and various salads. This was followed by tropical fruit salad and tinned cream. After coffee we headed for the airstrip carrying a bag of chocolates and some apples in case we got hungry on the plane. I had a jersey in case it got cold. It was a beautiful day, fine and hot with a scattering of clouds. As we headed down the Kalomo River flying at about 9000 feet the view was magnificent. There were a few bumps caused by air thermals, but nothing to worry about. The river at first wound its way through farms and then through uninterrupted bush. Soon we were over the escarpment which became increasingly rugged until it looked rather like the Grand Canyon. Now we were getting into the area where we should have been looking for the 'Amazon' village. Most unfortunately, by now I was feeling increasingly unwell. The thermals were becoming constant and severe. I knew I was going to be sick very soon. Bruce did not carry bags, but there were the chocolates, so I emptied them onto the back seat and used the bag. Unfortunately, the thermals got worse, and as there was nothing else I had to use the neck and then the sleeves of my jersey. Such was my condition that there was no question of a serious search for the village. Bruce told me that he had never felt sick in his life but by now he too was feeling sick. He decided to continue flying south eastwards and across the western end of Lake Kariba and we landed at a place called Binga, the district headquarters on the Southern Rhodesian side. As we got out of the plane, the outside air hit us like a blast from an oven. Having greeted an old boy keeping the grass down on the strip, we climbed back into the plane and headed off north across the lake. Over water there were no thermals, and the flight was blessedly smooth for a few minutes over the lake as we headed home.

Joe and I were never to make the trip because about March 1962 I was told I was to be transferred to Luanshya on the Copperbelt. When I went up to Lusaka to be briefed by the officer responsible for staffing, my mentor Peter Burles told me of the need for staff in the Copperbelt bomas to be strengthened in the light of increasing political activity with the onset of campaigning for the first 'one man one vote' national elections.

Before leaving for the Copperbelt, I was required for a special assignment, again connected with the forthcoming elections. The background to this was the overall intimidation and the threat of violence associated with political activity. The government had decided to mount a campaign to try to convince ordinary people that they should not doubt that their vote was secret. As I spoke Tonga, I was to be sent to a politically sensitive part of the Choma district as part of the campaign. I was to camp near groups of villages moving to a new place every day, while the public information van went round publicising the evening meetings that I would conduct. To attract the people, there was a cowboy film followed by an election film and I would round off the evening with a talk and answer questions. The theme of the black-and-white cowboy film was the usual of the hero and outsider taking on the local baddies. I remember when he put himself up for hire by the rancher, he sold himself with the words, 'well I don't kick dogs and I'm kind to old ladies'. The audiences loved the film. Any film went down well. This included the election film whose hero, Lazerus Pemtonya was his name, a worthy man, lived in a house with a portrait of the Queen on the wall. He clearly knew that *vote lyenu masiseke* (your vote is secret). The film began and ended with a song no doubt composed by the Information Department. There were three or four verses and I remember two of them.

> Oh listen to me, Oh listen to me
> Please take this matter seriously
> In October we hold elections
> Yes we are going in the right direction

> Oh listen to me, Oh listen to me
> We have our problems one, two, three
> All this talk of intimidation
> Is giving us a bad reputation.

The campaign went well though the heavily populated Choma countryside where I went could not compare with the wilds of Kalomo. Some proffered hospitality which I was not used to came one evening after the entertainment and before I went to bed. A girl approached Stephen who was clearing up the kitchen saying she had been sent by the headman in case I wanted company. I could hear the conversation with Stephen saying politely that the Bwana didn't indulge.

3

Miners and Tassle Tossers

I had never been to the Copperbelt before, with its six big towns, Ndola, the provincial capital, and the five giant copper mines at Luanshya, Kitwe, Mufulira, Chingola and Bancroft. When I passed through Lusaka, I called at the Secretariat and Peter Burles told me that the budget of the Luanshya Mine alone was bigger than that of the whole Northern Rhodesian government. Driving up on the Great North Road, the bush gets thicker and the trees larger as you get nearer the Copperbelt. At Luanshya, I went straight to see the DC, a dynamic New Zealander Phil Aldous. He put me in the picture on the local political situation which seemed mainly to involve supporters of the United National Independence Party (UNIP) led by Kenneth Kaunda, attacking the few overt supporters of the old nationalist party the African National Congress led by Harry Nkumbula. There were almost daily cases of ANC supporters being badly beaten up or killed. The very excellent Northern Rhodesian Police (NRP) was badly overstretched. The political temperature was rising as the October election approached. Our role in the boma was to plan for the election. There did not seem to be much else going on. Our relationship with the mine was underlined for me at a security meeting with senior mine staff at which the DC deferred to the general manager calling him sir. Soon after I arrived, there was a meeting for civil servants addressed by Sir John Moffat, a descendant of David Livingstone and a farmer from Mkushi. Sir John had founded a party which he hoped would bridge the gap between the black nationalist parties and the pro-federation United Federal Party supported by most whites. Because under the constitution a minimum of support from both racial groups was necessary for some urban seats, his moderate approach seemed a reasonable one. Worrying for some of us was the plunge not just to representative government but also seemingly beyond that to independence. In answer to questions, Sir John said that though he agreed that in an ideal world Britain should not be going so fast, the reality was that the British government was by now totally set on getting out of Northern Rhodesia very fast. There was no prospect at all he felt of it being dissuaded and therefore the best strategy was to accept this and try to provide a moderate political influence. I was taken aback by this analysis, feeling that this timing would be highly irresponsible and guarantee disaster for the future.

I did not stay long in Luanshya where I had been District Officer I and within a month, Stephen and his family and I found ourselves in the Copperbelt's biggest town Kitwe. There I was DO III. The boma offices were near the centre of the town and housed several government departments. Compared to a rural boma, it certainly seemed at first that there was little work to be done as I sat in my office looking out over the veranda and the lawn towards the Labour Exchange, wearing the urban DO's uniform of all-white shirt, shorts and long socks. One of my jobs was to get people who had lost the tickets for their dry cleaning to swear affidavits. I had time on my hands, so I determined that I would learn the Copperbelt majority language and the language spoken all over the Northern and Luapula provinces, Bemba, the language of Bwana Quick of Cambridge days. I wanted to try and go straight for the higher level exam, which would not only be useful but also entitle me to a £100 bonus. This would be very useful with overseas leave coming up the following year. So I set to work with my grammar book and had the messengers come into my office in rotation for practice.

The position on political violence and intimidation was even worse than in Luanshya although confined entirely to the nationalist parties. There was little violence involving whites. There were, however, two incidents at the time which I remember. One involved whites trying to prevent blacks going into a cafe in Kitwe. The situation was saved by a white member of the Northern Rhodesia rugby team, a giant front-row forward called Jumbo who single-handedly put a stop to the nonsense by physically throwing out a couple of militant whites. The other incident was the tragic murder of a white woman driving between Ndola and Mufulira who was set on fire by a mob following a political meeting and she and her dog were burnt alive in her car. Thankfully this was a one-off incident. Otherwise there was little or no public hostility towards whites. There were some burglaries, usually at night and I remember chasing and yelling at a man whom I had caught trying to climb into the bathroom of my little house. Another time my house was burgled while I was away for the weekend and the jacket of my best suit was stolen. I saw it a week later being worn by a man at the Kitwe market where I happened to be, a lone European amongst large crowds of Africans. I approached the man and asked him to explain from where he had got my jacket. He said he had bought it from a trader at the market. By this time a crowd of people had gathered around us. I asked the man to hand over the jacket. A murmur of approval from the crowd spurred him on and he handed it over. Theft of any hue is very much taboo in every African society I have lived in.

One day I was sitting in my office looking across to where the messengers sat and beyond to the Labour Exchange where there was a queue. Suddenly I saw the queue disintegrate and start chasing a man down the road. While I dashed for my car, I saw the second messenger, Smart was his name, leap on to his bicycle and ride off after the crowd. As I drove up behind, I saw Smart scoop up the man being chased. He stopped as the car approached and he and I each grabbed one of the chasers and the rest fled. It turned out that the man being chased was a Tonga from the Southern Province where they had not heard of the nationalist habit of burning identity books or *chitupas* as they were known. He had produced his to identify himself and might well have paid for this with his life. I remember the police had difficulty in knowing what charge to lay on the men we caught. My Stephen, being a moderate man and a Tonga, wanted to join the police reserve. I advised him to go and apply. He came back with a very nice letter from the officer in charge of the Kitwe police saying that much as he would have liked to take him on, he simply could not do so as Stephen was only just over five feet tall.

One episode I remember very well was the week I was sent on temporary transfer to Bancroft (now Chililabombwe). The town was smaller and newer than the other Copperbelt towns. I was needed to help out the senior DO at the boma while the DC was away on local leave. Keen on the prospect of new experiences I took off with Stephen in my car. I had packed minimal luggage as we would be temporarily accommodated in the modern house of the headmaster of the nearby school who was also away on holiday. I only remember one day at Bancroft. It was a day of so-called *cha cha cha*. This meant crowds of women blocking roads with dustbins while gangs of youths hurled stones at the police. Cha cha cha erupted regularly in the Copperbelt towns at that time and if it reflected protest, it was pointless as we were heading helter-skelter for independence. It seemed to us in the administration that it was mainly about bored urban women with not enough to occupy them in the urban environment. It had a sinister side though as there was often the scope for UNIP supporters to attack and injure, even kill, anybody they

suspected as non-members of the party. The freedom struggle was frequently
not very noble. By mid-morning I remember, reports were of widespread
chaos all over the large mine townships. The tough police mobile unit started
to arrive, and there were local police gathering outside the boma. We of the
administration were involved as technically we had a supervisory role over
the police. While the acting DC talked tactics with the police and mobile
unit chief officers, I found myself being handed a revolver and suddenly in
charge of a group of ten unarmed African policemen. We set off by Land
Rover for the township and then continued on foot until we started to see
roadblocks. We would approach these on foot and the crowd of women
would disappear as would the gangs of stone-throwing youths. For an hour
or so this was the cat and mouse pattern. We would approach slowly in a
line and the gang would disappear round a house or an anthill. I knew my
group was as keen as I to catch some stone-throwers. The next time the
latter disappeared instead of continuing at the usual slow pace, I told my
group to run hard, half going to the right and half to the left of the anthill.
Thus we burst into the clearing behind and there were the stone-throwers
who tried to scatter. We managed to grab about six of the youths who were
promptly arrested. Most unfortunately, I forgot to remember any faces, so
I was useless as a witness and I think most were acquitted when they went
to court.

Later on that day we caught a group of women. One of them was being hit hard by a constable who kept saying, 'I don't want to be your boy
friend.' It was the only time in all my years in Northern Rhodesia I had ever
witnessed violence and I was moved to intervene. By late afternoon the dis-
turbances had died down and the townships were quiet and the Mobile Unit
returned to barracks. I don't think there were any deaths that day mainly due
to the excellent work of the NRP, perhaps the finest police force in Africa.
Doubtless, our day of *cha cha cha* did not make the British press. Had it done
so I wondered whether the reports would have been all about the colonial
police brutalising the freedom-loving local population?

Considering all the violence that preceded it, the election when it came
in October was a wonderfully peaceful affair. Present at the count at the
Kitwe boma was one of the candidates for election, Sir Stuart Gore-Brown,
an elderly gentleman who had built his dream country house Shiwa Ngandu
near Chinsali in the Northern Province. He was well known, even notorious as far as whites were concerned, as an ultra liberal, but a hero to most
blacks for his unqualified support for African nationalism and UNIP. He wore

a monocle and came over as an old world figure unfailingly dignified and courteous. His failure to gain the minimum number of European votes he needed in terms of the constitution to get elected must have been a body blow for him and for many, a tragedy for the country. As the summer wore on I was thoroughly enjoying Kitwe. I had a girl friend at last, Margaret, and she would watch me play rugby or come camping with me up at Samfya on the great lake Bangwelu. In those days there was plenty of money around in Kitwe, thanks to copper prices, and there were four or five night clubs to choose from. Our favourite was the 'St Tropez' where we particularly enjoyed the resident tassel tosser. On other evenings we might go up past the mining town of Mufulira and into the Congo at Makambo where there were African run bars or shebeens where they played wonderfully rhythmic Congolese music and we met the locals, drank and danced.

At the office the DC John Adams, a South African who had been in the Nigerian administration, earned my eternal admiration and gratitude. Early in 1963 there was to be a national census and he put me in charge. It was delegation at its most effective. He briefed me thoroughly and then gave me my head saying, however, that I should not hesitate to come to him if I needed to. I felt here that for the first time in my career I was being trusted with an important complicated job by someone who had faith in me. This was hugely motivating and the exercise, which required a great deal of planning and involved training and briefing teams, each with their own leaders, went off very well. Kitwe at the time had the highest urban population in Northern Rhodesia (about 120,000) and I was singled out for compliments by the chief census officer in his report. After the census John Adams gave a party at his house to which were invited many leading Africans including teachers, traders, union leaders, civil servants and politicians. It was the first time I had been to such a gathering, and though most African men came without their wives, clearly they felt grateful and honoured to have been included. It struck me at the time and it strikes me now that though there were only a handful of South Africans in the PA, they were all outstanding and had a very clear understanding of political and racial realities. The way I saw it they seemed delighted to have had the chance of escape from the blind distortions of their own country.

About the same time the Provincial Commissioner Len Bean came to talk to boma staff about the implications of the UNIP victory at the elections. He explained that government in Lusaka would broadly be following the UNIP agenda from now on. Some of us were a bit taken aback. For me this was the event which fully brought home to me the fact of the British priority on an early pull-out. Any chance of a positive constructive forward-looking role in southern Africa disappeared for me at that point. I don't think that in hindsight the European population on the Copperbelt cared less one way or the other. Perhaps they were too preoccupied with making money or perhaps they were relieved that the dye was clearly cast. Certainly the Federation was doomed, but in the north with copper prices still high, optimism amounting perhaps to wishful thinking prevailed.

In mid-1963, I went on my first long leave to the United Kingdom. It was a pretty miserable six months, particularly after I was almost immediately ditched by Jane whom I had hoped to marry. Returning to Africa on the SS *Uganda* via the east coast we witnessed the exercise of British naval power in the form of the aircraft carriers *Centaur* and *Eagle*, which were instrumental in putting down the army mutinies in Tanzania and Kenya. Centaur had been in Aden harbour when we docked there and the news from Tanzania broke. She was gone by next morning. Forty years later, I met a retired admiral who had been serving on the ship. He told me the operation in Dar es Salaam had depended entirely on bluff and luck because the quartermaster had thought it was an exercise and the ship had sailed from Aden without ammunition.

4

Magic Lake

There was a lot to be said for a sea voyage easing you gently back into the reality of Africa. Seldom have I been fitter in my life with a combination of sea air, oppressive non-air-conditioned heat, lots of energetic deck tennis and a sleep in the afternoon after beers and hot curry. At Beira a crane lifted my Anglia estate off the Uganda's top deck and I headed into the Mozambique interior and on to Southern Rhodesia. After a night with my farmer friends the Valentines at Odzi near Umtali, it was two easy days' drive to Lusaka, where I learned at the secretariat that I was to be posted to Fort Rosebery, capital of Luapula Province. I had picked up Stephen en route and when I gave him the news, he was doubtful. 'Is it Bemba country?', he asked. 'Right in the middle', I said. I also learned that things had moved on apace during the seven months I had been away and that independence could come within a year. Anyway, off we set in the Anglia via Margaret in Kitwe and the Congo pedicle road. The pedicle is a strip of Congo territory about 40 miles wide that separates the Copperbelt from the Luapula Province. It was not dangerous to cross, but it was a tedious business coping with corrupt and shambolic officialdom whose only care was what they could extract from travellers in the way of bribes.

In one way I was delighted to be going to Fort Rosebery, as the provincial commissioner was my ex-DC from Kitwe, John Adams. I arrived on a Saturday afternoon and met the DC at the Fort Rosebery Club just after he had finished his round of golf. He helped Stephen and me settle straight into my new house in the leafy avenues housing the provincial capital's civil servants. I was not thrilled to be at the town boma, but there was plenty of work in the aftermath of Northern Rhodesia's first local government elections. Gone were the old Native Authorities, and in their place were local councils composed almost totally of newly elected UNIP councillors. Public expectations of them were sky high. Within a few days of my arrival, the

DC went on leave and the new DC – a senior DO from Kawambwa – Hugh Bown arrived. Hugh was a bachelor and a refreshingly original character. He was bright and forthright, but sometimes disorganised. When his *katundu* or goods and chattels arrived on the boma lorry from Kawambwa, it was noticed to general amusement that many of them were contained in drawers which had merely been pulled out and loaded.

I had been in Fort Rosebery only about two weeks when the provincial commissioner (PC) told me I was to be transferred to Nchelenge on Lake Mweru as district officer in charge (DO i/c). He said the present incumbent John Hart was going as DC to Samfya on Lake Bangwelu. I was thrilled. Nchelenge, a so-called sub-boma, was part of the very large Kawambwa district. It was known as probably the leading sub-boma in the whole country and contained two district councils, the erstwhile Shila and Bwila Native Authorities. It also contained the port village of Kashikishi on the lake where there was an ice plant and where the fish traders came with their trucks and lorries to load up with fresh and dried fish for the Copperbelt market. I was told that politically the Shila and Bwile were particularly militant and that councillors having been elected on the promise of no more taxes, were refusing to pass budgets. Getting on with them and persuading them on some of the realities of life was going to be the challenge. Before leaving for Nchelenge I drove down to Samfya for a detailed briefing from John Hart on the personalities and problems of Nchelenge. The next day I set off with Stephen and Bounder on the 100-mile journey to Kawambwa to meet the DC there, Ian Harper. Ian promised me all possible help and support. Technically, I reported to him, but the reality was that mainly one was on one's own and in many circumstances instructions or policy would come direct from the provincial commissioner in Fort Rosebery.

Stephen and I set off after lunch to drive the 50 or so miles to Nchelenge. Unlike the Southern Province, the population density in some parts of this province was high and we passed through a great many villages with suicidal chickens, lots of dogs and many more fruit trees such as bananas, guavas, oranges, pawpaws and mangos than in the drier south. Soon we were climbing through heavily wooded country and then we broke out and in front of us as far as the eye could see was the Luapula Valley with the massive Lake Mweru nearly 100-miles long and 30-miles wide, sparkling in the far distance. I have to admit to a wonderful stimulating feeling that this was all to be mine. Then it was down the hill to the valley bottom and the beginning of what was sometimes called the longest high street in the world, mile after mile of villages. Here the deep alluvial soil would grow rice and pineapples and I noticed giant avocado pear trees along the road.

Nchelenge was all that I had expected. The boma with its long veranda looked out over a well-tended lawn and flowerbeds. It was less than 100 yards to the lake shore. There, as at the seaside, waves lapped along a white sandy beach. To the right of the boma beside the lake, a road led to the stores, a prison and the messenger's lines. To the left along the shoreline were six officers' houses and a guest house. My house, which was nearest to the boma, was slightly larger than the rest. There was a stone-built archway covered with an abundantly flowering golden shower, leading to the garden and the front door. The lawn stretched through the trees to the water's edge. To me the setting was total perfection. Later, from my office where I sat talking to the two district assistants Francis Jere and Tim O'Hara and enjoying a welcome cup of tea, I could see the two government boats, *MV Mpumbu* and *MV Luapula*, riding at anchor.

One didn't have much time to settle in when moving to a new job in the PA. My first priority was getting to know my staff. I soon came to appreciate that the 17 messengers were a very fine bunch of men. Not long before my arrival, one of them, a big man in every way, had rescued a poor fellow who was being attacked for supposedly being anti-UNIP by a crowd at a gathering up the lake at Puta. He had entered the crowd, handcuffed the man to himself and led him to safety. He was on his own. It was a huge act of bravery and selflessness, typical of the wonderfully loyal and dedicated district messenger service. He deserved a medal.

Among the first things I did at Nchelenge was to take a walk with the dog away from the boma and along the valley road with its houses on both sides surrounded by avocado, guava and pawpaw trees. All along the way to my surprise, I found the people incredibly friendly and forthcoming. Of course the greetings were all in Bemba, so I could see that my language skills were going to be tested. I also visited Kashikishi and introduced myself to John Sillitoe, manager of the ice plant serving the fish traders who came in their trucks to take the local bream to the Copperbelt. We were to become good friends. He was the son of an ex-northern policeman, Percy Sillitoe who had once been stationed at Nchelenge and was to become Sir Percy and head of MI5. Kashikishi was the first example I had seen of teeming indigenous African enterprise. One example was the spotlessly clean restaurant run by Kazembe Chimfuntu, who also made bread and courageously refused to have anything to do with politics. It was not long before I went to his

establishment for a mixed grill. At Kashikishi too there was a hospital run
by the Roman Catholic White Fathers and I went and introduced myself to
the Mother Superior in charge. She was Irish and struck me as a thoroughly
down-to-earth person. It was not many days before I was to meet her again.

One evening a little after dark, I was sitting in my house when there was
a bang on the door and there was the messenger on duty at the prison in an
agitated state. 'All the prisoners were being sick', he said. It seemed that
they might have been affected by anti-mosquito spray. I hurried over to the
prison with him and there sure enough were all the prisoners, about 20 of
them, kneeling in a line-up against the wall and apparently vomiting. This was
extremely serious and as I leapt into my Land Rover to drive to Kashikishi
Hospital I had visions of a national scandal involving prisoners being poisoned
by the administration. At the hospital, it was the Mother Superior herself
who came to the main door. I breathlessly told her what had happened. She
seemed very calm, even slightly amused. 'Would you be dealing with the
problem from the top end or the bottom end?' she asked. 'From the bottom
end', I ventured. She gave me a dozen large bottles of clear liquid and advised
me to dispense about a quarter of a glass per man. By now of course, I was
conscious that I was in all probability a victim of one of the 'try-ons' which
new incumbents in all walks of life so often face in Africa. I was relieved but
mindful that I needed to get my own back. On my return to the prison, I
more than doubled the dose. From the fact that the next day there arose not
one further peep from the prisoners, I gathered the results had been pretty
volcanic.

Actually the prison at Nchelenge was a happy place. The regime was not
onerous and there was always the implied threat that any real trouble from an
individual would result in him being transferred to the prison at Kawambwa
where life was much tougher. With us, prisoners thrived on the standard
prison diet which included maize meal as the staple. This, instead of the local
cassava or manioc which had little food value by comparison, was combined
with fish, vegetables and fruit. Invariably, the prisoners put on weight. When
Margaret came up from the Copperbelt to stay, the prisoner who took her
for a row on the lake confided to her that it was even possible for a prisoner
at Nchelenge to have a woman. The prisoners who wore white floppy canvas
uniforms gave me no more problems or worries and they worked away in the
boma gardens and in officers' vegetable patches. In the Southern Province it
had been considered that the latter practice might be regarded as a sort of
corruption, but here in the Luapula, why should one break with tradition?

The prisoners were a cheerful lot and there was one man who I remember was always on light duties supposedly because of a bad leg, usually weeding the boma lawn. I can't remember his name, but he was a cheerful rascal. One morning I thought of a plan to get him. Walking across the veranda and onto the lawn where he was sitting weeding with his back to the lake, suddenly I shouted at him in Bemba, 'Jackson stand up and come here now.' He leapt to his feet and came running across the lawn towards me with no sign of a limp and to the great amusement of the messengers and other prisoners who were watching.

Of course Nchelenge could be lonely for a young bachelor whose thoughts when he was not too busy often turned to sex. The fact that one might eschew relations with local girls for reasons of the supposed dignity of one's position did not mean that one was not sorely tempted at times. One such occasion was when a couple with a baby came to stay in the guest house. The husband was doing an audit I think. One Saturday afternoon the couple decided to drive to the top of the lake leaving the baby with its nanny at the guest house for the afternoon. The nanny was a really beautiful local girl of about 16. Stephen had gone home after lunch, the guest house was empty and the nanny found reason to bring the baby over to my house next door. The weather was hot and the sultriness was matched by the general demeanour of the girl who wandered between the sitting room and the kitchen in a highly evocative and provocative way. She didn't say anything. She didn't have to. She knew perfectly well the effect she was having on me. She oozed sex appeal to match her come-hither look. I was literally sweating from the struggle within myself and came within an ace of cracking.

One event involving the prison was of real significance. Over the years as UNIP established itself as the only political party in the north, there were not too many people who were courageous or foolish enough to stand up against them. The two exceptions were the Lumpa Church, of which more later, and the Watch Tower or Jehovah's Witness Sect. The Jehovah's Witnesses' beliefs forbade them from political activity. UNIP did not take kindly to this and threatened that when they came to power they would find ways of getting their own back. So with the election of a UNIP local council, one of its first acts was to ban the Jehovah's Witnesses from carrying out the door-to-door preaching which was at the very heart of their beliefs. One day I was in my office when a chief's *kapasu* arrived with 13 prisoners, seven men and six women, several of whom had small babies or toddlers. They had all been given fines by the chief's court, which they had refused to pay, and so had been sentenced to three months in prison. I looked at the case record and asked the respectfully assembled people if in the event of my releasing them, they would continue to preach house to house. With a single voice they said they would. I felt rather like Pontius Pilate. However, I reduced the sentences to a single month and via provincial headquarters referred the case to the governor for a ruling as to whether the new council law was in accordance with the constitution. The prisoners all thanked me in unison and were led off to the prison. The problem was that there was not nearly enough room nor were there enough uniforms. So they all went off to empty houses in the messengers lines and were allowed to wear their own clothes. As the days and weeks passed, they showed themselves to be thoroughly nice, hardworking and God-fearing people. On the day of their release they came to thank me. That very day came the ruling from Lusaka that the new Lunda Council Law was unconstitutional, so I was able to tell the people that they were free to continue their house-to-house preaching. Thinking about it, the case which reflected very badly on UNIP should have attracted the attention of the local media, perhaps even the British press. We were still a British colony after all. The latter, however, seemed to me to show no interest or understanding of the difficult and sometimes dangerous job we were doing in the run-up to independence. Somehow in its eyes, we remained the oppressors.

Though by arrangement with DC Kawambwa I had dealings with Chief Kambwali who lived just up the valley road from the boma, and with the Lunda Council, my main responsibilities were the two erstwhile Native Authorities for the small Shila and Bwile tribes up the lake beyond Kashikishi. The Shila headquarters was at a place called Mununga halfway up the lake. The Bwile HQ was 40 miles further up the road at Puta, with its wonderful views of the top of the lake where it turns west towards the Congo. At Puta there was one of the oldest of Northern Rhodesia's old bomas, Chiengi. It was a large, well-preserved thatched mud brick house dating from the turn of the century. On my first trip up the lake, I called on the two chiefs as well as on the local authority staff. Chief Mununga was a crusty old man in poor health. I wrote in my diary that 'It must be galling for him seeing his power and his hold over his people usurped by what he probably regards as upstart elected members of the Shila Council'. He revealingly remarked to me how his grandfather had found it convenient to sell off local bad hats to Arab slave traders. The Shila regarded themselves as superior to the Bwile, of whom they would say dismissively *Babwile balalima panshi* or 'The Bwile plant their crops low down' (i.e. not on ridges). The Bwile Chief Puta was a younger, better educated man. At the local authority, the Chief Councillor Edward Chishimba Mumba turned out to be sophisticated, intelligent and switched on to local political realities. For the Shila and Bwile Councils, these were difficult times. All the councillors belonged to UNIP and had promised voters that when they were in power, there would be no more taxes of any sort. Since their election, they had spent most of their time at unofficial meetings at which they seemed to do little more than discuss and determine on the multiplicity of allowances to which they would be entitled. The basic problem was that they were refusing to pass a budget as that would involve raising money from taxes, which they had promised would be abolished. Their allowances were being paid from the government subsidy, which government was increasingly reluctant to pay. On the way back to Nchelenge from Puta, I passed the turning towards Mweru Wantipa, a vast area of lake and marsh between Lake Mweru and the southern end of Lake Tanganyika. Apparently, Mweru Wantipa has just about the highest concentration of crocodiles in the world and is surrounded by wonderfully wild and virtually uninhabited bush country. I resolved to get up there as soon as work pressures allowed.

Back at Nchelenge I was getting on particularly well with the District Assistant Tim O'Hara, who was very conscientious and hardworking. Others in the officers' houses along the lake shore were the Fisheries Officer Mbaye, who had recently graduated in India; Bill Mporokoso from a government training agency whose name I forget; Pop Adams from the Royal Society for the Blind and researching the locally very prevalent river blindness, and Francis Jere, graduate and the second district assistant. I found Jere lazy and lacking in motivation. He did not compare for effectiveness with Tim, and so I was astounded when all of a sudden he was promoted to shadow one of the top jobs in Lusaka. When I expressed my surprise to the PC, he said in effect, 'You ain't seen nothing yet.' Those were hectic days in May and June 1964. We kept getting ministerial visits which took up a lot of time. You never knew who the ministers were going to turn up with. It was the first time I had lived in a community including Africans on equal terms, and luckily we got on well together. Tim and I resurrected the tennis court which had become overgrown, using prison labour. Friends like Ewen and Jean Pinsent and their children would come up for weekends from Fort Rosebery to play tennis and fish. For them it was like a weekend at the seaside. The social highlight was the Governor Sir Evelyn Hone's visit. Then every road on the boma was picked clear of weeds, the trees along the avenue painted white at the base and the grass slashed all the way down to the beach. I had a flagpole put up in my garden and the Union Jack fluttered proudly as the 30 or so guests including civil servants, local politicians, chiefs and sisters from Kashikishi Hospital took tea under the trees beside the lake.

At work I was keeping things going while Tim was away with his fiancée Jane and her parents visiting the fabulous Nyika Plateau on the Northern Rhodesia–Nyasaland border. One day I had an unusual visitor. He was a British Army Major called Bruce Hamilton and he came with full recommendations from the Pinsents who had known him in Scotland and a request to be nice to him. We were in the interim period between the break-up of the Federation and independence, and Britain had reassumed responsibility for Northern Rhodesia's defence. We were right on the border, with the mountains of the Congo clearly visible 40 or so miles away across the lake. The possibility of trouble coming from the notoriously unstable Congo was ever present. There was a brisk trade with the Congo, mainly their bottled Simba beer for our dried fish. Bruce Hamilton and I got on very well. We started with a game of tennis in mid-morning followed by a trip in the *MV Luapula* across the lake to a nearby peninsular where the tiger fishing was particularly good. We had a picnic and beers and returned to the boma in mid-afternoon. Now we had duck shooting on the programme. I had my trusty, tough .410 shotgun, which was a rebored .303 service rifle with a bolt action. For Bruce we went to the boma armoury and picked up a double-barrel 12-bore police riot gun. Then we drove to a spot on the marshes where the Luapula River enters the lake. The little village boys ran beside the Land Rover shouting and waving their welcome. I had arranged a dugout canoe with two boatmen and Bruce and I climbed aboard. Soon we were out in deep water amongst floating islands growing with papyrus. There were a lot of ducks around on their evening flightings, mainly whistlers and knobnose. Then suddenly a pair of pygmy geese appeared flying very fast and parallel to us about 25 yards away. Bruce brought them both down with a left and a right. 'Wonderful', said the boatmen with one voice.

At work the main challenge remained to get the two local authorities to approve budgets and to start raising money. I had done quite a lot of spadework in this direction with council staff and elected members. When the Shila Council met at Mununga, members sat round a table spread with the Union Jack and the council passed a resolution to send loyal greetings to the Queen. After all this the budget was passed and shortly after the Bwile followed suit. My stock with the provincial commissioner rose.

Across Lake Mweru, only a few hundred yards from the Congolese shore lies Kilwa Island, so named by Arab slave traders after the island of Kilwa Msoko off the east coast of southern Tanzania. I have always been fascinated by islands and this one was the shape of an equilateral triangle, each side being about five miles long. The island was fairly well known for its resident herd of rare puku antelope. I wanted to go to Kilwa to see the headman and to call on the Congolese chef de poste at the little town of Kilwa Mulenga facing the island. I was reluctant to travel on the boma boat, the *MV Luapula*, which was said to be not very reliable and I was put off by its resident population of numberless enormous cockroaches all eating anything including each other. The opportunity of a much more agreeable means of transport came with an invitation from the Provincial Fisheries Officer Tim Carey to accompany him on the spacious and magnificent *MV Mpumbu* with its superstructure built on what looked like an old whaler. It was clean, reliable and flew the blue ensign. We embarked after lunch at Nchelenge transferring to the *Mpumbu* on its small boat. There was much amusement from the prisoners, all lake and river people, who were loading our gear, at Stephen's obvious terror at the first boat trip of his life.

By mid-afternoon we were at anchor in a small bay near Kilwa's main village. I paid a visit to the headman and was presented with lots of paw-paws and other fruit and was back on board with Tim well before sundown. There was almost no wind and a wonderful sunset, of the sort that requires just a little cloud near the horizon, was developing. We had a few casts for tiger fish, flinging our spoons with metal trace 50 or more yards. Within 20 minutes we had each caught two fish all between five and ten pounds with beautiful silver, red and black colouring and fearsome rows of sharp, pointed teeth like a cat. But by now the ducks were beginning to flight, so we put down our rods and stood with shotguns at the ready. We had some wonderful shooting and bagged several ducks for our, the messengers' and the boatmen's dinners. Then we sat on the deck in the fading light with our beers and the backdrop of the Congolese mountains and the verdant island. In this beautiful remote peaceful place, it was impossible not to be filled with almost perfect happiness. For dinner we had duck generously spiced with the tiny *piri piri* chillies. Slavers were reputed to have put their victims to a slow agonising death by feeding them a few dozen. The next day was something of a contrast. After breakfast we had a short trip in *Mpumbu* and then a row to the beach at Kilwa Mulenga town to call on the local administrator and the head of the army garrison. Though it was barely eight in the morning,

Off on tour on *MV Mpumbu*, Lake Mweru, 1964

we soon found ourselves in a local bar being pressed with a continuous flow of Simba beer. It was the first time in my life I had ever drunk alcohol at that time of day. I can't say I enjoyed the experience, but by the time we were able to extract ourselves after almost two hours, Tim and I were decidedly under the weather. As it turned out, it was in more ways than one. The wind had got up and following a choppy crossing in the small boat, we found the rather top heavy *Mpumbu* rolling and pitching at anchor. Never a very good sailor or indeed traveller, I felt increasingly ill as we headed off across the lake into the bad weather. Things got worse as besides the effects of the alcohol, we were seasick and worst of all the piri piri from the night before was playing simultaneously havoc with our constitutions. In short, the two-hour voyage to Nchelenge was the most uncomfortable of my life.

Mpumbu was soon to feature in a new adventure. The PC had been on the radio. 'Provincer here Jonathan', he said. 'Yes Sir.' 'We have been getting intelligence reports from the British Consulate General in Elizabethville that there are Muleleist rebels making their way south. There's no danger yet but they may eventually get to Pweto in the Congo at the northern end of the lake and I'd like you to check on the British missionaries there and at Lukonzolwa. You must get them to agree that if we tell them to evacuate they will do so.' So within a day or two, off I set up the lake in *Mpumbu* with blue ensign fluttering and with five or six messengers. We spent the first night in a sheltered anchorage off Puta and the next day crossed the lake to Pweto in the northwest corner near the place where the Luvua River flows out of the lake. It was a sunny morning when we dropped anchor just off Pweto from where across the white sandy beach I could see an official-looking building painted dark blue and white. As the messengers and I approached the shore in the dingy, I felt decidedly under-dressed. There drawn up in front of the government offices was the entire army garrison led by a splendidly attired and bemedalled officer. I was merely dressed in the standard shorts and knee-length stockings as for a day's golf at Woodbridge or Aldeburgh. After inspecting the military, there on hand was the administrator accompanied by a very small European woman wearing glasses. After the courtesies, I explained the purpose of my visit to the administrator in very general terms, taking care not to give him the impression that I thought a Muleleist invasion was imminent or even likely. I did say, however, that if at any time there was to be any trouble, we in Northern Rhodesia would not tolerate anybody, refugees or others, bringing arms into the country. The administrator accepted my point and I turned to the lady missionary. She immediately invited me to lunch and to spend the night at the mission after I had been shown around the town by the administrator. As we did our tour all seemed peaceful. There was not much in the shops, however, apart from tinned food clearly marked as being the gift of various aid agencies. Given the prevailing rate for my sterling area pounds, it was incredibly cheap.

Up at the mission, the four British ladies told me that they were the only qualified staff at the hospital. They had been working there through all the traumas over the past four years since independence. There had been the Katangese military and the Congolese army, and Katangese rebels and the United Nations. Though occupied at times by various factions, they had been able to continue working. They made it clear that being used to dire times, they would be most reluctant to leave. However, they promised to do so if we told them it was absolutely necessary. Before leaving next morning for Lukonzolwa, I lined them up for a photo which, I remember thinking, would be useful in the event of some tragic development. Back in *Mpumbu*, we headed along the Congolese coast past the gorge where the mighty Luvua, which becomes the Congo further downstream, leaves Lake Mweru. The shoreline is pretty dull along the western side of the lake. It slopes steeply for the first hundred or so feet before reaching a flat shelf. We anchored opposite a path leading upwards. I took a couple of messengers and we climbed up and up, and then suddenly we emerged into an English rose garden. To go with this was an elderly, very English looking lady with her back to us apparently pruning the roses. Suddenly, she stood up and turned and said, 'Good God a white man.' We introduced ourselves and she said she was the head of the mission, Miss Salisbury. She said she and her deputy, also British, were the only Europeans left on the mission following the traumatic years after Congolese independence. The nearby large thatched house where they lived had been built before the turn of the century when the mission was founded. It seemed that the mission hospital now run by the younger woman following the departure of the male doctor was the only hospital in the Congo for literally hundreds of miles. I was asked to dinner and to stay the night. Miss Salisbury said she was particularly pleased to see the messengers, whose presence even for one night would have a steadying influence in the sometimes volatile atmosphere of the compound.

Over dinner I heard of continuous war, chaos, brutality, fear and suffering. Following the departure of the doctor, the younger woman frequently had no choice but to carry out as best she could the most difficult and sophisticated surgery. It was often the only hope in the face of certain death. As we talked, I became increasingly conscious of the truly extraordinary dedication, selflessness and bravery of these two outstanding women. Their motivation was pure love and compassion. When the conversation turned to politics, they said that reluctantly they had, after much agonising, reached the conclusion that white supremacy South African style was the only answer for Africa.

Back at Nchelenge, we were soon to face problems of our own. Chief Kambwali, the Lunda chief who had sentenced the Jehovah's Witnesses, had had a visit from a certain Alice Lenshina a few years before. Alice Lenshina, the leader of the Lumpa Church, was a charismatic character with firebrand skills as an orator and rabble-rouser. Lumpa followers combined Christian doctrine with African spiritual beliefs. In common with Jehovah's Witnesses, they refused to become involved in politics. They had had the courage to stand up to the all-powerful UNIP. As with the Jehovah's Witnesses, the party had said that when it gained power, the Lumpas would pay for their intransigence. With the advent of a UNIP government, trouble loomed, particularly in the Chinsali, Isoka and Lundazi districts far to the east. It was said that Alice Lenshina, who was supposed to have special powers, had come to see Chief Kambwali in connection with a cure for his gonorrhoea. While she was in the area, she had converted significant numbers of people living along the long valley high street to her religion. Several Lumpa churches had been built along the stretch of road near Nchelenge.

With the troubles getting worse and the flare-up of Lumpa/UNIP violence in the Northern and Eastern Provinces leading to several deaths, the army had been brought in to the worst affected areas. It also looked as if the Lumpa Church was likely to be banned. The story of the Lumpa troubles has been told by John Hudson, who was DC Isoka at the time, in his fascinating book *A Time to Mourn*. There was dreadful violence and the police and army were involved in trying to keep the two sides apart and restore order. Many villagers, both UNIP and Lumpa Church followers, were killed. Aside from the troubles, of great interest to me was the way the new government saw and faced up to them. We remained in mid-1964 a British colony and protectorate, but UNIP was in power on the ground and directing policy at the centre. The question that arises is whether without UNIP involvement the Lumpa problems would have or should have been dealt with differently, so as to avoid the eventual very heavy death toll. As it was, following the bloodiest period in Northern Rhodesia's history, peace was restored, Alice Lenshina was incarcerated in Zambia and many of her followers were exiled to the Congo.

For us at Nchelenge there had been no trouble, but as a precaution, two companies of the Northern Rhodesia Police Mobile Unit had been sent up from the Copperbelt. They arrived a couple of days before the government announced the banning of the Lumpa Church. The mobile unit had the reputation of being tough and well disciplined, but neither officers nor men were necessarily chosen for their intellect. The banning became effective on a Saturday. Though the unit was on standby, one of the two European officers called in for a drink at my house at lunch time that day. As we sat on the lawn under the trees, he told me that following the banning announcement, UNIP officials had asked him to provide a police presence that afternoon while they organised party workers in the demolition of the churches. I said, 'What?'

or some stronger expletive and jumped into the Land Rover and drove down to Kashikishi at breakneck speed. There I found all the main UNIP officials sitting in a circle near the fish market drinking beer. This was the audience I needed. With little ceremony I told them that if anybody so much as laid a finger on one of those churches or on the Lumpa followers, there would be monumental trouble for the individual, for them as a group and for UNIP. There were no questions or comments. None were needed. I got back into the Land Rover and drove back to the boma. We had no trouble, and within a week the mobile unit had returned to the Copperbelt.

We remained very worried about what was going on in the Congo. My sister Veronica and her husband David and two-year-old son Charles, happened to be on a Unilever-owned estate at Elizabetha on the Congo River downstream from Stanleyville. If we had cause for concern more than a thousand miles to the south, surely there was great cause for concern about the area around Stanleyville. I mentioned to the sisters at Kashikishi Hospital that Veronica was expecting a baby in August and they very kindly suggested that I should invite her to come down and have the baby with them. Veronica, for understandable reasons, declined the invitation. Apart from anything else, the travel logistics were pretty horrific. It was, however, not long before to my horror I heard that the Muleleist rebels had taken Stanleyville. It was a month or so later that I learned that on the Elizabetha estate, they heard that the rebels were moving down the river and an immediate evacuation of all whites was necessary. Veronica and Charles were flown out by the company to Kinshasa, where she immediately gave birth to Jessica. David and colleagues evacuated themselves by barge provisioned with a case of champagne.

Meanwhile in Fort Rosebery as well as Nchelenge, concerns over the Congo were growing. I was called to the radio to speak to the PC, who told me that intelligence reports indicated that it was time to tell the missionaries at Pweto and Lukonzolwa to evacuate as the rebels had reached Albertville on Lake Tanganyika and were moving south. I promptly sent off messengers bearing the necessary instruction. After a few days, back came the messengers with a letter. The missionaries were very sorry not to be able to stick to their undertaking, but their information was that the rebels were a long way off and presented no immediate threat. And that was it. The rebels never got down to Pweto. I was about to move on.

5

A Valley and a Dam

One morning in August, the PC came on the radio again to tell me that I had been promoted and should travel down to Gwembe in the Southern Province and take over immediately as DC. I was thrilled and exhilarated. Gwembe was a very important district, stretching some 200 miles from the Mulola River downstream of the Victoria Falls (where I had camped two years before) right down to the confluence of the Kafue River with the Zambezi. It took in the whole northern side of the Kariba Dam, then the world's biggest man-made lake held back by a dam built to provide hydro-electric power for the Federation as a whole. There were government programmes for resettling and training people for their new life. These included the Gwembe Special Fund whose money came from the Federal Power Board. Many thousands of people of the Tonga tribe had to be resettled only four years previously to make way for the spreading waters. I knew that many problems remained following resettlement. I knew too I was highly honoured to get the job. In the normal course of events I could not have aspired to such promotion. But independence was approaching and many senior officers were due to leave the country. I was still only 27 and had been serving for less than four and half years. Having been able to cope at Nchelenge, I was sure I could do the job.

Of course Stephen was thrilled at the news. He was such a genuinely nice man that contrary to his early fear, he had got on very well at Nchelenge. Now he was going home again. I left him to pack my goods and chattels onto the boma lorry whilst I went to stay with Margaret at Kitwe for a day or two so that my arrival at Gwembe would coincide with his. And so it transpired.

Gwembe boma is a mere 15 miles from the Great North Road and the line of rail at Chisekesi near Monze. It is at 4400 feet and literally on the lip of the Zambezi escarpment. From the boma the road descends steeply into the valley via the old Native (now Local) Authority headquarters at

Munyumbwe and down to the port of Chipepo at just over 1600 feet. There were roads along the valley bottom to the two sub-bomas. The latter were down the lake at Siavonga near the Kariba Dam wall and 60 miles up the lake at Sinazongwe. Originally the inhabitants, the Valley Tonga, had lived mainly along the alluvial flood plain of the Zambezi. Now they were resettled in the mainly dry infertile interior. On arrival at Gwembe, I stayed in the DC's charming guest house in the garden of what was to be my new home. My predecessor Bill Oliver and his wife, a doctor who worked at our local Gwembe hospital and nearby leper colony, were most hospitable. I gathered that they were not unhappy to be leaving. Bill suggested that we set off more or less immediately for Chipepo where we would board the famous *MV Guimbe* the DC's 47-foot motor launch and go up the lake to Sinazongwe and thence to visit my counterpart at Binga, the Rhodesian district on the southern side of the lake. We were driven down to the lake by driver Benjamin Shipopo and were accompanied by Head Messenger Mwene Falls. It being now mid-August, Gwembe was getting hot but the temperature was mild compared to the valley heat at Chipepo. Still, I never feel too hot beside water and we set off from Chipepo harbour with Mwene Falls and our crew of two and with the Union Jack fluttering at the stern. It was a three-hour voyage to Sinazongwe where we called for me to meet the District Assistant in Charge Sandy Macdonald. Then we carried on for another three hours to Binga. Along the way we passed numerous islands, some with game on them. The most notable of these was Chete, 30 miles square with plenty of elephants on it in those days and very close to the southern side. It was ours because the border was the old line of the river which had flowed through the Chete Gorge between what is now the island and the Chete Peninsular. By now it was mid-afternoon and we got on to the VHF lake safety net radio to alert Binga of our arrival. There we met the DC Ian Findlay whose house was at the township way up on the first rung of the south's much gentler escarpment. Ian and his wife, Pat, proved very hospitable; tea was followed by gins and tonics. Ian clearly thought that Northern Rhodesia was on totally the wrong track and was keen to indicate sympathy for us as our independence approached. We demurred but conversation revolved around what was best for Africa and whether it would not soon be overrun by the Chinese. Meanwhile Bill had said he wanted to get back to Sinazongwe that night from where he could drive to Livingstone where he had been summoned to see the PC. More gins followed and when finally we had been persuaded to spend the night, he was saying that he 'never liked the bugger anyway'.

The Olivers left Gwembe within a day or two and I settled into my lovely house with its large avocado pear tree laden with tiny fruit the size of hen's eggs and the most delicious I had ever had. There was a wonderful view right over the escarpment hills. The house itself was large, with a long wide ve randa at the front behind mosquito gauze. Beside the house were a disused swimming pool and an equally disused tennis court. The guest house was charming and made of wood. At night there was the wonderful rippling call of nightjars which send me to sleep even faster than the call of frogs. Not quite so lulling was the regular nightly call of a hyena which used to come to clear up the offal and other remains left by the butcher who operated at the compound a quarter of a mile away. The boma offices were pretty standard. I had a large office which made me feel very important with a large green coir mat carpet. I had a secretary. Her name was Tuppy Mitchell; she was married to the agricultural officer, Crighton Mitchell, and she came from an old pioneer family. Crighton was a grizzled Scot and steeped in experience of the valley resettlement. Tuppy wore the trousers in her quiet way. She came over at first as not having much to say and when she did, of being gruff and monosyllabic. I soon learned that this was only the exterior. Still, I was a bit of a pipsqueak of just 28, and she knew far more about the country and the district than me. I stood to gain from her experience and of course I was keen to take advantage of this and of her advice if I could get her to give it. The chance came within a few days. Between the boma and the officers' houses, the compound, the hospital, the leper colony and the prison was open park-land. The grass was kept short by regular slashing by prisoners and a small seven-hole golf course had been laid out there with sand greens. Regular attention meant that the grass though short was pretty lush. I noticed that there were 30 or 40 cattle which appeared every day to graze it. I asked Tuppy if they had a right to be there. She said 'No' but that my predecessor had felt that relations with the nearby headman to whom the cattle belonged might be damaged if anything was done to remove them. Clearly Tuppy saw things differently and so did I. So I sent a messenger to ask the headman not to graze his cattle on boma land. The next day they were back, so I arranged for them to be driven there and then 15 miles to the public pound in Chisekesi. There they would be available for collection on payment of a shilling or two per beast. I never saw another cow on the boma and I earned a good mark from Tuppy and developed excellent relations with the headman.

A few days after the takeover, examining the contents of my desk, besides a rhino horn, I found a file stamped 'W'. This was the designation for files mainly concerned with security which it had been considered necessary to burn prior to independence of Zambia and the handover of power to a new nationalist government. The file contained copies of correspondence about all the problems of displacement and resettlement of the Valley Tonga people to make way for the Kariba Lake. All the correspondence sent to DC Gwembe was there. There were letters from the Northern and Southern Rhodesian governments, the provincial commissioner in Livingstone and the DCs at Kariba and Binga, as well as records of meetings. It was obviously an historical document of great interest. I decided not to burn it, and I have it to this day.

It was not difficult to settle down at Gwembe. Jim Michie, the DO, was very helpful and of course Tuppy was a mine of background information. Moving between districts in Northern Rhodesia was always made easier by the uniformity of systems and procedures and of course the backbone of the district administration were the district messengers. Mwene Falls, the head messenger, was a man who was always cheerful, positive and thoroughly straightforward. I knew from the start that he would say what he thought, not what he thought I wanted to hear. From him, Jim and Tuppy, bit by bit I gained an appreciation of the size of the challenges which confronted me and the enormity of the responsibility with which I had been entrusted. Before the Kariba Dam was built a few years before and had started to fill in 1960, the Tonga people had lived for centuries in their villages along the banks of the great Zambezi River, between Devil's Gorge, below Victoria Falls and the Kariba Gorge 200 miles to the east. The low altitude, nearly 3000 feet below the cool plateau, meant there was a different climate down there. It was one that had discouraged European visitors, even missionaries and it was only the odd intrepid district officer who ever ventured down there. Left alone thus to live their lives according to their age-old traditions, the Valley Tonga valued their privacy. For them life along the Zambezi flood plain was relatively easy. After the flood waters had receded, they planted their mealies, millet and especially their giant sorghum in the rich alluvial soil washed down by the river in the annual flood. The Valley Tonga had cattle too, tough beasts well acclimatised and not dependent on the sparse grass because they browsed the leaves of the trees and bushes. Were the valley cattle to be taken up to the plateau, they would die.

Although they enjoyed their privacy, the valley people were not anti-government. Quite the contrary. From the days of David Livingstone whose travels took him through the valley, they had regarded Europeans as their protectors from the Arab slaver traders or Matabele cattle raiders. Besides going bare-breasted and smoking their huge 'hubble bubble' gourd pipes, the women stuck a short piece of wood through the lower part of their noses where it meets the upper lip. They also knocked out their front teeth. All this was regarded as enhancing their beauty but the habit may have originated in a practice designed originally to do the very opposite and make them less likely to be taken off by the slavers. Few valley women ever ventured out of the valley. The young men did occasionally and by tradition, many used to work at the Bulawayo power station for the money to pay their taxes and little else. Only a very few ventured up to the Copperbelt mines or even Lusaka.

With the decision to build the Kariba Dam destined to become the biggest man-made lake in the world, life for the Valley Tonga suddenly changed forever. All the people living along the river, in seven chiefs' areas, had to move, either into the interior, or to Lusitu downstream of the great dam and the Kariba Gorge. For the Valley Tonga, as it would be for any African living in the region, this was a step that could barely be contemplated. Besides the loss of their land, there was the prospect of leaving the burial sites of their ancestors whose spirits governed their lives and their future prospects. Besides, they were not inclined to accept that the river could ever be tamed by building a mere wall across it. They wanted to believe this was impossible and were persuaded by nationalist politicians that the white man wanted to steal their land. Back went the district officers whom they had always trusted, to persuade them that their land would be flooded and that they had to move. Once persuaded, however, back came the politicians to tell that what they wanted to hear. And so it went on. The district officers persisted and gradually the people began to move, loading their belongings on to lorries provided by the government. It was only in Chief Chipepo's area that there was a serious confrontation and a stand-off between villagers and the police mobile unit. Tragically eight villagers were shot dead but the resettlement of some 30,000 people was completed. By contrast, on the Southern Rhodesia side of the river the government there had not attempted consultation. The people there were firmly told they had to move, and they did. I would be seeing a lot of them in 16 years' time in 1980.

Though life was incredibly busy in the run-up to independence now set for 24 October, it was top priority to get around my district, get to know the men in charge of the sub-bomas and visit the chiefs. I think that my appointment had gone down well with them as they were worried not by the prospect of a new government led by UNIP but at the prospect of losing still more power to local politicians. My job was to try to reassure them and demonstrate continuity. To get around the district there was the *MV Guimbe* for the journeys to Sinazongwe and Siavonga, but most of the chiefs lived inland and in between, so most of my travels were by Land Rover. My companions on these journeys were Mwene Falls and driver Benjamin Shipopo. Both were men about 50. Though both spoke only Tonga with me, they knew a little English. Mwene Falls had already rejected the option of early retirement when I assured him that I really needed him and would strive to maintain standards in every possible way. Benjamin spoke less, and I wondered if perhaps there was more than a hint of antipathy towards me, the young upstart, in his attitude as I perceived it. Whether there was or not I consulted Tuppy who told me straight out that he was one of the nicest people she had ever known. Tuppy around 50 years old was Northern Rhodesia born and bred and a more straightforward person it would be impossible to find. Perhaps her revelation affected my attitude to Benjamin. He and Mwene Falls became not just companions but real friends.

It was not just me who wanted to reassure the Gwembe chiefs about independence. The Prime Minister and President-elect Kenneth Kaunda came to stay only a few weeks after my arrival. I had seen him up in the Luapula but I had not really talked to him. This time I was highly impressed. We had a party for him in my house and the boma ladies did the catering and it went off swimmingly. They and everyone else were highly impressed by the PM's charm and courtesy. We travelled together down to Sinazongwe in the back of his official car and talked about the country and the future. He told me that one of his major worries was that he did not know whom to trust. I said straight away that he ought to trust us, the British. After all we knew the country and were committed to it. Britain no longer had any ambition to dominate in Africa. He seemed to take my point, but I think the question continued to trouble him. He was a man who seemed to be interested in everything and gave the impression that he was much influenced by what you had said. I think he had been, but no doubt he was getting all sorts of conflicting opinions. Unlike leaders like Kenyatta, Nyerere and Banda, he did not really know or understand the British and our culture and way of life. I remember him pointing to the sports cartoon in the *Northern News* newspaper following a cricketing victory by England over Australia. He asked me to explain the picture of a kangaroo nursing a bandaged tail. Thinking particularly about the horrific inter-party violence I had witnessed on the Copperbelt, I asked him how long he thought it would be before real democracy and tolerance of the other man's viewpoint became the norm. 'A very long time', he replied,

Down at Sinazongwe there was a crowd to greet us at the sub-boma. I stood beside the PM. Not being a Tonga speaker he gave a short address in English with me acting as interpreter.

During the day at a series of meetings he was welcomed with great courtesy and respect. I concluded that the government would avoid deliberately upsetting the Valley Tonga by forcing things on them that they did not want. I hoped that I would be able to stay on for a few more years to demonstrate to those apolitical and law-abiding people that government was happy to maintain the status quo.

As DC, I reported to the provincial commissioner in Livingstone. He was a great big bluff man called Haji Bourne who had been DC Gwembe in pre Kariba resettlement days. His reputation for toughness came partly from the days when he had sought to impose a rule on all villages that they had to plant a minimum number of cassava bushes to act as an insurance against drought when all crops except for cassava were liable to die, producing a series of serious famines in the valley. The prospect of these being particularly severe had increased significantly now that all villages except those downstream of the Kariba Dam wall were now away from the lake in the dry infertile interior. Haji's policy on growing cassava had not succeeded, with the Tonga showing great determination in resisting the new order which went counter to their customs and traditions. The DC had been equally determined and had even sent in the mobile unit, but to no avail.

Now PC Haji Bourne was about to retire. He came not just to see me, but to meet old friends like Mwene Falls and Tuppy and Crighton Mitchell. I think he also wanted to try and reassure himself that his beloved Gwembe was in good hands. I hope I conveyed the stimulus I felt at all the challenges of my new job.

Haji Bourne was succeeded, a bit before independence, by another big man Colin Rawlins. Colin was vastly experienced and was ideal for the newly created post of resident secretary reporting to a new political appointee at provincial level, the resident minister. Into the latter position came a man called Sakubita, a teacher who had hitherto never been involved in politics. Because of this perhaps, he would irritatingly try to assert himself at every

Colin Rawlins, Mike Southcombe and Mwene Falls, Siavonga 1965

turn. He came to Gwembe and wanted to go off on the lake in the *Guimbe*. The name of the boat arose from the original spelling of the name of the district. His only preoccupation after the visit was a change in the spelling of the boat's name. Meanwhile Colin told me Sakubita asked why it was that people generally seemed to respect him (Colin) more than himself. Colin said he would have to consider the answer carefully, and eventually, tactfully and diplomatically he ventured the biblical saying that 'a prophet is not acknowledged in his own country'.

The weeks in the run-up to independence were extremely busy. It was a matter of having to face up to change and change again and this was challenging and stimulating. As to the medium and long-term future, I was very worried. I quote from my diary entry of 23 October on the eve of the big day

> I am going to be terribly sad about independence. . . . Britain is stepping out at a time when in the cut and thrust of the modern world she should be doing all she can to maintain her strength and position here. The people who are ashamed of the empire are saying that the policy of giving independence is winning friends. Time has shown and history will I think confirm that this is not the case. Colonial people will have contempt for our weakness and our enemies in the wings will rub their hands gleefully and shout "neo colonialism" at our future efforts. We could not have and would not have wanted to hold our colonies in a perpetual state of servitude. We could have done so much more and finished off the job . . . and also by making it a Commonwealth effort. Now all we can hope is that the empire having gone, the Labour party has the gumption and idealism necessary to make the commonwealth mean more than it does at the moment. I would not be surprised if SR declares her independence at the same time as Zambia gets hers. We shall see.

An immediate preoccupation on the day before independence was that I was determined that for the first and last time I was going to wear my colonial service uniform. It was all white with gold buttons, a large traditional ceremonial pith helmet and a sword. I had inherited it all from the portly deputy PC on the Copperbelt a couple of years before and had never had the chance to wear it. I phoned up Reg Thompson, DC at neighbouring Mazabuka 80 or so miles away to ask him how the sword was worn. 'You're not going to wear it, are you Jonathan?' he exclaimed. I said I certainly was. 'Be it on your own head', was his response.

We had planned our main celebrations for Munyumbwe in the valley. They were organised by Jim Michie the DO who was about to retire, and David Smith, the Accountant for the Gwembe Special Fund which had been set up to finance resettlement projects with the large sums of compensation money provided by the Federal Power Board. Jim and I drove over to Chikuni mission on Independence eve to borrow some loudspeaker equipment he needed for Munyumbwe the next day. We stayed for the mission's celebrations culminating in the flag lowering and raising ceremony at midnight. I think they were broadcasting a live commentary on the main ceremony at the national stadium in Lusaka. I had not thought about how I would react when the moment came. Lit by floodlights the Union Jack came down and up went the new green, red and black flag of the new nation incorporating a fish eagle. The bird was minus the fish it had carried in the Northern

Rhodesian coat of arms. That had come to symbolise the colonial power holding the country in its talons. Now the people were free. The new flag fluttered proudly. I had not expected my reaction. I found myself exhilarated at
the hope that the new flag represented but at the same time with tears pouring down my face. To quote again from my diary 'found myself more deeply
moved than I have ever been – also sadder. It was like losing a loved one or a
dear friend. I was not ashamed to shed a tear for everything that this country
and the Empire had stood for and for all that so many good men have put
into it; not for personal gain but especially because they loved the country,
the people and the job and believed in what Britain stood for'.

I had the feeling that unlike the ordinary people the new hierarchy would
simply not understand or care about what we had been trying to achieve. I
also felt that in granting independence before the country was ready for it,
we were letting down the ordinary people and civil servants like the district messengers who had had total faith in us and had shown us exceptional
loyalty. I felt I was lucky that I was likely to be in a position to continue to
preserve these traditions and relationships for at least a year or two.

6

The New State

On the big day, it was hot at Gwembe boma as it usually is at the end of
October before the rains. Still 90 degrees was cool compared to what
it would be like at Munyumbwe. The main celebrations were to involve
a massive beer drink, the roasting of oxen and lots of dancing, with a large
number of people jumping up and down in unison blowing cow horns. Before
going down to Munyumbwe, however, there was my own little ceremony to
perform involving my uniform and the flag-raising. Most of the messengers
were at Munyumbwe, so there was a lineup of only five or six when I arrived
at the boma, sword clanking and the white topee just about obscuring my features. There was a small gathering including Jean Nixon, my new secretary,
with a cine camera to record the event. (Crighton and Tuppy had just been
transferred.) As I prepared to inspect the messengers, I looked up and was
horrified to see that the Union Jack on the flagpole was flying at half-mast. I
had been determined that if a flag was to be raised, another had to be low-
ered. No doubt the duty messenger had thought that it might be considered
politically incorrect to fly the Union Jack in the normal way on Independence
Day, even for a brief ceremony. He was probably right and I never mentioned
the subject.

Down at Munyumbwe it was like stepping into a furnace. There was a
lot of traditional beer around and everyone was happy. ANC and UNIP councillors walked around hand in hand and an atmosphere of immense goodwill
prevailed. It was a day for contact and celebration with the ordinary people.
The valley men dressed and looked like their cousins on the plateau. The
women though, particularly the older women, were very different. They
went bare-breasted and invariably carried their great pipes made from gourds
filled with water. There were groups of people jump dancing and raising
clouds of dust. There were running races too; I fancied my chances and joined
the young men in a 100-yard dash, but slipped at the start and came in last. It

was a great day full of goodwill, hope and pride. It was not a day for doubts. There would be lots of time for them later.

Back at the boma it was a time of change. I was about to lose my DO, Jim Michie, who was due to carry on with the Colonial Service in the South Pacific. I was missing Tuppy Mitchell and her unflappable good sense. Sadly, Crighton had been transferred to the Kafue Polder project. Tuppy's replacement Jean Nixon was married to Nick Nixon, who was in charge of our local Gwembe hospital and the separate Leper Colony. Though he was not qualified as a doctor, he had massive experience both as a medical administrator and in medicine itself. He was totally committed to his job and was acknowledged as a world expert on sleeping sickness. He was also a very worried man because the talk coming from Lusaka was of his being replaced at the hospital because of his lack of qualifications. The authority tried to reassure him by saying that he would still be needed, but it was only as head of the laundry unit at the new Lusaka teaching hospital. This was a body blow for a very proud man. Before long he was to commit suicide.

Meanwhile, change was gathering pace; I lost my responsibility for law and order when a police post was established at Gwembe, and for the Native Authority at Munyumbwe responsibility for which went to the new department of local government. I was now called district secretary. All the same I seemed to get busier and busier with two sub-bomas and eight chiefs to look after, not to mention all the problems in the aftermath of resettlement. Jim Michie was replaced by a newly promoted African DO who, the Resident Secretary Colin Rawlins said, had failed miserably in another district. He said the new man Simon Basikolo needed close supervision, which he felt I could give.

One night shortly after the police post had been established, I was woken up a bit before midnight by a messenger to be told that there had been a murder. I pulled on some clothes and we jumped into the Land Rover and drove to a bit of open ground near the compound where there was a female body on the ground with head wounds. Standing nearby was a man holding a blood-stained brick. He said he was very sorry, but during a quarrel he had lost his temper and killed his wife. I told one of the bystanders to go and call the inspector in charge of police who arrived fairly soon and I left the matter in his hands. Some weeks later I was amazed to hear that the murderer had been acquitted. The experienced magistrate had apparently said that he had no choice but to acquit for lack of evidence or any statements. Such incidents were inevitable with the lack of Zambian experience. The government response to problems tended to be to appoint more and more people to more and more specialist departments. There were signs too that it saw the politicisation of the administration as being the way forward. I was sure that the people of Gwembe did not see things that way. In fact I started to get messages from the chiefs that they had not seen the DC or DO for months and would appreciate a visit. Despite an almost overwhelming workload back at the boma, I tried to accommodate them with short visits and by encouraging the officers in charge at Siavonga and Sinazongwe to do the same. On one trip I drove up the valley road deep into Chief Mwemba's area and camped near a village on his side of the Mulola River opposite Madiongo where I had camped in Kalomo days. This time the new Zambian flag with its fish eagle minus the fish fluttered from a pole near my tent. The visit was much appreciated by the surrounding villagers.

Sometimes I travelled to the sub-bomas by the main road via Kafue in the case of Siavonga and via Choma in the case of Sinazongwe. Otherwise there were more direct but very rough roads along the valley bottom, and in each case the journey could take the best part of a day. When going by boat I would take a boma Land Rover straight down to Chipepo harbour on the lake with Mwene Falls and Benjamin Shipopo and sometimes with Stephen if we were going to camp on an island. By this time Stephen was quite at home on the great wide waters of the lake. The islands were wonderful, all uninhabited in those days and some of the larger ones had small populations of game. Chete Island near the Rhodesian shore (the boundary followed the old line of the Zambezi River) hosted a herd of elephants. On the islands I would usually sleep out in the open under a tree listening to the owls and the nightjars and the lapping of the waves on the lake shore.

One morning shortly after dawn, I went for a swim off a lovely sandy beach before carrying on to Sinazongwe. Next day as we passed the island en route back to Chipepo, a very large crocodile slid into the water from the same beach. I became a lot more circumspect after that but reasoned that as the lake was new there had not been time for a significant crocodile population to build up. Amongst my trips on the *Guimbe* was one to a fishing co-operative, about 50 miles up lake from Sinazongwe. Co-operatives were all the rage in the years following independence and the government had plenty of money to dish out to them. The one I had been invited to visit was run by people from Lake Mweru or Lake Tanganyika I think. They certainly seemed to have political connections and I was welcomed by the chairman and the vice chairman and his secretary and his deputy and other officials, about a dozen people all wearing togas. This garb was not traditionally Zambian, but the politicians fancied them as they indicated transcontinental nationalist solidarity. Anyway when I asked to see the workers, I was shown just two lonely looking local valley Tonga men mending nets.

Another time I was invited to call on Ian Findlay across the lake at Binga. The journey must have been nearly a hundred miles up lake. The lake was calm and with the Zambian flag fluttering from *Guimbe*'s mast we made good progress westwards down the middle of the lake with the northern and southern shores each several miles away. All of a sudden the calm was broken by an earth-shattering roar. We must all have leapt a foot in the air and then perhaps fallen down, but when I looked up again there was a Hawker Hunter jet fighter of the Rhodesian Air Force. It had come up behind us at near supersonic speed and was only a few feet above our heads. Having contacted DC Binga on the Lake Safety Radio, he met us at Binga harbour. Mwene Falls saluted him as we went ashore, and he and the crew were taken off to the billets in the civil service compound. I was taken up the hill to the DC's house and this time there was much more time to get to know him and his wife Pat. Apart from the odd illegal crossing of the narrow upper part of the lake, there was the subject of the rains and crops to discuss. There was also the looming probability of a Unilateral Declaration of Independence (UDI), which I was sure would be a disaster. I did feel some sympathy for the Rhodesians, however. They had run a successful, incorrupt and efficient country, albeit with the white man's interests firmly to the fore. Unfortunately, successive British governments had failed to assert themselves over obviously unacceptable and untenable Rhodesian policies on race, nor had they convinced the Rhodesians that they would not be abandoned to African nationalism. Clearly the Rhodesians were less than ever prepared to trust the British. I found myself being lectured to by Ian Findlay on how in his view Africa and Africans would become easy prey for the communists as the West withdrew from the continent. Apart from the Findlays, I met a few other Europeans at Binga, notably a delightful couple called Angus and Hazel Van Jaarsveld who were traders and had just started to breed crocodiles for their skins. I was to see a lot of them in Binga 15 years later in 1980.

Binga was the only place where I ever went ashore on the southern side of the lake though I always used to call the hotel at Bumi Hills, a hundred miles to the east, on the Lake Safety Radio. Always the friendly female voice would reply, 'Hello Northern Rhodesia how are you?' Another time I went up the lake well beyond Binga and the little holiday hotel at Milibizi up to the gorges at the top of the lake. I was checking on the notorious Kariba weed, which I had seen on the desk of the then PC at Livingstone five years before. Now it clogged bays and river estuaries and threatened to put paid to prospects of a viable fishing industry on the lake. There had been great hopes for fishing, and during the construction of the dam wall, great swathes of country had been cleared of trees by dragging massive metal balls linked by huge chains across the bush. Thus it was hoped, there would be areas where in future years trawlers would operate. Apart from the weed, things were looking very promising with tiger fish, bream and other species growing very quickly to massive sizes sustained by all the food in the growing lake. Now chugging up the gorges I was hoping to reach the point at the very top of the lake where the Zambezi flows in. It is also where the Mulola River joins, and I had camped there in Kalomo days in 1961. Now the weed was getting thicker and thicker and we were forced to turn back.

Back at the boma, by November 1965, whereas there were fewer Europeans with the departure of the Smiths and lately the Grays (he had been a fisheries officer), life carried on pretty much as normal. However, my social life, such as it was, tended to revolve more around Monze, 30 miles away where I played tennis with the magistrate, Steve Morgan. The head of the agricultural training college there, Tony Philips and his wife Lorna used to visit me for a game of squash on the boma court followed by supper. Then it was usually Tony and me versus Lorna who tended to be supportive of Ian Smith and the approaching UDI.

Meanwhile life carried on and I remained very busy in the office. It was depressing at night though to hear Basikolo's periodic incoherent drunken rantings. I had asked the new Zambian resident secretary for him to be removed, but a decision was taking a long time to reach me. By 9 November I was particularly keen to have a break as there was always business at the sub-bomas needing my attention. I radioed Sandy Macdonald at Sinazongwe saying I intended to come and see him the next day on the *Guimbe*. So, early next morning, Mwene Falls, Benjamin, Stephen and I drove down to the oven heat of the valley. The road descended the ten miles to Munyumbwe very rapidly and then more gently another 30 miles to Chipepo harbour. Amongst the escarpment hills was one which had a flat top and rose steeply nearly a thousand feet above the surrounding countryside. There was a spring up there I was told, and a lot of game. I always intended to go up there and camp on this island in the bush. By 8 am we were down at 1690 feet at Chipepo harbour and set sail. It took us about four hours to get to Sinazongwe. I concluded my business with Sandy over lunch and by early afternoon I was back on the lake heading for Chipepo. It was a lovely evening and as always, despite the intense valley heat, it always felt cool on the lake. As planned we stopped at one of my favourite islands, which had some attractive trees amongst sparse grass and of course wonderful views across the lake to the mainland on both sides. While Stephen set up camp, I took the dogs for a walk around the island. At about 6.30 pm before settling down to a beer I decided to give DC Binga a call. I think I was aware that the Lake Safety Radio was attended round the clock. I was surprised when the operator told me that the DC was in his office and very soon he was on the air. There was no particular reason for the call, but we talked about crop prospects and stray fishermen and the like and said goodnight. It did not occur to me that it might be unusual that he was still in the office at 6.30 pm. Next morning we carried on to Chipepo, got into the Land Rover and were back at the boma by mid-day. It was 11 November and I was home for lunch; I switched on the radio to listen to the news. Immediately there was Ian Smith, obviously with a heavy cold speaking of the 'rights of man' and his country's destiny and in short declaring UDI. It was a depressing moment but not unexpected. This would have major implications for our region, but there was nothing in particular that needed to be done. The resident secretary rang to ask whether the population in the valley needed reassurance. I advised that no special measures were needed, that posting troops to the valley would serve merely to upset ordinary village people. I was worried on my own account about likely fuel shortages arising from possible international sanctions against Rhodesia which would inevitably affect us, given our dependence on the railway to the south for most of our imports. After work that afternoon I looked around the sheds at the back of my house and found an empty 44-gallon drum with a conveniently placed tap at the bottom. I put the drum in the back of the Land Rover and drove straight to Chisekesi. At the Couvaras's filling station I had it filled to the brim and then drove back home. I was thinking of an invitation to go and spend Christmas with friends in Lusaka and the fuel my Anglia Estate would need. I never regretted filling up that drum. Within a week or two fuel rationing was announced and when Christmas came I was one of only a handful of cars on the road to Lusaka.

Apart from the need to conserve fuel, UDI made no immediate impact on the population. I did decide to go to Siavonga to see Mike Southcombe. We drove to the dam wall where there were soldiers dug in on both sides. I certainly did not want to cross over to talk to the Rhodesians. I had been

over a few weeks before and in the presence of the affable DC Kariba, had
to listen to a tirade from an officious little immigration officer who kept on
about 'my government this' and 'my government that'.

Of course after UDI the world's media descended on Zambia and Mike
and I went down for a drink at the motel with the major commanding the
Zambian army soldiers at the dam wall, a British army secondee. In the pub
there were journalists from several British and one French newspaper. We
somehow managed to have a drunken and at times contentious evening with
them without letting on who we were.

Back in Gwembe I had a puzzling visit. By now it was the beginning of
December and two police special branch officers from Lusaka came to see
me in my office. They were both thoroughly affable, assured me that there
was no particular problem but said they wanted to go down to Chipepo.
They talked of it as a routine visit following UDI. When they came back
they again assured me there was no problem. It was only afterwards that
I learned that they had been interviewing the two crewmen on the Guimbe
who had obviously reported to somebody, possibly the party, that I had been
speaking on the radio to the Rhodesians on the eve of UDI. The two officers
must have satisfied themselves that there was nothing sinister about my talk
with Ian Findlay with whom of course I had now ceased to have any contact
at all. I was probably lucky that all this came before all the British special
branch officers in the Zambian police were suddenly sacked. A few Irishmen
remained. I still don't know what was behind the sackings which seemed an
unnecessary, divisive and unjust step which got rid of highly competent and
loyal officers. It inevitably caused bad blood for the Irish officers. From about
then on, the question sometimes arose as to whether officers who had stayed
on were sometimes too keen to tell the new powers that be what they wanted
to hear at the expense of the truth.

One of the results of UDI was that Zambia needed to look to its self-
sufficiency in various ways including the supply of vital coal for the power
stations and smelters on the giant Copperbelt. They relied on a particularly
high grade of coal from Wankie, about 70 miles down the railway south of
Victoria Falls towards Bulawayo. Zambia had a deposit of low-quality coal at
a place called Nkandabwe in the valley near Sinazongwe. A presidential visit
was planned to have a look at the deposit, which fleets of bulldozers were
beginning to expose. I was down on the lake camping on an island near Sinazongwe and once again before the sun set decided to use Guimbe's rarely used
radio. This time it was not to be the Lake Safety net which still linked only

Guimbe on our side with the Rhodesian stations. This time I decided to try out the long-range shortwave radio linked to police HQ in Lusaka and theoretically with every sizable police station in the country. So I switched on the set and started calling 'HQ Lusaka this is MV Guimbe calling'. Eventually there was a responding voice 'Hello MV Guimbe this is constable Bwalya at Police Headquarters'.

The conversation proceeded more or less as follows, 'Hello constable, I am the district secretary at Gwembe on board the boat Guimbe and I am testing out our radio because the president is due to visit us next week, have you got that?' 'Affirmative sir, affirmative', replied Bwalya. 'By the way constable can you do me a favour?' 'Yes sir.' 'Can you telephone Miss Dorothy Fowler at the British High Commission on 72717 and tell her that I won't be coming to Lusaka at the weekend. Have you got that? Thank you constable. Over and out.'

About three weeks later I received a letter from Lusaka on State House writing paper; it was from the president's private secretary who had been a fellow district officer. I wish I had kept the letter, but it read something like:

Dear Lawley,

It has come to our notice that not only have you been instrumental in a waste of ZRP time at police Headquarters but that you have been consorting with a foreign power.

Last Friday evening while I was at State House, I received a phone call from a constable at police headquarters quoting a Lusaka telephone number and telling me that the President was on Lake Kariba. This came as a considerable surprise as I knew that at that time the President was dining with the Mayor of Lusaka at the City Hall. Fortunately I recognised the telephone number as of a young lady at the British High Commission.

I must warn you that any repeat of such conduct and you will be sent on immediate transfer to Mwinilunga.

Yours sincerely
Mike Merrifield
Private Secretary to His Excellency The President

I don't think it had anything to do with the radio incident, but the question of the future of the *Guimbe* suddenly came to a head. With Colin Rawlins gone, I got scant support from the new Zambian resident secretary in my struggle to keep the boat. Though it was unreliable, we did have a telephone line to Lusaka and one day I had a phone call from Gavin Barr, another ex-DO now dealing with police matters in the president's office. The conversation was short but not sweet. He ordered me to hand over the *Guimbe* to the police. It was pretty blunt and totally unexpected. I refused point blank. I guessed that police high-ups in Lusaka wanted the boat mainly for weekend recreation. Two or three weeks passed and I heard nothing more. Then one day Gavin appeared in person asking me to accompany him down to Chipepo to inspect the boat. He explained that because of potential security problems along the border, the police were insistent that they had to have a boat. However, he said she would remain based at Chipepo and I would have the use of her whenever I wanted, provided I gave a few days' notice. There was nothing more I could do, and though I disliked the letters POLICE painted on her sides and she was no longer mine, I have to admit that the arrangement worked well enough. Gavin Barr though was not my favourite person at that point. We were destined to meet again seven years later in the Congo under circumstances which again were hardly likely to endear us to each other.

Before I lost my boat, my parents came to stay all the way from Iran where my father was working for the United Nations. They came north having been winding up their affairs in Salisbury. I was pleased to give them a chance to get a feel for the atmosphere in Zambia, and I took them to Lusaka by a circuitous route first on *Guimbe* to stay the night with Mike Southcombe at Siavonga and then on by Land Rover. They were most impressed by all they saw and heard. They told me that the post-UDI atmosphere they had found in Salisbury was 'lets get back to the good old days'.

Perhaps by now I was travelling to Sinazongwe more often by Land Rover than by boat. One day Benjamin, Mwene Falls and I were driving back to Gwembe and were just starting to get into escarpment country when we saw beside the road a villager in a state of some agitation. There beside him lay the body of what at first looked like a large dog. As we got out of the vehicle we could see that it was a hyena. With incredible calmness under the circumstances, the man told us that a few minutes earlier as he walked along the road carrying his spear over his shoulder in the traditional way, the hyena had suddenly appeared and attacked him. Though he had received several nasty bites on his arms, he was able to fight the animal off with his spear and kill it. Despite his wounds he continued to stand there and give us the details. It seemed highly likely that the hyena had been rabid. Despite its enormous strength and potential to overwhelm a man on his own, even one

Author and his mother on board *MV Guimbe*

armed with a spear, an attack such as this would not be normal behaviour. I told the man that we would take him up to Choma Hospital immediately. He was most reluctant and wanted to continue on his journey to his village. Full of admiration for his incredible bravery, we persuaded him to climb into the Land Rover. We also loaded the dead hyena into the back, with Mwene Falls and Benjamin taking the legs and me the tail. When we reached Choma Hospital, we dropped the brave villager off for his course of injections and the hyena for tests on its brain and returned to Gwembe. The next day I received a call from Choma Hospital, the hyena had been rabid and Mwene Falls, Benjamin and I should return immediately to Choma for a course of injections. I protested that I had merely touched the tail which was hardly likely to have had saliva on it. Anyway I had no cuts on my hands. I was able to get out of the injections which, because they are given into the stomach muscles, are unpleasant and painful. Mwene Falls and Benjamin were not so lucky.

By mid-1966, I was the only ex-PA expatriate still in charge of a rural district in Zambia. This in itself possibly made for difficulties. I had no problems with the local UNIP officials, but there had been the problems with Basikolo by now thankfully transferred and the suspicion of spying arising from the call to Binga from the *Guimbe* the night before UDI. 'There is no smoke without fire' could well be the sentiment I was not too surprised when I was informed at the end of May that I was to be transferred to Lusaka. My feelings were very mixed. Of course I was delighted that I would be seeing more of Sarah Pelly, a girl I had met on the banks of the Kafue River over a weekend with friends. Like me she was born in India. We had much in common and she had been to Gwembe and the lake several times. Now I was sad that the chance of sharing with her the sort of bush life that for years I had longed to share with the right person was probably gone forever. On the plus side, life was getting pretty lonely at Gwembe and it was becoming harder to maintain standards. I did chair a meeting of the district 'team' in early 1966. Many years later I heard from Thayer Scudder, the American who had written *The Ecology of the Gwembe Tonga*, that it had not been convened since then.

Although I knew I would miss Gwembe and the life and work, at that stage I had no intention of leaving the country. I was confident that there would be interesting opportunities in Lusaka. There were two other factors both involving money. It may sound insincere in retrospect with the massive salaries needed to persuade people to go and work in mildly uncomfortable circumstances around the world. However, I did not know a single member of the provincial administration or indeed other government departments in Northern Rhodesia who was mainly motivated by money. After independence, however, there were incentive schemes to try to get people to stay and one did begin to get the feeling of being treated as a mercenary. In my case, before I was promoted from Nchelenge my salary was a little over a thousand a year. In Gwembe I became aware that my salary had more than doubled. I was never one to bother about what particular grade or salary band I was on. I just knew I was being paid more than enough to cater for my needs. One day the ex-senior DO dealing with staff matters in the president's office rang to say that ever since my promotion I had been paid at the wrong rate. In fact I owed the government nearly a thousand pounds, a huge sum for me. I was flabbergasted and having resisted the initial suggestion that I must have known, agreed a rate of repayment which put a heavy burden on me just as I was contemplating marriage. The other financial consideration was that at long last I had won the argument with HMG that my home base was not in Southern Rhodesia and therefore I was eligible for UK-funded incentive payments. In short I was a 'designated' officer and that made all the difference in the world.

When my replacement arrived in Gwembe for a week's handover I was shocked. He was an ex-clerk and he told me straight away that he was most unhappy about being sent to Gwembe. He said he would be missing out on the sort of promotion opportunities from which his friends and colleagues were benefiting in Lusaka. The new man showed no interest in what was one of the most important, interesting and challenging districts in the country. To compound all this, from the word go he took my Land Rover to Chisekesi every evening and got drunk. After a few days the UNIP secretary came to see me in the office. He said that he and the party had been pleased and excited at the prospect of a Zambian national taking over the district. Now, having seen the new man, he was deeply worried and unhappy. I tried to set his mind at rest, but I shared his feelings.

I wrote a sort of lament in my diary saying that I would no doubt be the last white man in my lovely house with its flagpole, its little wooden guest house with the long veranda, its lawn, slashed short every day by prisoners which gave way to bush and long views over the Zambezi Valley and the delightful avocado pear tree with its delicious fruit the size of a hen's eggs.

I travelled to Lusaka in my car with Stephen and Mwene Falls, while the boma lorry loaded with my luggage followed with Stephen's wife and children and about ten prisoners and a pair of messenger escorts. When we got to the block of flats in Birdcage Walk, which as a bachelor was all I rated, I overheard the prisoners discussing my new situation. Looking at the large three-storey building, I heard one remark, 'The Bwana must be coming up in the world. Look at the size of his house.'

7

Dividing the Fuel

L usaka in mid-1966 was jumping. There was plenty of money around, new Zambian ministries were springing up all over the place, new embassies and high commissions were being set up and business people of all sorts came pouring in. The social life was often hectic. Though the old hierarchy of senior civil servants was disappearing, the second stringers like me could hardly step straight into their shoes. The new top dogs were various international presidential advisors and of course the diplomats. Amongst the latter, the British were top of the pile and most numerous. Their relationship with us long-standing colonial civil servants, was a strange one. On our side, as always, there was the feeling that the British from Britain did not really understand. On the other side, remarks such as 'we see our job now as clearing up the mess that you people made' was hardly likely to get them loved and got passed around at great speed. There were one or two British diplomats who presumed on loyalties to which they thought they were entitled and pressed colleagues for inside information. Hopefully, they never got it. At the same time, I got an ever-stronger feeling of a divide amongst civil service colleagues between those who were ready to tell the new government what it wanted to hear and the rest.

Officially, the new government took a very moral stance over the illegal regime in Southern Rhodesia, now calling itself simply Rhodesia. However, there was a great deal of pragmatism – even hypocrisy – around, and the Zambia government found itself explaining why we were still importing ice cream from that country or having our shoes repaired there. There were of course, fundamental issues of how far Zambia should go in risking damage to its own economy through taking principled stands against Rhodesia, particularly over trade and trade routes. We were after all landlocked and the vast bulk of our imports and exports passed up and down the railway line to the south via Victoria Falls. I saw a bit of this in my first Lusaka job with the

Ministry of Commerce and Industry. I started there working on a scheme for price controls and saw at close quarters how an expatriate under-secretary, an economist, was tearing his hair out over measures such as the vastly increased pay forced on the mining companies for their workers by the British-led Brown Commission on wage levels in the industry. These were bound to damage the economy and the country in the medium term. However, for the time being the economy remained buoyant, thanks to high copper prices and the fact that the new government had inherited full coffers.

Having arrived in Lusaka nearly two years after independence, I felt at first that I had missed out on the more attractive posts which might have been going in government; in the game department or in tourism promotion perhaps. In the run-up to the celebration of the second anniversary of Zambia's independence on 24 October 1964, I found myself in a team of six ex-colonial service expatriates organising the 1966 celebrations. There was a great deal of work to be done. I particularly remember teaching the Lusaka milkmen how to march as proud Zambians with their heads held high and a spring in their step at the independence parade down Cairo Road. Other memories are of the military tattoo organised by a British army officer attached to the Zambian army. He did a wonderfully impressive and professional job with impeccably drilled soldiers and mock battles and lots more. On the night I sat next to one of the government's VIP guests – the artist David Shepherd whom I had been asked to look after. He was a connoisseur of tattoos, and he told me ours came up to top international standards. Apparently, President Kaunda was highly impressed too and said that the British had made their point.

Sarah and I settled into Lusaka life quickly and I started to feel less awkward at the numerous cocktail parties. It was a strange time. I had most in common with ex-PA colleagues, all of whom I knew by reputation even if we had not actually met. There was little social interaction with Zambians, although some whites made efforts in that direction. A problem was that people who had been invited to functions would not show up and they seldom brought their wives few of whom had much education in those days. The Chief Justice's wife told the story of how she had invited two senior male Zambians to dinner and they had accepted but did not show up. She came across them a day or two later and inquired as to whether there had been a problem. 'Ah Lady Blagden', said one, 'we thought about your kind invitation to dinner, but we were not hungry.'

For Sarah and me there was the question of where we were going to live after we were married in August. Despite the acute shortage of housing I was allocated a charming little house off a quiet side road beside Church Road. We were pleased as was Stephen and his family as there was a servant's quarter at the back. It had a lovely garden but the gardener was living in the shower, so he had to go. We were soon deep into wedding preparations and were offered the use of the Msamba Club outside Lusaka where there was a lovely garden and bar. We spent a lot of time there over weekends. A problem arose, however, when the manager asked if we planned to have any Zambian guests. I replied in the affirmative as we had already asked several Zambians, most notably Benjamin Shipopo and Mwene Falls from Gwembe and the assistant district secretary from Siavonga. So in the interests of preserving the Msamba Club's status as a refuge for expats, we had to agree to squeeze the reception into our modest garden in Church Road. At least the guests had to drive only a couple of hundred yards from the Anglican Cathedral and we had a very happy wedding. Both our mothers came, Sarah's from Wiltshire and mine from Iran. We motored down to Rhodesia for the first part of our honeymoon, spending the first night at Makuti on the other side of the Zambezi escarpment. The next day we carried on via Salisbury to the Eastern Highlands and the Troutbeck Inn which stands beside a lake at nearly 7000 feet. We planned on some trout fishing and golf. The sixth hole down the hill and over a burn on the superb little nine-hole course was described by the late great Henry Longhurst as one of the best par threes in the world. That first evening we sat down for a drink in the main lounge beside the fire and were joined by a middle-aged couple. It was Mr and Mrs Ian Smith. I asked him if he remembered our conversation in the car between Bulawayo and Salisbury nine years before. He replied that he certainly did, remarking that one could be forgiven for being misguided in one's youth. He was very interested when I told him I had been working in the Zambezi Valley and we went on to discuss its considerable tourist potential. We spent four nights at delightful Troutbeck with its log fires in the bedrooms which by tradition were never locked. Then it was down through the Rhodes Inyanga National Park to Umtali and on the 190 miles to Beira in Mozambique. We had another four days there, eating giant prawns and drinking Portuguese wine. Beira was all bright lights and night clubs with a multiracial clientele and totally Portuguese. The last night of our honeymoon we spent with my very old friends, the Valentines back in Rhodesia at their farm near Umtali. I had known Richard at school in Bulawayo and South Africa and had been his best man. His wife Heather was intelligent and artistic and I wondered how she would cope with life on the farm.

At work, after the independence anniversary celebrations, I was appointed chief rationing officer (petroleum products) in succession to ex DOs Jamie Broughton, who had set up rationing after UDI the year before, and his successor Ross Smith. The new job carried the rank of senior principal and involved a bit more money, which was a great help as I was feeling pretty broke with wedding expenses and all the money I was having to pay back to government as a result of being overpaid for nearly two years.

As chief rationing officer I had a small headquarters staff at the top of UNIP house which housed the Ministry of Commerce and Industry. I reported to the Permanent Secretary Goodwin Mutale via the under-secretary in the ministry, Mick Wagner, one of the few senior colleagues still in the country. I had an excellent second-in-command, a huge rugby-playing Scot called George Gardiner. We ran a simple but tight scheme with rationing offices in all the main towns including Lusaka. At headquarters we dealt directly with very big users like the mines and the contractors building the pipeline to Tanzania and diplomats including my friend from the Czech embassy who was over the moon about the Prague Spring. When I mentioned the Russians and Hungary in 1956, he said that that was altogether different.

The main centres were the key to our effectiveness. My man in Lusaka, Wally Walford, was over 60 and learning to fly. He was an enthusiast and highly efficient. On the Copperbelt, I had a coordinator – a Mr Campbell – but it was the tough Afrikaans ladies running the Copperbelt offices who really kept the lid on fuel consumption. They did not much like answering to old Mr Campbell, but after he very sadly died, they would have nothing at all to do with his successor – a bright, young, highly efficient, female graduate. They preferred to report to me. They were under enormous pressure. A typical case was Mrs Venter who ran the Kitwe office phoning me to say that someone with political connections was in her office, telling a lot of lies and threatening to report her to the minister for not giving him what he wanted. 'Can I throw him out Mr Lawley?' she asked. 'Throw him out Mrs Venter', I replied. 'Thank you Mr Lawley. I knew you would say that.' On another occasion I remember George coming into my office red in the face and obviously very angry. 'There's a man in my office who has just called me a racist.' I accompanied George to his office, spoke to the man – an Asian businessman – and told him to leave immediately. He blustered and left saying he was going straight to the minister. I immediately phoned the Permanent Secretary Mr Mutale, who said he would throw the man out himself. That was the end of the matter. I always got wonderful support. It was an irony that as rationing continued and got stricter, I still had some petrol in the 44-gallon drum in the corridor beside the kitchen in our house at 44 Church Road. Rationing had been pretty strict, but our reserve meant that we could spend the odd weekend out of Lusaka down at Siavonga, where we borrowed a cottage and spent the time having barbeques with friends, water skiing or just swimming and sunbathing.

Though I was getting used to life in Lusaka, I missed the bush and of course I regretted that Sarah who would have been the ideal DO's wife had not been around to share that life with me.

One weekend we decided to try and rekindle something from that life and Sarah, Stephen and I set off by car for the Lusitu area about 40 miles downstream from the Kariba Dam wall. We took a bush track with which the Anglia Estate could cope and drove down to one of the resettled villages near the river. There we explained ourselves to the headman and Stephen secured accommodation for himself in the village and we drove to a point on the river a few hundred yards away and set up camp under the trees. It was a lovely place with the mighty river fast flowing below us. In the evening I went off to talk to the headman, while Stephen prepared our supper and Sarah went for a walk up the river. I insisted that she take my rifle. When I got back to the camp later, she told me how she had been followed on her walk by a group of South African policemen on the south bank of the river, whistling and passing remarks. She had also had to confront a troop of aggressive baboons. That night we could hear the lions roaring from across the river.

Towards the end of 1967, I was invited to Sunday lunch with President Kaunda. Government House was now State House and as I went in at the front entrance past all the security, I remembered how a few years before I had just walked into the same hall to sign the visitors' book as required of all district officers visiting Lusaka. It was on the table amongst the governor's hats and walking sticks. Now there was barbed wire and a security fence. Barbara Castle, who visited Kaunda shortly after independence, assuming that these barriers were inherited, suggested that now he could take them down. In fact, they had only just been erected. The lunch was most agreeable. My fellow guests were the Vice President Simon Kapwepwe and the well-known Presidential Advisor Simon Zukas. Kaunda was his usual very charming self and open to all ideas. I had never met Kapwepwe. His image was of a rather sinister left winger and a potential threat to Kaunda. I found him quietly perceptive. The only bit of conversation I remember was on the need for villagers to change traditional agricultural practices. Kaunda and Kapwepwe felt that if Zambian extension officers delivered the message, it would make all the difference. I was not sure. The lunch was delicious and we washed it down with South African wine.

8

Diversity Stillborn

In April 1968 the fuel situation had improved to the extent that at last I was allowed to go on leave and join Sarah at her mother's house on the Wiltshire Avon. We spent the six months fly fishing and buying a Suffolk cottage.

We returned to Africa on the magnificent Pendennis Castle, first class. Though she was pregnant, Sarah and I being young won most of the deck games competitions. At Cape Town we got all the usual help from the Crown Agents to HMOCS officers returning from leave. Then our new car was unloaded and we drove north via the Garden Route, the Transkei, Swaziland, the Northern Transvaal and Rhodesia. Back at work, George Gardiner had been running fuel rationing and now I was back to wind it up. The oil pipeline from Dar es Salaam terminated at Ndola, where there was a refinery. I went to Ndola for the opening by President Julius Nyerere of Tanzania, who made a witty speech and I was much impressed. I remember him saying what had at first been labelled a pipe dream had turned into a pipeline. Before I finally closed the office I received a visit from my Czech diplomat friend who told me he had just got back from Prague. 'I now understand what you were talking about when you mentioned Hungary', he said.

Though rationing had come to an end, I was confident that there was no shortage of interesting government jobs to be had. Though being in charge of fuel rationing had been very hard work and sometimes stressful, I had thoroughly enjoyed the challenge of running a successful and economical scheme. Though I was fairly sure we would eventually have to leave Zambia, I was in no hurry to go. Life was interesting and enjoyable, I was well paid and we had plenty of friends. In some ways life was pretty well idyllic. People would say how, though they had opposed the rush towards independence, things had turned out far better than they had expected. There was still a lot of sensitivity about anything that could be perceived as racist attitudes and you had to be very careful not to do or say things that might be taken the wrong way. The head of my bank was deported after he had presented a politician's wife with a frozen turkey which went bad after she refroze it and she accused him of giving her 'a rotten chicken'. Nearly all senior members of the old provincial administration had now gone but the vastly expanded government machine was still delivering the goods. Fuel rationing had been economical and effective, and ex-PA colleagues set up the new national registration scheme, the national lottery and hospital building programme, the new game department and tourist promotion and generally showed their versatility. Even so, the government felt it could afford to bring in a lot of outside expertise. We old hands were a little cynical about this. The new people, in our view, lacked commitment to the country, cost a very great deal and, due to their lack of background knowledge, took the country down paths, which seemed to reflect their ignorance as well as their political preconceptions. There was the Brown Commission from the UK on wage levels in the mining industry. It reported that miners were not receiving a living wage and the resultant doubling of wages effectively destroyed Zambian industry's export potential. At first such things were not seen as a worry, but as the tendency to overspend grew, one could see real dangers ahead for the country.

I managed to engineer a transfer from the Ministry of Commerce and Industry to the new Ministry of Rural Development where a young live wire and recently qualified Zambian engineer Andrew Kashita was permanent secretary. I managed to secure a new post with the job title of development plan coordinator. The government had started to commit large sums to projects which would help diversify the economy and move it away from its huge over-reliance on copper revenues. The idea was that Zambia had vast agricultural potential and it was a matter of getting projects going to show the way forward with a variety of potentially profitable crops. As an ex-DO I had plenty of ideas about agriculture, the need for change and the difficulty of changing traditional practices. As a young DO it had all seemed so logical. Just explain to villagers how they would benefit from things like crop rotation or spreading manure on crops to save the soil and people would see sense and change their ways. To the locals we must have sounded rather like British politicians such as Tony Blair or Gordon Brown visiting Africa sound today. I had discovered that even when there was a so-called improved farmer to give a good example, it was never that simple. Now in 1968, I was mindful of a conversation with Monsieur Andre Dumont, author of a book called *False Start in Africa*, when we flew up to Mwinilunga together while I was still looking after fuel rationing. At the old-style rest house with its magnificent views over the mighty Lunga River, we had talked long into the night after dinner. It had been wonderful to be back in a good rural rest house, spotlessly clean, and where the old man in charge stuck to the highest standards. M Dumont's theory was that if there was to be progress in African agriculture, farmers needed to go through the various stages for them to be lasting and sustainable. It was just not possible to go from the kindergarten stage to the university stage in one leap. For example, progress from turning over the soil with a hoe had to be via ploughing with oxen before ploughing with a tractor could be attempted. Nyerere had apparently made the book required reading for his ministers. Now Dumont had come to Zambia bearing the same message. Kaunda certainly accepted the logic. Part of his problem was that with plenty of money around and the availability of tractors in the form of overseas aid, it was difficult to resist the clamour in rural areas to be allowed the tractors. Unfortunately the machines tended to be used merely for transport and then broke down for lack of spare parts or proper maintenance.

The new development plan, however, was a reality and whatever the difficulties of getting things going, there was a need to monitor progress and apply lessons across the board. I felt I was very lucky with my new job. I had total freedom to travel where and when I liked to projects all over the country. With Andrew Kashita's backing, I felt it would be possible to achieve a great deal. I can't remember where I went first. It may have been to the cotton-growing project in the Petauke district along the Great East Road. The idea was that refugees from Mozambique living there in thousands would grow cotton profitably under expert supervision. What I found was some cotton badly overgrown with weeds and unreaped. Any work done had been by project employees. The refugees did not seem to be involved at all. They just sat around. It was more or less the same story at Mwinilunga, where a reputation for growing good pineapples had led to investment in a canning plant. This was never going to be economic because of the lack of fruit in sufficient quantity to keep the plant working and because Mwinilunga in the far north-west was much too far from potential markets. The same story applied to the banana project up near Nchelenge. Clearly there was a need to rethink these and other projects which were destined to waste a great deal of money.

I had been in my new job for only a couple of months when in January 1969 came a bolt from the blue. One day there was a letter in the post from government's Establishment Division to say that I was being retired 'in the public interest'. Enquiries around Lusaka revealed that a number of people had received similar letters. All had recently returned from overseas leave. I was outraged. Had not Kaunda promised there was room in government service for people who were committed to the country and who had adapted to the new circumstances? I can't remember the logic behind the reference to the public interest, but it applied to all of us and was a device to save government having to pay us our full severance dues. As we were all members of HMOCS, the British government was involved and we all protested vigorously to the British High Commissioner. When I went to see him full of indignation not just at the way we had been treated, but at the logic of getting rid of people whose help the country clearly needed, he made me feel better by likening our situation to a young man going for his first job and finding that his boss was his old housemaster from school. It also made me feel better when I learned that the Establishment Division had not caught up with the fact that I had recently started an important new job. So there it was. I had six months to serve before we had to leave Zambia. Soon there were more notices to leave and within a couple of years, nearly all ex-members of the PA and other British civil servants would be gone.

About the time of the letter our first child was born. When Sarah was in labour at the Lusaka General Hospital, I went in to look for her and going down a darkened corridor I heard her voice. I knocked on the door and said who I was and the female Irish nurse said, 'Come in, grab a leg and tell her to push.' Very soon Juliet appeared. It was a thrilling experience for me and a case of instant and intense love. She was not Juliet to start with. We had called the unborn child 'Sixpence', a well-known name in Zambia. While Sarah was nursing her and talking to her, a Zambian girl in the next-door bed said, 'you can't call her Sixpence, Sixpence is a boy's name'.

The feeling that one was being treated as a mercenary had been growing since independence. Nevertheless I still loved Zambia and I would love to have stayed on. I suppose I was nervous about a plunge into the outside world. I suppose too that we felt cushioned and general opinion had it that the world of commerce was ferociously efficient and competitive. Yet I was confident that I had been able to handle a lot of power and responsibility at a young age and that it was going to be a matter of adapting to new challenges. I was only 32 after all.

Meanwhile we had time to serve out. I was determined to use my position to see parts of Zambia where I had never had the chance to go. The first of these was the fabulous Nyika Plateau in the far north-east described by Laurens van der Post in his first book *Venture into the Interior*, which I had loved. Juliet was only a few weeks old, but she was strong and healthy and so was Sarah, so we set off leaving Stephen behind. We drove in my own car via the capital of the Eastern Province, Chipata, on to Lundazi and the North. Sarah was breast-feeding Juliet, so there were no feeding problems. We just took plenty of water, a few tins of baked beans and bullied beef and of course plenty of gin and bottles of tonic water and a few lemons. We also had a camera and I remembered to pack my trout rod and some flies. It was a long first day's drive to Lundazi, and I did all the driving. When we stopped along the way, there were always Zambian women with their babies and Juliet attracted much interest and some admiration. Certainly she was the big talking point though I wished that my limited Chinyanja, the local language in the east, had been more fluent. Though unpaved, the roads were good and after a very early start we got to Lundazi by early evening. We called at the boma to talk to some messengers who were delighted to see us and then drove down to the castle via the messenger's lines consisting of extraordinary little houses built in the Rumple-Stilt-Skin style. They together with the castle had been the idea of an extraordinary former District Commissioner Errol Button. Mr Button's castle was a real one with its turrets and battlements and it stood beside a small lake and extensive parkland full of very tame antelope. The castle was also a comfortable rest house. Amongst the ornaments was a pair of the biggest elephant tusks I had ever seen; they must have stood six or seven feet tall.

The drive from Lundazi to Mzuzu in Malawi was on rougher minor roads. From there to the Nyika the road crosses and recrosses the frontier with Zambia until it starts to climb the plateau which goes up to over 9000 feet in Malawi. Whoever decided on the original border must have had considerable imagination to include this bit of unique upland country in Northern Rhodesia. The road to the main part of the plateau runs right through it. We found ourselves climbing up through thick bush. Higher and higher we went until at about 7000 feet we broke out into spectacular open grassland with massive views and little valleys containing pockets of thick forest. The road carried on upwards till we reached the turnoff on the left to our destination, the Zambian rest house. We had heard a lot about it and it came up to expectations in every way. The rest house was another creation of the very creative Errol Button, builder of Lundazi Castle, and stands on the highest point in Zambia at just about 8000 feet. The building itself is plain and unobtrusive as befits its location in this wild and beautiful place. We arrived to be welcomed enthusiastically by the housekeeper, an elderly man of the old school who did not compromise on standards. Although he was not expecting us (there was no telephone or radio, and messages to and from district headquarters at Lundazi would take days unless there was a visitor arriving by car), he made us feel very welcome. Soon there was a fire roaring in the lounge with its vast views towards the Isoka boma about 50 miles to the north-west. On that side of the building there is a rough lawn where we rolled around playing with Juliet for a time. A path descends from the rest house through grassland full of wild flowers into a wooded valley where there is a clear fast-flowing stream. Down there is a small centrifugal pump which provides water for the rest house, and in the dappled shade under the large trees, we noticed several species of butterflies and an amazing variety of birds. The Nyika valleys are a unique ecosystem and contain flora and fauna found nowhere else in the world. Climbing back up the hill with Juliet on Sarah's back in the African style, we started picking some of the many different wild flowers growing in abundance until we had a good bunch. Back in the rest house with Juliet in a cot we sat down to enjoy our drinks and the spectacular sunset on the Zambian horizon 60 miles away and 4000 feet below us. The rest house had a small library and I read Judith Todd's book about her fight against oppression in Southern Rhodesia where she went on hunger strike and was force-fed. We also had a good look at the rest house guest book, which read almost like a Who's Who of central and southern Africa top people like Sir Humphrey Gibbs, governor of Southern Rhodesia, and the last governor of Northern Rhodesia Sir Evelyn Hone. They all knew a very special place when they saw one. The next day after breakfast we set off for the Selinda Forest plantation well into the main Malawi part of the plateau. The rough dirt road was only just passable for my Cortina Estate and ran up over vast grassy meadows and then down into valleys to cross fast-flowing streams. On the rounded hills were large herds of game, which turned out to be mainly eland and zebra. Down in the valleys, the pockets of thick forest waited invitingly to be explored. It was a half-hour run to Selinda, where there was a Malawian Forest Department office and huts for visitors amongst the pine plantations. I wondered about the economic potential of the plantations. They spoilt an otherwise untouched wilderness area I thought. At the Forestry Office I bought a permit to fish and we were persuaded to go and try our luck in the adjacent small dams. Sarah and I took it in turns to fish and look after the baby but had no luck and so decided to go and try some river fishing. We drove back along the main road and stopped at a bridge. I walked downstream until I came to a straight run of water above a waterfall. I cast a wet fly and let the current take most of the line before starting to reel in. Almost immediately I felt a fish take. It felt like a big one, but I was not sure because of the current; my leader was only four-pound breaking strain. Then there was not much line to let out, but I let the fish take me before the line eased and I started reeling in. I was beginning to wonder whether I had lost him when suddenly the fish made a run and the reel screamed. Again I started to reel him in. That fish took over half an hour to land and was a superb rainbow trout weighing nearly seven pounds, bigger than any other trout I had seen in southern Africa or the United Kingdom. That fish sticks in my mind, but I think Sarah and I caught a few more before, at sunset, we began our drive back to the rest house. As we drove along in the blackness we could see lots of eyes caught in the car headlights. They may have been jackals, hares, serval cats or even leopards, but we did not get a clear view of an animal until there in the middle of the road right in front of us was a porcupine. It shuffled along ahead of us with long quills stacked on its back. It turned towards us a few times before turning off the road into the long grass.

At the rest house the fire was roaring in the sitting room and we sat in front of it and reviewed our day while the smell of cooking trout filtered invitingly from the kitchen. Next day after taking some photos we set off on the long drive back to Lusaka and so-called civilisation.

I had taken many trips up the Zambezi River during my days in the Kalomo district. However, I had never been further than the border with the Sesheke district, which is in what had then been known as Barotseland. This protectorate within a protectorate was always regarded as a very special place by the officers who served there. It was entirely rural and dominated by the mighty river which when it flooded caused the traditional ruler, the *Litunga*, to move his capital in a traditional ceremony called the *kuomboka*. The people of Barotseland, the 'Lozi', spoke a language called 'Silozi', which is almost identical to the languages spoken in Botswana and Lesotho. I knew the main greetings because three of the Kalomo chiefs had an ethnic Lozi population and there were a lot of Lozis in Livingstone, the provincial capital. I had always adored the river from the days when I had been to Kazangula with my parents and then had toured up and down it in the Kalomo days. There are quiet stretches where the river is divided by great islands of forest often holding populations of elephant taking advantage of the lush vegetation. To camp beside the river is to be lulled at night by honking of hippos and what for me is the soporific night sound of the calls of hundreds of frogs. The bird life is spectacular with skeins of rare skimmers which fly in formation dipping their beaks into the water to pick up small fish or other edibles. On patches of weed or water lilies commonly seen are the beautiful jacana or lily-trotters with their nut brown, light blue and white colouring, long legs and widespread feet. More than any other animal, they look as though they are walking on water. Of course there are crocodiles aplenty, large numbers of duck of all sorts, Egyptian geese and quite a few massive spurwing geese. Now that we were leaving Zambia I wanted to get back to the river and combine this with a trip up to the interior of Barotseland, where I had never been. I hatched a plan with Peter Fullerton, an ex-Kenya DO who had joined the Foreign Office and was now a first secretary at the British High Commission in Lusaka. The plan was to take my nearly new Ford Cortina Estate down to Livingstone and then drive up the river to Mongu, capital of Barotseland, and from there all the way back to Lusaka.

It was over 300 miles from Lusaka to Livingstone, where we arrived in the early afternoon. Peter would have loved to have crossed the Falls Bridge, but there was an official British government ban on civil servants travelling into rebel Rhodesia, so he stayed at the Mosi Oa Tunya hotel very close to the Eastern Cataract of the Victoria Falls on the northern side while I crossed the famous Falls Bridge to collect a picture I had had commissioned from a well-known Rhodesian artist Joan Jocelyn at Victoria Falls village. The picture was a life-size head-and-shoulders portrait of a Valley Tonga woman in her full regalia of thick necklaces and bracelets, the stick through her nose and of course the hubble-bubble gourd pipe. It is a splendid picture done in pastels, which I have to this day.

Next morning Peter and I set off up river past the turnings to Chief Sekute's village on the right and to Katombora Reformatory on the left, and I thought of the many times I had been up and down there since my first tour with John Durant. Later we passed the turning down to Kazangula and 'Freedom Ally' at the point where Zambia, Rhodesia, Botswana and the then South-West Africa meet. At the Mambova fishing village the good road stopped and we carried on along a bush track towards Mulobezi where there was a sawmill to exploit the so-called Rhodesian teak and other hardwood timbers in the local forests. Along the way we crossed and recrossed the famous Mulobezi railway line where the trucks loaded with timber were pulled by the ancient timber-burning steam engines much loved by railway enthusiasts including the artist David Shepherd. As it ran mainly through the Kalomo district, I had toured in the area and remembered my amazement the first time I had seen old Anglian motor cars fitted with metal wheels zipping up and down the line at a fair speed. In Mulobezi we went to see the management of the sawmill and were shown around while I made notes for my report to the ministry. So far we had no problem with the car despite the rough but dry roads. The dust was bad, but we left that in clouds behind us and we saw no other vehicles. We were making for a remote Forestry Department rest house halfway to Sesheke. We were delighted to find a substantial house, double-storied and thatched, with lovely views over the dambo and forest and as isolated and deep in the bush as it is possible to be. I could see we were going to be very comfortable and we had steaks for the cook to prepare as well as beer, wine and some Camembert.

Well nourished and rested we carried on the next day to Sesheke on the mighty Zambezi, had tea with the District Governor Princess Nakatindi in the wonderfully sited old DC's house and carried on into the heart of what used to be Barotseland towards Senanga. A hundred miles upstream where the road crossed the river there was a pontoon, and there we came across two Russian military trucks from Angola apparently loaded with arms and heading south, presumably for Rhodesia or Namibia due soon to become conflict zones. We had basic camping equipment and stopped that night at the beautiful Sioma Falls where the wide river breaks into a series of rapids and low waterfalls. In the warmth of the evening air, covered in dust the first thing Peter and I did was to strip off and luxuriate in pools under the cascading torrents.

The Barotseland trip was my last into the bush. Soon the farewell parties began.

We gave away the two dogs, which had become inseparable, to a family who were due to go to Botswana. For me perhaps the biggest wrench was parting from my faithful manservant and friend Stephen. In lieu of pension, besides clothes, money and an airgun (mea culpa), I agreed to put his daughter Bweda through secondary school at Chikuni Mission.

When we left Zambia in mid-1969 with six-month-old Juliet via the Kenya Coast for a few days, I wondered whether we would ever see Africa again. I don't think that I realised the extent to which Africa was in my blood. One thing about the PA was that it certainly prepared you to accept change and to look on it as a challenge rather than a threat. We had a house in England to return to and at 33 the prospect of an exciting new career beckoned. First of all though, under the terms of our contracts with the Zambian government, we designated officers could retire anywhere in the world. So, my little family and I had tickets to New York. I swapped the onward portions from London, and while Sarah and baby Juliet went to my parents in Malta, I took off to visit friends and relations across America. First stop was San Francisco where I got in touch with Elizabeth Colson, now a much respected Africanist professor at the University of California, Berkeley. These were the days of anti-Vietnam War and anti all sorts of things especially amongst academics. I did not really know Elizabeth all that well, but she seemed delighted to see me and we spent a wonderful evening speaking Tonga, listening to Tonga music and drinking in bars with young academics and students. Inevitably, the conversation turned to the supposed iniquities of colonialism. I was surprised and delighted to find Elizabeth wholeheartedly supporting my general line in every conversation we had about Africa, colonialism and so on. She had seen and experienced too much of the realities on the ground in the Gwembe Valley and from the likes of Crighton and Tuppy Mitchell to go along with the heavily biased and ill-informed American viewpoint. From San Francisco I flew on to Santa Barbara to see Brian Fagan; we talked about the good times we had shared in Kalomo and Livingstone and went for a sail in his yacht with its painted mermaid with two tone nipples at the prow. It was clear though that his career had moved on and he was no longer interested in Zambia and Africa. On I flew to stay with my American friends Charlie and Sally with whom I had shared the five bottles of champagne in Taormina during my first leave in 1963. Now they were clearly doing well in their careers as academics at Harvard and lived in a large house in suburban Boston. They had changed though. No longer were they models of the American establishment. Charlie had grown long hair and they were vehemently against anything and everything the American government did or stood for. I found myself defending basic American values, even democracy, to them. In Sicily they had been interested in talking about Africa, but now were simply not interested in any views I might have. They had invited some interesting friends, mainly fellow academics, one or two pretty eminent I gathered. The evening was totally ruined for me when in the absence of my wife and anybody else I knew, I was persuaded that everybody else would be on 'grass' and that I should try some. It was one of the most miserable experiences of my life. Simply, I could not 'go with the flow' and I would not try it again for anything. Finally in America I went to stay with my cousin Shirley, who was married to Beverly Byrd, brother-in-law of the well-known Senator Harry Byrd (of whom more later), on a huge apple farm near Berryville, Virginia. I had a wonderful few days hunting to hounds (with Shirley leading me round any jumps) and taking part in a pigeon shoot, over the huge estate. It was an extraordinary set-up as Shirley worked like a beaver getting black children into school and doing good works while Beverly was telling me that his two political heroes in Africa were the arch-exponent of apartheid: the South African Prime Minister John Vorster and the Prime Minister of the then rebel Rhodesia, Ian Smith.

Back in the United Kingdom things certainly looked promising. With the help of the Overseas Resettlement Bureau operating out of the old Colonial Office building in Great Smith Street, a number of attractive alternatives came to my attention. My guru there was a delightful retired colonial civil servant who encouraged me to prepare an alternative CV in French and to mention my interest in *pêche à la mouche* (fly fishing). In 1969, the staff was expert in getting one interviews with leading companies where retired colonial civil servants had a good reputation. For me though, top of the priority list was the Foreign Office where I was accepted for the final interview stage for entry into the Grade V level, which was pretty senior. My interviews were held within a few days of arriving in England and were a nightmare.

To begin with, I was staying in London with my sister, and as one of her children was crying all night, I did not get much sleep. Worse though was that there were tests of the sort that you did for 11+. The trouble was that I had never taken the 11+ and was panicked by what at first appeared to be pretty simple tests of my intelligence. The result I fear must have been abject failure and I must have come over as totally stupid. Another thing was that aside from 18 months in prep school and a year at Cambridge I had never lived in the United Kingdom and, whereas I could have named the Vietnamese foreign minister or the leader of the Canadian Conservatives, I had no idea who was the deputy general secretary of the TUC.

So the Foreign Office was blown. However, there were other prospects. I had excellent interviews at Rolls-Royce at Derby and at Lansing Bagnall at Basingstoke. These interviews were preceded by an altogether unhelpful talk with an Overseas Resettlement Bureau consultant whose main aim, rather than boost your confidence at a difficult time, seemed to be to pull you down a peg or two and convince you that even though you might have had huge responsibilities in the colonies you were of little potential use to commerce and industry. For me this sort of talk was totally unhelpful because I think most of us had got it into our heads that industry was incredibly efficient and up to date and we would be very lucky to get in. I soon came to see British industry in a very different light. However, despite the good interviews my problems were far from over. Lansing Bagnall proposed a day for a third interview. I said that that day did not suit as I had an interview with Rolls-Royce. That was a mistake as I suppose it was seen as name-dropping. Anyway I had a phone call to say they were no longer interested in me. Good news soon followed, however, and I received an offer from Rolls-Royce to work in their Personnel Department in Derby. I was delighted and the company agreed I could go on a one-month course at Ashridge Management College to which I was being sent by the Overseas Resettlement Bureau, before joining. On the course one of my friends was a man from Rolls-Royce in Derby. One day during the course, it was October 1969, I had a phone call from my contact in Derby saying that unfortunately the company was in trouble and the offer of employment was being withdrawn. I was thunderstruck. I knew that an offer made and accepted constituted a contract and I saw the offer of three months' pay as totally inadequate particularly in the light of all the promising job prospects I had abandoned. I consulted my friend on the course from Derby, who advised me to write to the Chairman Sir Denning Pearson asking for a minimum of six months' pay. I got it and we carpeted the cottage.

Meanwhile, another friend on the Ashridge course was from the IBM company and he offered me a job looking after the sales of office products in Suffolk and Essex. The attraction was that we could continue to live in our cottage and I would get an excellent sales training from a company which was seen at that time as the byword in progressive modernity. So I accepted and after some failures and lot of adjustment, had one of the most lucrative years of my life and attained the sought-after IBM 100% Club. I had received a first-class sales training and a lot of hard experience. I came to appreciate that nothing sells itself and that the days of empire and an automatic market for British goods were well and truly over.

By now in late 1970, Sarah and I were settling into Suffolk life and had another child Ting (Juliet's corruption of Shilling). IBM had taught me a lot including how outdated was so much of British commerce and industry. One could almost smell the conservative attitude and practices when one walked in the front door of many companies. There was talk of 'Mr John' and the clack-clack of manual typewriters could be heard in the background. It would hardly have surprised me to see an old clerk using a quill pen. No wonder Britain was failing to punch its weight in the world. It seemed to me that instead of being encouraged to go and work in things like the new government training boards, or as school bursars, ex-colonial service colleagues should have been encouraged to join commerce and industry where they could bring into play the ability, for instance, to see the whole picture rather than only a small part of it.

Anyway after a year with IBM, since there were no immediate prospects of promotion into the management, I was persuaded to join a neighbour's company which made small jet engines at Harwich and become his general manager and sales director. Meanwhile, we bought a brand new luxury car and went skiing with the children plus a nanny. After getting back from skiing I drove to Harwich for my first day's work only to be told that because of the collapse of Rolls-Royce, sub-contracts had fallen through and there was no longer a job for me. I resisted the temptation to go back to IBM and started job-hunting afresh. The problem was that whatever my view of my own abilities, after instant success with IBM, for potential employers I only had a single year's experience in sales. I found, however, that my fluency in French was saleable and this got me taken on in London as the personnel manager designate on a large mining project in the Congo, shortly to become Zaire. So after less than two years away, we were going back to Africa.

9

Malachite Hills

Soon my new employers sent me out to Lubumbashi, the old Elizabethville and capital of the Katanga province, to join a project inspection team sent by Anglo-American in Lusaka. One of the men from Lusaka was Gavin Barr, who had deprived me of my beloved boat MV Guimbe, five years before. Now through a quirk of fate we both found ourselves appointed to the same job as personnel manager (designate) on Socotef's Tenke Fungurume mining project on the Katangan Copperbelt in the Congo Republic. This was perhaps symptomatic of the whole set-up of the project where it was often unclear who was responsible for what, and where the decisions were being taken. Socotef, soon to become SMTF (Societe Miniere de Tenke Fungurume) when the Congo changed its name to Zaire, was an international consortium formed to exploit the copper deposit at Fungurume, said to be the richest in the world. I had been taken on by the project's leading partner and manager, Charter Consolidated, which was based in London and effectively the international arm of the Anglo-American Corporation of South Africa.

President Mobutu had removed the concession to mine at Fungurume from the state mining company Gecamines, formally the Belgian-owned Union Miniere, and given it to Charter, because he hoped for a more progressive approach particularly over the training of indigenous Congolese. The real significance of this whole investment was that it linked South African capital and expertise with the natural resources of a part of Africa outside its traditional sphere of influence in the south. The trouble was that at that time, blacks had made no progress at all into the skilled trades, much less into technical management in any southern African country. That afternoon in Lubumbashi was a revelation to me. I had not expected to find Lubumbashi, the former Elizabethville of the colonial era, so prosperous and sophisticated. The mainly Belgian expatriates enjoyed a very good lifestyle with high tax-free salaries, frequent overseas leave and some of the best restaurants in Africa. Most of the food and wine was imported on the overnight flights direct from Belgium. The priority that Belgians give to their food certainly extended to those living in Lubumbashi, where besides having excellent restaurants, they occupied large villas and enjoyed facilities like the Club Hippique and a magnificent 18-hole golf course with an American professional.

The mine site at Fungurume was a surprise too. The well-established mining township reoccupied in 1970 mainly by Charter geologists was set in spectacular bush country well back from the railway and the main Lubumbashi–Kolwezi road. It was dominated by the green hills where the copper lay. Though that September the rains had yet to break, part of the green of the hills came from the copper deposits including malachite – the semi-precious bright-green stone which is itself 95 per cent copper. There was a club, including a bar, swimming pool, tennis court and squash court. From the surrounding bush and into the gardens emerged a fantastic variety of birdlife to take advantage of the lawns and flowerbeds covered with colourful butterflies. Frequently, a bateleur or other large African eagle soared overhead as we sat round the club pool. On that first visit, Gavin and I were not yet sure how the job issue would be resolved. I think we both thought Fungurume would be an ideal place to live and work.

Fungurume, it turned out, had been as far as Cecil Rhodes's Benguela Railway had reached in 1916 during the First World War. It was the jumping-off point for an extraordinary African story, the story of 'The African Queen'. The real story, though it lacks the romantic element, is more interesting and dramatic than the fictional film version starring Humphrey Bogart and Katharine Hepburn. Peter Shankland in his fascinating book *The Phantom Flotilla* (also a TV drama documentary) tells how in 1916 the Royal Navy under the command of a Captain Spicer railed two gunboats, the 'Mimi' and the 'Toutou', from Cape Town to the railhead at Fungurume and dragged them with steam traction engines up the steep, heavily wooded Mitumba Mountains to the Lualaba River which becomes the mighty Congo. The Mimi and the Toutou were put on barges and floated 500 miles down river to the railhead at Kabalo and then railed down to Albertville on Lake Tanganyika. There, after a number of skirmishes, they blew the German navy out of the water. The colourful story features Spicer's habit of wearing a skirt and at the end describes the role of a detachment of tearaway Rhodesian soldiers.

Before going to live in the Congo, which changed its name to Zaire while I was on that first visit, I spent some months getting used to the Anglo-American/Charter Consolidated way of doing things at their offices near Chancery Lane in London. I gathered that the Anglo group had ambitions to become a global player in the mining field through its international arm, Charter. It had had a failure, because of inappropriate technology, it was said, in Mauritania, but had high hopes for the Congo and Fungurume. Charter was staffed largely by people who had worked in the Zambian Copperbelt pre- and post-independence. Clearly, it was felt that with their experience of a black African country, they had the appropriate background for a project in the Congo. The feeling was that they would have much more appropriately progressive ideas and policies than the Belgians who were the mainstay of Gecamines management. At the time, nobody questioned the fact that until Zambian independence, only seven years before in 1964, African advancement on the Copperbelt had been comprehensively blocked by the white trade unions. After independence, the management's prime task had been to emasculate these unions and introduce programmes of every sort to train Zambians. In the Congo, as I was soon to discover, racial prejudice and discrimination under the Belgians had taken a different form. There, there were plenty of skilled black operators on the mines. There were even some black technical managers, a genus which our management preferred not to even contemplate.

I was intrigued by the flavours of management style I got at Charter headquarters in London in 1971. Clearly the Anglo group was an Oppenheimer family company and it made no bones about that. It meant that if you had links to the family, you were in a position of clear advantage. It also meant that there was a lot of name-dropping, and employees talked of knowing someone who knew someone who knew the family. All this made for a very hierarchical company, which was reflected specially in the lunching arrangements. I ate in the 'B' dining room one up from the ordinary staff dining room. We had drinks before lunch and a waitress service, but no wine with the meal as in the 'A' dining room. The director's dining room, it was said, had haute cuisine of the highest order. Non-technical managers at Charter were members of the Prospecting and Mining (P & M) Department and were typically young men of good public school and Oxbridge background. I think the company was using SMTF for young managers to cut their teeth on. Although several showed promise, few had any experience of Africa or of genuine management responsibility. One was so arrogant and offhand when

I introduced myself to him that I resolved there and then to have as little as possible to do with him from then on. I think his behaviour reflected feelings of personal inadequacy. It was a different problem with the technical hierarchy, which provided the in situ mine management. They were mainly experienced mining men ex Zambia. To my recollection, none spoke French and were certainly not versed in the sensitivities and complexities of the infinitely corrupt and chaotic Congo.

I had no qualifications in personnel management and had only been taken on because of my French and my experience of post-independence Zambia. I was supposed to be trained in my new 'technology' at Charter. My mentor for this was Mack Hunter, the man who had masterminded the emasculation of the European trade unions on the Zambian Copperbelt over the independence period. Mack was very much a company man loyal to its methods and what it was trying to achieve, and not afraid of being unpopular. He was convinced that Anglo/Charter personnel and training policies were highly advanced and that we had been brought in to supplant what he perceived as the out-of-date Belgian ways being followed by Gecamines in the Congo.

Before going out to live in the Congo, as part of my training and induction, I was sent for a month to the massive Nchanga Mine on the Zambian Copperbelt. There, despite recent nationalisation, the Anglo influence was still very strong. I was taken aback by the sheer scale of this massive operation with its open pit about half a mile in diameter and a thousand feet deep. Great trucks with electric motors in their ten-feet-high wheels descended slowly into the open pit where the dust was kept down by smaller sprinkler trucks. There they were loaded with 200 tons of ore by diggers taking 20-ton bites. The Copperbelt was a very different place from when I had lived there in the early 1960s. However, there were still thousands of whites employed on the mines. Now the whole emphasis was on training. There were massive, generously staffed training schools carrying out both technical training and general education. The latter was necessary to bring people up to the level of a full primary school education. This was generally accepted to be the minimum necessary for a man to be able to absorb the training in technical skills. There was no programme to develop indigenous technical management. I don't think Zambia Consolidated Copper Mines (ZCCM) saw this as a problem even though at this stage the mines were entirely dependent on white technical management.

My month-long stay at Nchanga Consolidated Copper Mines (NCCM) was very eventful, and I learned a lot. Despite the enormous efforts made towards improving black skills, it would obviously be several years before there were significant numbers of Zambians in the higher echelons. Something that struck me quite forcibly at the time was the existence of multiple social levels dependent on seniority. It was quite extraordinary how the mine captains and the wives socialised with each other but not with the shift bosses below them or the underground managers above them. Most talk was of shop even with wives and I overheard one spouse remark, 'it is NCCM this and NCCM that. If I have NCCM tattooed on my bum, perhaps he will pay more attention to me'.

When eventually we moved out en famille to live in Lubumbashi, we found ourselves in a nice airy white house with a medium-sized garden and a small swimming pool. We were near the delightful golf course which I joined immediately. Neighbours were mainly Belgians, either business people or working for the state mining company Gecamines. Juliet aged 3 and Ting 2 went to a local nursery school where they picked up French in what seemed just a few weeks. We started to lead a good social life with dinner parties, children's parties and golf for me. Sarah played bridge and did some sailing on the local Lubumbashi reservoir. All the expatriates seemed to have plenty of money and a high proportion of this was spent in some of the best restaurants I have come across anywhere. It was not just the food, such as foie gras, the Dover sole or fresh asparagus flown in from Brussels. That was matched by the finest wines, nearly all French, from Bordeaux, Burgundy and the Rhone. We learned to eat well, and though I developed a taste for oysters, I could never get to like frogs' legs. The Belgian preoccupation with food was such that even on the golf course it tended to be the main topic of conversation. All this was a far cry from the British colonial eating tradition which tended to revolve around mixed grill or the occasional Indian or Chinese restaurant. So obsessed were the Belgians with their own European culinary traditions that they neglected some marvellous local fish, venison and game such as guinea fowl, which could have been available.

Lubumbashi in 1972 was still a beautiful city with broad tree-lined avenues and modern-looking public buildings, some pockmarked by bullet holes from the post-independence troubles. Most of the houses occupied by Europeans had high walls and massive gates. Gardens were smaller than in the ex-British colonies. The streets, however, were in a very poor condition with numerous potholes, some massive and a foot or two deep. They had probably not been maintained since independence. The police, who were indistinguishable from the army, were awful, scruffy, aggressive and greedy.

The reason, I suppose, was that they seldom received any pay. They lay in wait at stop streets and demanded money if the unfortunate motorist was an inch or two beyond the by now almost invisible painted lines. Such bribes were called *matabiche* and were demanded by so-called public servants at every opportunity. This included when one wanted to make an overseas phone call. It was sometimes necessary to meet the operator in the park near the telephone exchange and hand him his fee. When we first arrived, the crime and security situation was quite good despite high unemployment. This was apparently because a recently caught robber had been hanged in public. Altogether the atmosphere was of reasonable security and stability. I think people were so frightened of returning to the chaos and bloodshed of the years following independence that there was a determination to stay peaceful. A stabilising factor was the fact of employment for a high proportion of the population in the mines, the railways and a significant number of expatriate-owned enterprises. The majority of the population seemed pretty well fed mainly by regular 'Affretair' flights from rebel Rhodesia loaded with maize meal and beef.

I was very busy at work planning for the future mine. It was obviously a good idea to gain a good understanding of Gecamines policy and practice and to pay regular visits to liaise with the management at Fungurume and particularly with Gavin Barr. There was also the considerable input from our personnel guru at Charter Consolidated headquarters in London. Mack Hunter was a man of considerable force of character and charisma. He was imbued with the idea that Anglo group policies and practices were what our project needed. Belgian ideas were in his opinion, backward and inappropriate. I was coming to see the very opposite. I was meeting some very impressive senior managers both Belgian and Zairois and was aware that generally speaking, localisation in Gecamines was being carried out from the bottom up rather that from the top down as was the case in Zambia.

Vital Belgian skills were being retained through the payment of high salaries, part of which were paid in Europe free of tax. We at SMTF also enjoyed high salaries but had no concession over tax despite the fact that every penny of the money for our pay had to be brought into the country. This situation was of our own making and arose from the desire to be seen to be doing everything by the book. The local Belgians found this rather amusing.

The family and I liked Lubumbashi. I found it relaxing that I did not have the emotional relationship with the country that I would have had in Zambia. Meanwhile we could get on with enjoying all the advantages of a very different and very beautiful African country. I had yet to see anything of the wonderful unspoiled and seldom-visited national parks in which the local Belgians showed little interest. I started playing a lot of golf, Sarah improved her sailing skills on the town dam and the children became even more fluent in French. In the early days, I could not believe my ears when late at night I heard the familiar and unmistakable sound of a lion roaring. I could not believe that a lion would approach even to within a couple of miles of Lubumbashi suburbs. Yet there it was. The country was certainly special. It was only the next day that I learned that Lubumbashi had a zoo.

On another occasion over the weekend, Sarah was with friends at the sailing club at the dam when down the road leading to the slipway came a car being driven at speed by a middle-aged European male. The car hurtled down and into the water where the momentum carried it a long way out into the lake. There it remained floating steadily out into the middle. Sarah leapt into the water and started swimming after it. She got to it to find it quite dry inside; she even slid in through the open back window. The white man was slumped over the wheel, conscious and apparently unhurt. She then got out into the water again and started back to shore calling for a rope; the boatman swam past her with a rope in his teeth. They attached it to the car's tow bar and swam back towing it slowly. The crowd that had gathered pulled it back up the ramp. There was only a little water in the car which had come in via the pedals. It turned out that she was due to meet the man later that day through a friend. He was a Monsieur Waters, the head of personnel on the railways, and had decided on drastic action on learning that his wife had left him for another. He had presumed that his car would sink and he with it. Now safe and sound he was apparently glad still to be alive. He was also grateful to his saviour Sarah, with whom he endowed all sorts of wisdom. He was sure that she was predestined to advise him on what best to do in his marital predicament. The downside of all this was that for a few weeks there were interminable sessions at our house, with Sarah urging him that his wife should have her divorce despite his Catholic upbringing. We heard later that he had divorced her and was very happy living with his son.

After six months in Lubumbashi, Gavin Barr and I carried out the pre-planned job swap and our family went to live in Fungurume. Gavin's house in the old Belgian geological prospectors' camp was a lovely old one with a beautiful view of the green malachite hills and the garden running down to the swimming pool and club. The old Belgian houses had been supplemented with half a dozen modern Zambian-style houses. Otherwise the houses were all prefabricated, so-called terrapins. I had assumed that part of the swap arrangement would involve an exchange of houses. Gavin did not see it that way and in accordance with his own waiting list system, had allocated his house to an Italian geologist with an outspoken wife. I disputed the allocation and the upshot was that though I got the house, the wife never spoke to me or Sarah from then on. This was not the best of starts.

I was aware of Fungurume's main problem, which arose from the fact that it was the end of a long hierarchical chain of commands. Although we were supposed to be managed by Charter in London, which led the international consortium, everyone knew that it was really Anglo-American at its headquarters at 44 Main Street in Johannesburg which called the shots. After London there was the political office in the Zaire capital Kinshasa and the company headquarters in Lubumbashi. Our man in charge at the mine site, Dave Harries, reported to the Project Director Trevor Lee Jones in Lubumbashi.

The problem was that the whole decision-making and command structure was confused. The Charter people in London and in Ashford Kent were out of touch and in any case uncertain of the scope of their authority and how it related to Johannesburg, the international partners or the Lubumbashi office or what was going on the spot at Fungurume. Trevor Lee Jones in Lubumbashi told me that he was not there to make decisions as he was a consultant. From my point of view, the result of all this was that a huge and unfair burden fell on our boss Dave Harries at the mine site. This did not matter too much in the early days as we were still basically an expanded prospecting camp. However, after the main contracts had been awarded, senior staff from the main contractors began to arrive. These were the French contractor Dumez Afrique for the housing and Fluor Utah of the USA for the plant and other engineering work.

At all stages it was difficult or impossible to know who was responsible for what. In this situation Dave Harries performed marvels, but inevitably all the uncertainty affected the morale of expatriates who were working in a difficult and potentially insecure environment. Yet it was difficult or impossible to identify someone to blame for all the little things that inevitably went wrong.

In such circumstances, I have found, people latch on to mundane issues and for lack of anyone else to blame, they blame the personnel department. Though Dave Harries did not seek this, I had to absorb a lot of flack as did the man responsible for housing, Gerry Rees. Problems did not just come from employees. Wives with little or nothing to do were the main troublemakers. They could cause difficulties for their husbands too. One husband came to confide in me about the exhaustion which was affecting his work. It arose, he said, from the physical demands made on him by his bored wife who demanded sex at night, in the morning and at lunch time too. One couple came to disturb our family Christmas lunch to ask what I proposed to do about the fact that he had seen a snake in his garden. 'Nothing', I replied. Another couple demanded that the children of their Zairois neighbour, my assistant Mr Chiwengo, be stopped from playing games that involved clapping. One day in the office, I received a letter full of mouse droppings.

Despite the problems and frustrations, we had a happy expatriate community at Fungurume.

Social life revolved around the club and tennis and squash courts. I loved being back in the bush which surrounded our camp and came right up to the boundary fence. A huge variety of birds were in our garden all the time. The views over the hills where the copper lay were a constant inspiration and in the evenings numerous bats flitted amongst the houses and gardens and nightjars took up their wonderful lulling call. Considering that we were now living in one of the most beautiful and least spoilt parts of the whole of Africa, the pressures of work were such that we did not see as much of the deep bush as I would have liked. However, Sarah took the children and dog out in the car most afternoons. We had invested in a nearly new Toyota Land Cruiser and one weekend took our little girls along a bush track which had probably been cleared by labourers making way for the steam traction engines dragging Mimi and Toutou up into the Mitumba Mountains on their way to engage the German navy on Lake Tanganyika. It was September and still the dry season, but the trees in the forest we passed through were quite the most magnificent I had seen before or since anywhere. They were significantly bigger than those I was used to in Zambia, and there was a great variety of species. What made them really memorable, however, were the spring colours of their new leaves which varied from yellows to every shade of green and on to oranges, reds and purples. We crossed a rushing stream. Behind us were magnificent views of endless rolling bush several hundred feet below. We carried on to the top of the escarpment and were suddenly out of the forest and looking over a vast grassy plain. In the distance we could see prancing oribi antelope. It was the first time I had seen oribi since Kalomo days, ten years before.

I have overwhelmingly happy memories of Fungurume days because we were 'en famille' and the girls were at a wonderful age. I got several bouts of bronchitis due mainly, I think, to a combination of smoking and the thick dust from the camp roads. I had to have antibiotics to get me right, and I remember the wonderful dancing sessions, mainly jumping up and down with the girls, as I got better. Sarah was pregnant with Tom; otherwise she and the girls would have come with me into the bush when one day the desire to be out there became overwhelming and I went off and camped in an area about ten miles north of Fungurume on my own. The noises of the night including those from nightjars, frogs and a variety of owls as well as a distant leopard were wonderful. Next morning I went for a long walk and found a porcupine quill near my camp and saw plenty of signs of elephant but apart from a lone bushbuck, nothing else.

About that time I had my first experience of the wonderful vast Upemba National Park; I went with friends via the cement-manufacturing town of Lubudi where we stopped off to visit the cemetery which is or was still maintained by the Commonwealth War Graves Commission. There must have been fighting near there during the First World War. It was a long day's motoring, 300 miles or so to the main camp where we were booked in for a couple of nights. The park was well run and the poachers had been kept away despite all the troubles since independence. The visitors' book had only two pages of names, covering the previous 40 years. I can't remember much about that trip except that there were plenty of elephants and we saw a wonderful pride of young lions and my appetite was whetted for further visits, next time with the family I hoped. The park is roughly divided into two by the Lufira River, which runs between the plateau country to the north and east and a vast area of low-lying bush country bordering the great Lake Upemba in the west. The western part was virtually untouched in those days. There were no roads and I never met anyone who had been there. The area was rumoured to be inhabited by two mutually hostile tribes. I imagined the lake and its environs to be inhabited by vast numbers of waders and other aquatic birds.

It was in the rainy season when we went on our first family holiday from Fungurume. We would like to have gone to Rhodesia, but the direct route via Zambia and the bridge at Chirundu being closed by the Zambians, we decided to go to Malawi and revisit the Nyika Plateau for some fishing, spend a few days on the Lake at Selima and then go onto the Zomba Plateau beside the old colonial capital for more fishing. It was a very long journey. Our system was to put our luggage into cases in the well of the Land Cruiser and then put a mattress on top for the girls. On the way we played games and sang songs and Sarah and I told stories. We got to the Nyika in three days and found the Zambian rest house as welcoming as ever. Shortly after our arrival, a fire was roaring in the living room. The next day both Sarah and I caught trout and the girls were thrilled by the zebra and eland on the undulating grassland not very different from the Upemba.

After a couple of days, we were rested enough to move on via Mzuzu from where we headed straight for the lake. We had met the head of the Malawi tourist office at the rest house in Mzuzu on our way north and he had advised us to use the nearly completed lake shore road on our way south. The road as yet untarred was, however, wonderfully smooth until all of a sudden we hit a big ditch dug right across the road. We all hit the roof hard. There were no seat belts in those days. The children wailed, but as the car came to a halt, I was most worried about Sarah, who was seven-months pregnant. Thank heavens we were all okay, and we carried on along the otherwise silky smooth road to Selima 150 miles further on.

Selima was where Colonel David Stirling's Capricorn Africa Society's famous conference had been held in 1956, and Africans, Europeans and Asians met and talked about a non-racial future for the region. For many of the participants, this was the first time they had met people of another race on a basis of equality. Capricorn's idea was to get away from considerations of race and build a society based on mutual respect and shared higher values. There would be no need for black nationalism nor for white racism and all would live happily together. The implications were of a leading role for Europeans. It was pie in the sky stuff and not much to do with real politik, but believers were passionate. Now Selima had reverted to a charming lakeside hotel with bedroom huts under the trees, a sandy beach and the clear clean waters of the great inland sea that is Lake Malawi. Apart from lying on the beach watching the fish eagles, I remember the superb local fish called *chomba*, even better, if that's possible, than yellow-bellied bream. However, after two days of doing nothing, Sarah and I were bored stiff and so we all piled into the car and drove down the lake and inland to Zomba, the old capital of Nyasaland, a delightful town with colonial bungalows and lush colourful gardens right under the Zomba Mountain rising 3000 feet above us.

Up the mountain we drove with the powerful little box-shaped Land Cruiser making light of the slopes. It was a narrow one-way road and soon we were in cloud and it began to rain. We recited 'up the airy mountain down the rushy glen, we daren't go a hunting for fear of little men' as we drove up and up about 2000 feet till we reached the welcoming delights of a really comfortable country hotel, the Ku Chawe Inn. It was all dripping pine trees and mist rolling over the large gardens on the slope and down towards Zomba hidden by the cloud far below.

We were all happy but dog tired and the girls went straight to bed after children's supper. Sarah and I wanted to taste the benefits of civilisation and chose a bottle of South African red wine with the unpromising name of 'Grand Cheval' for dinner. It turned out to be utterly delicious and went very well with the game patè if not with the *chomba*. Up there on the mountain there were no sounds in the night apart from the steady rain on the roof, the dripping gutters and the swish of the wind in the pines.

The next day was a revelation as we drew the curtains to reveal a seemingly endless view across Africa towards the magnificent 10,000 feet of Mount Mlanji a hundred miles away. It was a wonderfully clear sunny day and already there was a multiplicity of butterflies and birds in the colourful hotel gardens. We were up at more than 6000 feet and heard that the trout fishing in the mountain streams was very good, so off we went in the car, taking our rods. The girls were happy to play beside us as Sarah and I fished wet and caught several trout. Later we explored the area near the hotel and found the weekend cottages used by staff of the British High Commission in Zomba and the British army trainers of the Malawian army. Another day we drove down the mountain to Zomba and had a game of golf on the charming little nine-hole course, all part of an historic old sports club with its delightful echoes of the colonial past. We met someone working for the government who played squash and I proposed a game and got a thorough pasting. I might have been Fungurume champion, but he was the top player in Malawi.

Back at Fungurume the decision to go ahead with the project had been taken and the pace of life began to quicken. Advance teams of Americans from Fluor Utah, the main plant contractors, and the French firm Dumez Afrique, who were building the housing, began to arrive. Those of us on the spot had to give them the benefit of our experience and tried to ensure that policies, particularly over the employment conditions of local Zairois, were co-ordinated as far as possible. At the same time, two senior Americans – Messrs Robinson and Hagan from the major project partners Standard Oil – arrived to be on the spot to keep an eye on their investment. As the numbers of expatriate staff built up, so did the number of Zairois workers. There was no room for the expatriates in the original geologists' camp despite rows of new terrapins, so they occupied the houses on the new low-density area as Dumez made them available. There was no housing for the Zairois workers and gradually an enormous squatter camp grew up around Fungurume. Security, particularly against theft of both private and company property, became a problem.

It was a relief that the project had started, but employees still felt they were being kept in the dark about what was going on. There was a hunger for information and for communication which management on the spot was unable to satisfy. Nobody was prepared to take responsibility for this and the intense frustration was frequently turned on us in the personnel department. High-level visits from senior managers in London brought the prospect of news. Just the chance to talk to someone in the know would have been enough. On more than one occasion, London high-ups arrived in Fungurume with their wives. There was a slap-up lunch and then everyone went away again. It was on one such visit that the managing director of SMTF based in London came to the personnel department and spent nearly an hour talking to my deputy, David Phillimore. I was certain that he would want to see me too; there was a lot I wanted to talk about, despite my resolve two years before in London never to have anything to do with him. To my intense frustration, off he went and I never saw him again on that visit.

In many ways Fungurume was a rough, tough place. However, despite all the frustrations, there was a good atmosphere in the camp. We had some great parties and the community laid on a number of plays and concerts which went down very well. Squash and tennis were much played and some of us used to practice our golf on a vast area of flat ground destined for some part of the treatment plant for the copper ore. A number of us golfers used to travel every Saturday either to Likasi or to Kolwezi to play golf on their excellent little courses where we frequently scooped the prizes. It was 40 miles to Likasi and 60 to Kolwezi and the roads were dreadful with potholes 2 or 3 feet deep. More of a nuisance were the roadblocks put up by the army or the police. It was difficult to tell which was which. They were purely out to get *matabiche*. We learned that the easy way was to pay but that every time you paid, it would make it more difficult for you or someone else next time. Refusal to pay sometimes led to being taken off to the police station. This just meant waiting for half an hour or so until you paid up or the soldiers lost hope of getting any money out of you. One factor which worked in our favour was that the message had got over to the police and the army that SMTF was not to be seriously harassed for *matabiche*. The wife of our engineering manager, a feisty young woman, pushed her luck beyond what might have been considered prudent. She was driving back on her own from a shopping expedition to Zambia when she was stopped at a roadblock manned by soldiers. She was ordered to open the boot of the car but refused. 'Then give us 250 zaires' (about 250 pounds), said the soldier. 'No' was the response. 'Then give us 100.' Again she refused. 'Well make it ten.' Again no. 'Well give us a beer.' 'No.' 'Can you spare a cigarette?' 'No.' 'Thank you madam', said the soldier saluting as she drove on.

About this time, Zaire seemed to be doing well and Mobutu Sese Seke Nkuku wa Zibanga (the cockerel which is never satisfied) was boasting that the local currency, the Zaire, had an even higher value than the pound. Metal prices were high and he had attracted the very significant investment from the international consortium, which was SMTF. Ironically but with the aim of encouraging local indigenous enterprise which was pretty well non-existent, he dealt a massive blow to the economy by effectively dispossessing the Belgian, Greek, Lebanese or other expatriate owners of local enterprises. Though the former owners often moved aside, the whole exercise was a massive failure and, on top of the examples from Uganda and Zambia, should have served as a warning to the likes of Zimbabwe and South Africa that taking from one group to give to another has a history of failure. In the Congo's case, it was a significant step along the path towards national disaster.

We did not only go to Malawi on holiday. Three times over the years, we went to Rhodesia always by road via Zambia where we stayed with Malcolm and Judy Mitchell in Lusaka. Malcolm's parents had been in India with mine. He had joined HMOCS in the very last intake of cadets into Northern Rhodesia in 1962. Now he was the director of elections, the last ex-member of the provincial administration still working for the Zambian government. His presence in 1973 showed that whatever his faults, Kenneth Kaunda still valued free and fair elections. On we went down the Great North Road over the mighty Kafue and then right turned into the Southern Province. We passed through Mazabuka, where I had played rugby in Gwembe days. Then through Monze and the turnoff to Gwembe at Chisekesi. On through the farming areas of Choma, Kalomo and Zimba, which all looked much as I had remembered them 14 years before. It is all Tonga country and I still spoke the language whenever I had the chance and was agreeably surprised how fluent it remained. Each conversation I had provoked an almost ecstatic reaction of goodwill and the desire to be of service. We could see that there were obviously a lot of European farmers around; though on this occasion, there was no time to call on old friends.

At Livingstone we turned right and drove up the familiar road to Mambova past the turning to Chief Sekute's village and on to Freedom Alley at Kazangula on the Zambezi. The crossing was as I had remembered it, and we drove the Toyota off the pontoon and on to Botswana territory. From there it was only about ten miles into the Chobe Game Park where we were booked into the very modern Chobe Safari Lodge. The modernity and sophistication of everything was such a surprise. Normally I prefer unadulterated wild Africa, but with three hungry children to feed, dirty clothes to be washed and the modern facilities with the bedroom radios tuned in to the BBC World Service, it was all wondrous after the rigors of the road and Zaire. Sarah and I settled down with long gin and tonics to appreciate the views over the Chobe River and the plains and swamps towards the Zambezi. The children were fed by the hotel staff and Sarah and I were left to enjoy a good dinner washed down with an excellent bottle of Zonnebloem.

Next day we were told we could not possibly miss the chance of an early morning game drive, so we set off before breakfast in the Toyota. Almost immediately we saw one of the great sights of the wild. It was a female elephant with tiny twins only four- or five-feet high. Though we were very close and I was worried about her reaction to us, she continued to graze. The girls were thrilled. After breakfast we set off for the Rhodesian border crossing. The officials there were friendly and efficient and were happy to stamp a piece of paper rather than our passports. Then it was an hour's drive to look at the Victoria Falls presenting wonderful sights with the river yet to rise too much and block out the view with drenching spray. We called in at a familiar stamping ground, the Victoria Falls Hotel, still at that stage property of Rhodesia Railways, a high point of colonial sophistication and reeking of history. We had a long day ahead of us as we wanted to get well beyond Bulawayo on our way to the Eastern Districts. En route we passed the great coal mine at Wankie and the turnoff to the southern part of the Zambezi Valley. Throughout that area, Tonga is understood, so I had more chances to practice and to get an idea of the state of race relations more than eight years after UDI. We found that to our surprise everybody we came in contact with was friendly. It was ever thus in Southern Rhodesia. Despite the discrimination and prevalent racial slurs, there was never a general atmosphere of antipathy, much less the hate and fear that I found in South Africa.

We stopped for a drink at the Gwaai River Hotel nearly halfway to Bulawayo and would have loved to have stayed in this friendly little bush hotel with bedroom huts under the great riverine trees and the wonderful food and superb friendly service. The concept of service is something with which to their credit Africans do not have a problem. We shot through Bulawayo in the early evening and kept going towards Gwelo and as we approached the outskirts, we spotted a neon sign off the main road, which said 'Motel'. So as the children were tired and hungry, we stopped and booked into a family room. The place was run down, but clean and managed by a middle-aged white couple. 'Where do you come from?' the friendly wife asked Juliet. 'Zaire, where do you come from?' she replied. 'Scotland', came the reply. 'Oh that's where people say coo when they mean cow', said Juliet. 'Oh no they don't say coo, they say coo', came the reply.

Our first stop with friends was with the Andersens in Salisbury. Chris was still in the law and doing extremely well. He was also a member of the Rhodesian parliament and apparently destined for high office. As in 1966 when I had attacked him for the country's move to the political right, he would have none of it. Even so compared to most whites, his views were liberal. After Salisbury we carried on eastwards to stay with the Valentines on their farm in Odzi district near Umtali. The road was fairly empty due to the shortage of petrol and diesel, thanks to international sanctions. However, as tourists we were allocated plenty and I gathered that rationing was pretty nominal with fuel stocks good, thanks to the pipeline from Beira in Mozambique to Feruka near Umtali. The shortage was alleviated too by the substituted fuel produced from sugar grown in the eastern lowveld. Altogether nearly nine years after UDI, Rhodesia seemed to be doing pretty well. We learned that the country lacked practically nothing, thanks to enterprising locals producing anything from tomato sauce to squash rackets to wine. Thus were foreign exchange and employment created and the culture of self-sufficiency developed. There seemed to be plenty of foreign cars, particularly French and Japanese, and the banks made it easy for visitors to cash cheques, thanks, I was told, to arrangements with Switzerland. In short, sanctions did not seem to be biting at all and the only country losing out seemed to be Britain; certainly that was how the local whites liked to see things.

On the farm, employees whom I had known since I had first stayed there more than 20 years before were as friendly as ever. Richard was an excellent farmer and wonderful with people. He had a good joking relationship with the workers and he was aware of their personal needs and problems. As a result he was well liked and respected. Again thanks to effective sanctions-busting, he and other tobacco farmers were making a lot of money.

He had also diversified into peas which he was selling to the canning factory in Mutare. Richard's parents were still on the farm with his father Phil, who had opened it up in the early 1930s, still involved and living in the main house. Richard and Heather and their two little girls were in a similar but smaller thatched house with wonderful long views through the trees and over the green lawn to the Odzi River and the mountains beyond. During the days, I would accompany Richard on his rounds. He proudly showed me new methods of reaping and curing the ripened tobacco leaves, which he had developed. In the grading sheds where most employees were wives of farm workers, he knew all their names and made them laugh with some remark in a version of Chilapalapa with more Shona grammar than the usual kitchen variety. I always tried to persuade Richard to become fluent in Shona, which would have gone down very well, not just with his employees, but also with all local Africans. I had seen how the use of this semi-language Chilapalapa had fallen away in Zambia, where it was identified with white domination. But then the whites in Rhodesia did still dominate in early 1974.

At weekends we played tennis at the delightful Odzi Club where the members, nearly all farmers, were friendly and welcoming, perhaps seeing our presence as support for them in their country's struggle for international recognition. As Richard and Heather knew, I was supportive of them mainly in the context of our friendship. I always told him and Heather what I really thought and this included that I was sure that however rosy life seemed in Odzi, things were bound to change. Meanwhile, before heading on the long road home to Zaire, we had a few days playing golf and fishing at the Troutbeck Inn nearly 7000 feet up in the Inyanga Mountains, where we had spent part of our honeymoon. It was wonderful and full of visitors including a few from Britain. Though no longer running it, Major Macilwaine, who had taught most of Rhodesia to fish with a fly, retained an interest. He was a great big man and had played rugby for Scotland both before and after the First World War.

In mid-1974 we left en famille for the United Kingdom on long leave to be followed by a spell on secondment to the Industrial Society in London. The plan was to fly via Nigeria, where we had friends ex Zambia, and then to Portugal via Ghana. I had never been to West Africa and we stayed in Apapa near Lagos with Tony and Lorna Phillips, who used to come and see me at Gwembe for squash and supper. Sadly our plans were thrown awry by Juliet developing hepatitis. It was diagnosed by a doctor in Lagos who advised us to take the child straight to England. At the airport, some official manufactured a query over our tickets, no doubt looking for *matabiche*. Zaire experience came in use in the argument that followed, and we paid nothing.

Back in London we hired a car and headed straight for the doctor's surgery in Amesbury near where Sarah's mother lived. The doctor was horrified. How could we possibly be so irresponsible as to bring a child with an infectious disease on a crowded aeroplane? He did not know Lagos. Poor Juliet went off for a miserable week in isolation at Odstock Hospital.

We settled into our cottage in Suffolk and after two or three months' leave, Charter gave me a large modern luxurious flat in Wimbledon, from where I commuted daily to the Industrial Society. I stayed in London during the week and went home to Suffolk at weekends. The six-month secondment was designed to turn me into a so-called personnel and training professional. Whether it did or did not I am not sure, but it was fascinating getting insights into the industrial relations chaos which was Britain in the mid-1970s. The secondment was just about over and I was playing squash on a cold winter's Sunday morning at RAF Wattisham in Suffolk. Suddenly it felt as if my right leg had been clubbed from behind with a baseball bat. I fell to the ground and saw my opponent and a few friends in the gallery looking anxious. I had broken my Achilles tendon.

After the operation to sew the bits together, we hurried back to Zaire with me still in a walking plaster. I had been told that I was badly needed back at work. This turned out to be an exaggeration. However, I had been away for nearly a year and things had moved on. A new man from London had come in to take charge of personnel, and I was to take over the planning and setting up of the enormous training function. This was good news because it was quite clear that for a long-term future, training was as good as anything, particularly for someone totally non-technical like me.

It was wonderful to be back in our lovely house in Fungurume with the birds and beautiful views. The house had been well looked after, except that a case of **Châteauneuf-du-Pape** of the fabulous 1961 vintage had been drunk by the house sitters. The camp was hardly changed, but outside it the massive crusher was under construction, the plant site had been cleared, a vast new suburb had been built in the woods to the north and work had started on an 18-hole golf course. Now there were dozens of Americans too from Fluor Utah and French from Dumez Afrique.

While we had been in Europe, SMTF had acquired a farm in the area north of the new township and near the airstrip. It had been owned and run by a Belgian family up to Congolese independence in 1960. It was a beautiful farm with a good mix of arable land and woodland. It was crossed by a clear-flowing small river. We appointed an assistant geologist to manage it, a Dutchman who had started his working life as an assistant on a Rhodesian tobacco farm near Odzi. What impressed me at the time was the enthusiastic support we received for the farm project which included plans to grow several crops and train local people, from village people including the local chief. He insisted that we hold a ceremony with him of traditional blessing for the project and the land.

With all the money around and all the jobs to be had, some fairly rough elements moved into Fungurume and there was a lot of bawdy singing and the odd brawl down at the club. Apart from my assistant Chiwengo and two or three black Rhodesian geologists, the camp and club remained entirely white. Outside the camp though, beside the main road the squatter camp grew and grew. The reason was simple; the prospect of a job was something new for Zaire, and people came from far and wide. When they were unsuccessful at first, they camped with relations or friends and waited for better luck. We were able to reengage our former house servant Ilunga but not our nanny, a beautiful girl who now earning much more as a part-time prostitute. We engaged a new gardener Daniel, who was young and small; the first time we paid him, his wages were taken from him by thugs outside the gates and he was beaten up. We complained to the SMTF admin manager, who next time smuggled Daniel out of the camp in the boot of his car, but he was seen and beaten up again.

Security overall was becoming a real problem with large-scale theft from stores both within and outside the camp and the guards on the camp gates were under enormous pressure. So we took on a senior policeman just retired from the Royal Ulster Constabulary and things got a lot better for a time. As yet, we were a long way from producing any copper, so every penny spent on the project by SMTF itself or by the contractors had to be brought into the country. It was all going to be worthwhile in the end, we were assured as the Fungurume copper deposit was the largest and richest in the whole world. There was a snag though. Half of the ore was sulphide and the other half was oxide. So the process of extracting the copper had to be very sophisticated and expensive. So too the complicated plant to deal with it. Components had to be imported by sea mainly to Lobito Bay in Angola and then railed from there up the Benguela Railway line. The alternative was greater distances and complications on the railway from South Africa via Rhodesia and Zambia. It would have been possible to devise simpler cheaper ways of extraction, but they would have resulted in throwing away a lot of copper and our management considered that this would not have been acceptable to the Zairois authorities. This decision was misguided as surely we held all the cards over the future mine. I think we were worrying needlessly about alternative investors. So instead of generating a cash flow, we carried on full steam ahead spending vast sums of money in the expectation of huge profits to come. But there were other worries, particularly over the supply route to west coast when Angola in May 1974 wrested independence from Portugal and a civil war was starting between the main nationalist parties, the Popular Movement for the Liberation of Angola (MPLA) and its rival the National Unions for the Total Independence of Angola (UNITA).

On the work front, I was relieved no longer to be involved with expatriate morale. I retained responsibility for industrial relations and for dealing with the trade unions, thanks to being able to deal with them in French. My main function now, however, was to plan and set up the massive training function. In late 1975 once again I was sent to the Nchanga Mine in Zambia for a month's attachment. The head of training, 'Mama Training' as she was known, was an old Rhodian Petal O'Brien, who like me had read French at the university and had then gone on to the Sorbonne in Paris. She was enormously helpful in my quest to become a mining trainer. This time I concentrated on the practicalities, especially the crucial training of operators of massive diggers scooping up blasted ore in the open pit and drivers of the 100- and 200-ton haul trucks. The latter with their massive electric motors in their huge 10-foot high wheels would be loaded up in the open pit and driven to the crusher. To operate these goliaths required highly skilled, well-motivated and reliable operators. It had been found that the best candidates for such work were young men of about 19 or 20. Nchanga in Zambia, like Gecamines, had a large-scale programme for training these people and maintaining standards. It also had an extensive programme providing basic education for young recruits to bring them up to the basic standard required for any recruit if he or she was able to absorb the skills training.

Back in Fungurume, we put a priority on recruiting and training the young men we needed. To achieve this we came to an agreement with Gecamines at Kolwezi that it would train our first intake which would be accompanied by their supervisor designate, a young geneticist from New Zealand, Paul Lupi. This was a totally new challenge for Paul, but he was really enthusiastic about it. He had picked the dozen or so young men and underwent exactly the same training as them at the training school serving the massive Kolwezi open pit which was about the same size as the one at Nchanga. It was over this period that I became aware of how sophisticated and advanced was the Gecamines training programme. The company was giving a high priority to an area of activity untouched at Nchanga and at that time not part of our plans. This was the question of the development of indigenous Zairois technical management potential. I got to know the head of the section responsible for this, Raymond Braibant, who with my friend at Kolwezi Louis Desmaele, who was head of mining, convinced me how important it was to provide for the future in this way.

After some weeks in Kolwezi, Paul and his trainees returned to Fungurume and I was amazed at what they had achieved. Without exception all the trainees had achieved marks in both the theoretical and practical sides of their training in the high 90s. I was reminded that given the chance with good motivating leadership, there was no limit to what young Africans can achieve. To my mind, no aid of any sort could possibly achieve such stunning success in terms of long-term benefit.

Fungurume's problems of uncontrolled population growth and other worries about theft and rough expatriate elements were compounded by a total lack of direction from our top management sitting in London or Johannesburg, we knew not which. Despite the reliance and loyalty to the project of people on the spot, who by the late 1975 had been at Fungurume for nearly five years, the continuing uncertainties about the project's future were affecting morale. This included employees of the main contractors Fluor Utah and Dumez Afrique just as much as SMTF and its many secondees from Charter Consolidated. The trouble was that nobody told us anything and the clear impression gained ground that really nobody was in charge. Certainly there was no leadership coming from the Project Director Trevor Lee Jones whom we seldom saw. He continued to maintain he was a consultant. It was a case of power without responsibility. Whatever he was, he was not based on site at Fungurume, where the two Standard Oil men Robinson and Hagan were based. It was well known that their confidence in Charter as project managers was low. Standard Oil decided to send a senior man out from America to see for himself what was going on and to report back. The man sent was called Rudi Schneider and all he needed to do was to move around the Fungurume offices and talk to the occupants. He soon got the full story from people demoralised by continuing uncertainty and longing to talk to somebody who was interested and seemed to have real authority and influence.

It was in January 1976 that the thunderbolt struck. The Exim Bank and other funders decided they were no longer going to support the project. This was officially because of the recent fall in the price of copper and the problems with our main railway supply route via the Benguela Railway and Lobito Bay due to a developing civil war in newly independent Angola. If morale was low before, now it was rock bottom. The fact was that most people associated with the project had come to be passionate about it. This was a special and beautiful part of the world with friendly motivated people and an expatriate community without the hierarchical divisions which were the norm on mines in southern Africa. The most significant factor of all was the effect on the local economy and the local population. My young haul truck driver trainees for instance; just as their lives and careers were about to take off, they would suddenly be unemployed. The way things were in Zaire, the likelihood was that despite their talents, intelligence and energies, they would never ever get another job. This was a major African tragedy.

Here was the biggest, richest deposit of copper in the whole world lying abandoned. Here was the first significant attempt to bring together South African technical expertise and capital to a part of Africa outside the traditional sphere of South African economic influence in Rhodesia, Zambia, Botswana and Namibia. It was our opinion on the ground that outside circumstances notwithstanding, the project's failure was in large part due to management failures including ignorance of the environment and a misplaced assumption that our approach to managing people was better than the successors of the old Belgian Union Miniere company. Errors of approach and planning were compounded by the priority we gave to a complicated expensive extraction process over getting a cash flow going even if this meant throwing away a lot of copper (which could have been reprocessed much later). Most significantly, the Anglo group had failed to bring in the modern and appropriate people management policies for which the government had hoped. Very sadly, the whole project had been a case study in failure with Charter as the main culprit.

It was not long before people started to leave Fungurume amidst an atmosphere of great sadness. I remember the farewell parties and the gloomy Burns Night dinner. The bitter pill was sweetened somewhat by the Zaire authorities allowing us to take anything we liked out of the country without limit and the company agreeing to pay for the shipment. One French employee went way over the top by buying up huge quantities of ivory and malachite. His haul transported free came to several large cratefuls. The company

Lawleys and Moores, Upemba National Park 1976

and the government had agreed that we could send out all our money at the official rate of exchange. So people were selling their personal possessions in a sometimes frenzied and unseemly attempt to accumulate money. At the same time, incidents of thefts from houses in the camp jumped dramatically. I sold for cash my own trusty light-green Toyota Land Cruiser, which was in good condition. Most fortunately, on receiving it, I immediately entrusted the considerable sum to our chief accountant's company safe. That evening, Sarah and I went out of the camp to the railway station to say goodbye to the American John Hagan who was returning home via the Zaire railways and river ferry system. When we got back home, we found that the locked drawer of my desk had been forced by persons unknown, in the belief that the money might be there.

There was a staged and, as I remember, well-organised departure from Fungurume. My family and I were due to be amongst the last to leave. A small presence was due to be maintained mainly to look after the considerable material assets including bits of crusher, plant, vehicles, railway locos and of course newly built houses. Before leaving I wanted to return to the wonderful Upemba National Park. The plans I had had to go up to the park and on to the great unknown Lake Upemba with colleagues John Horn and Paul Lupi had of course to be abandoned. However, it was possible to go for a few days with three families, the Blairs and the Moores and ourselves accompanied by the ever useful Paul Lupi and a geologist Sue Connolly, a Charter secondee. We set off in four vehicles with me driving the brand new company Range Rover, the first in Zaire. The new site manager Tony Smith was keen for me to put it to the test.

We packed beds and tables and chairs and food and drink for four nights. Once again we drove up to the park via the cement-manufacturing and railway town Lubudi and followed the road running for about 80 miles up the eastern side of the park. After a night at the main camp, we squeezed in our two Zairois game guards and headed for the park interior. The drive was spectacular and a great revelation. We were on a high plateau with the road crossing grassland dotted with clumps of thick bush including big trees. Heading south we passed spectacular views of the land falling away towards the east with wooded river valleys way below us. We could see a herd of elephants moving towards the river through a patch of grassland. Further on we stopped to admire a blaze of purple in the form of thousands of wild irises growing on the plain. A little later we found more irises, this time snow-white. Our little convoy continued driving south until we reached a point where the plateau terrain fell away suddenly and we could see that again there would be some magnificent views. We stopped and got out. We really had no idea of the general lie of the land when we started, so it came as a wonderful surprise to see not just a view but a panorama stretching perhaps 50 or 60 miles over uninterrupted bush stretching away 2000 to 3000 feet below us. Of human habitation or activity, there was no sign. In the very far distance, we saw the sparkle of what was clearly a great body of water. It was the mysterious Lake Upemba.

We pushed on westwards until the game guard indicated that we should leave the main track and follow a barely defined trail through the long grass and intermittent trees. Ahead of us we could see wooded hills about 500 feet high with gently sloping sides. Then through more trees and suddenly we were beside a river. It was a most delightful river with deep clear pools divided by stretches of fast-flowing water. This was to be our campsite and its situation seemed utterly idyllic. Soon the game guards were clearing the long grass for a camp fire, while the families sought a corner of nearby bush for their beds and unpacked. The weather was hot, so the river looked very tempting for swimming. There was no danger of bilharzia up here many miles from the nearest human habitation. I did, however, wonder about crocodiles, though there was no spoor on the river bank. I asked the game guards and they reassured me; so everyone donned their costumes and jumped in.

After the general swim we sat around enjoying the wonderful remote pristine environment and watched the woodland birds and the occasional martial eagle soaring above us. We looked forward to our drinks around the camp fire as the raucous call of the francolin and the familiar nagging notes of guinea fowl gave way to a leopard barking from up on the hill and a lion roaring from somewhere along the trail between us and the main track. Dinner was a combined effort from the four parties and was washed down with superior claret. After some conversation around the fire, we settled down into our camp beds not too near but not too far from each other. That was everybody, except the Blairs. It was their first time in the bush, and they decided to squeeze themselves into their vehicle as the lions continued an intermittent roaring. Lulled, as is my wont, by the soothing calling of nightjars, I slept like a top.

The next day we decided on an expedition down to the great Lufira River, which runs through the park before going on to join the mighty Congo. Retracing our way back along the main track, we turned off it to the right and found ourselves descending rapidly from the high plateau. The further we drove, the hotter it became until the track came to an abrupt halt by the edge of the great river. And there, there was a boat. Although the river was deep and fast flowing, it was only about 50 yards wide where we were. The boat normally used by game guards on patrol looked waterproof, so Paul and Sue clambered aboard, took up the paddles and were soon across. They then disappeared in the deep bush for long enough for me to start worrying about them. They eventually emerged looking happy and no questions were asked.

We spent another night at our wonderful camping site and a day driving around looking at the abundant game. It was amazing that we had this wonderful place all to ourselves. In 1976 there were no tourists at all and the mainly Belgian expatriates in places like Lubumbashi and Kolwezi did not seem to be interested in getting away into this unspoilt wonderland. In the evening we set off to return to the main camp for the last night in the Upemba. It must have been an hour or so before sunset and the track was straight with tall grass on either side. All of a sudden, there in the middle of the track was a small mammal running in front of us. It was a dark russet colour and had a very large bushy tail. None of us including the guards had ever seen anything like it. The little animal continued to run a few yards in front of the car. I took out my camera and photographed it through the windscreen and again as it veered off the road. The photos turned out moderately well and in the years ahead, I never found anyone who could identify it including the staff at London Zoo, where my ex-provincial commissioner in the Southern Province of Zambia, Colin Rawlins, was the director. I also drew a blank a year later with the WWF headquarters at Gland near Geneva.

The next day we rose early and after breakfast drove out of the Upemba towards the main road. There was a poignant moment as we passed a small village and a woman dashed out onto the road in front of us clutching a small copper cross. I was aware that these crosses used as a store of value in the region in pre-colonial times were now rare and valuable. She wanted to sell it for about ten zaires, an enormous sum for her but a small one for me. It seemed so sad that circumstances were forcing her to sell the only thing she had which might be valuable to us Westerners. I still have the cross about three inches by two.

And so we left Zaire with heavy hearts. Again the company plane took us to Chileka Airport in Malawi for a family holiday. There at Club Makakola, we were about the only guests, but we enjoyed the environment and were able to concentrate on the children. The only negative factor was that our family room was full of mosquitoes. They were the *anopheles* variety, with their rear ends pointing upwards. We were not unduly worried as we were all taking weekly anti-malaria tablets. From Malawi, Sarah and the children flew back to England via stop-offs in Nairobi and Cairo. I went south to Johannesburg determined to unburden myself of the real story of Fungurume to someone in authority at Anglo-American. I chose Peter Leydon, an ex-colonial service district officer with whom I used to play squash in Lusaka days. Now he was near the top in De Beers – the diamond mining company which in those days was run in closest collaboration with Anglo-American. Peter sat me down with a cup of tea and asked me to tell him exactly what had gone wrong with SMTF. Of course I let rip with my views on everything including the arrogance, the ignorance and above all the dreadfully weak, confused management. I did not spare Trevor Lee Jones. As I was in full flow, who should walk in but Trevor Lee Jones himself. He had recently been appointed as deputy to Peter at 44 Main Street in Johannesburg. It was said at the time that in the Anglo group if you were one of the favoured few, you could do no wrong.

10

A Taste of War

For the sake of continuity over Rhodesia, I want to go back to Christmas 1975, a few months before we finally left Zaire. Spending Christmas Day at Chileka Airport, Blantyre in Malawi, was more fun than Sarah and I could have possibly hoped. We had brought presents with us on the company plane flight from Lubumbashi, and when these were opened with ceremony, the girls Juliet and Ting, aged seven and five, played with the friendly immigration and customs officers while Tom, aged two, tried repeatedly to escape onto the runway. I can't remember what we had to eat apart from outsized peanuts, but we were all happy as we waited for the evening flight down to Salisbury in the then rebel Rhodesia.

We were on our way before dusk and, in about an hour, had touched down and were in a taxi to the Monomatapa Hotel. It was lovely to be in Rhodesia again with its friendly efficiency and first world standards. We had of course been coming to the country regularly over the years, in my case 27 years since 1948. Now, despite all the apparent calm and prosperity there were an increasing number of reports of the guerrilla war starting to affect rural areas particularly in the north-east. Several white-owned farms had been attacked and the country was beginning to go on to a war footing.

We were going to stay with the Valentines on their farm at Odzi near Umtali in the east. Before leaving for the farm we saw other friends and relations in Salisbury and gained the impression that nobody was taking the security situation too seriously. The whole picture had of course been changed by Mozambique independence two years before so that a friendly neighbour had now become a hostile one. The Rhodesian army and security forces, comprising a majority of black soldiers and policemen, with elite white units, were well trained and motivated and could surely cope with any threats coming from shambolic Mozambique. Moreover, Rhodesia was powerful and prosperous, with coffers swelled by profits from the sale of food to half of

Africa. With business booming from the sale of tobacco and chrome and countries such as France and Japan ignoring UN sanctions, to Rhodesian eyes they seemed well placed to win their battle for the world to recognise their independence. Besides, Rhodesia was the world's biggest producer of chrome, and sanctions busting sales to its largest consumer the United States were able to continue. This was thanks to the Byrd Amendment proposed by Senator Harry Byrd of Virginia, who by coincidence was the brother-in-law of my first cousin Shirley Byrd (now Shirley Cammack). There were worries about the South Africans from whom the Rhodesians felt entitled to full support for upholding civilised standards as they saw it. What they were getting seemed to them to be only half-hearted and tempered by hefty cuts being taken as the price for help in sanctions busting. This was a source of irritation and there was much talk of 'Friends of Rhodesia plus 10%'.

The atmosphere on the farm was as relaxed as ever mainly because Richard, following in the footsteps of his father Phil, got on extremely well with the labour force. They were mostly ethnic Malawians who had been there since the 1930s and now knew no other home. As I accompanied Richard on his early morning rounds, he had a word for everyone. There were many female employees, wives or daughters and they would double up with laughter at some joke which showed not only Richard's sense of humour but also his interest and insights into people. That morning, like every morning on the farm, work started at 5.30 with a knock on the door and tea produced by one of the housemaids. Actually for me it had started at least half an hour before with Odzi Farm's wonderful dawn chorus. This began with a single bird which was soon joined by a few more and then more again until the morning air was awash with hugely varied and incredibly beautiful song. One of the reasons for this was the large garden with its mixtures of massive native and exotic trees, flowering shrubs and bushes and banks of flowers. In between there were swathes of lawn pointing to long views of a ring of immense granite hills and mountains about 15 miles away. In the middle distance looking east was the Odzi River, one of the very few in Zimbabwe which runs all year round. This makes the farm particularly suitable for irrigation. Beyond the river beneath some tall gum trees and about a mile away as the crow flies was Peplow farm house. Peplow now converted to a small country hotel was well known for its good food, its English country house atmosphere and its genteel service. Phil and Mary Valentine, Richard's English-born parents, were particularly fond of it and they took us all there for Sunday lunch. As the children played in the swimming bath, the

adults sipped gins and tonics on the veranda with its view back towards the
Valentine's farm and beyond. It was the sort of scene which Harold Wilson
may have imagined when he predicted in 1965 that in the face of sanctions
which affected their way of life, the Rhodesians would abandon their rebel
lion in weeks rather than months. Now ten years later it was still going strong
and no doubt Wilson was constantly being reminded that there were more
on the Rhodesian list of priorities than a gin and tonic lifestyle. That Sunday
lunch time, amongst the people we talked to on the veranda was a young man
wearing the uniform of the BSA Police Reserve. He said he was about to go
on temporary posting to the farming area of Concession. His presence was
a reminder that incidents arising from armed incursions from Mozambique
along the north-eastern border were becoming more frequent. I am not sure
quite why I remember that day so well. It was sunny and peaceful and delightful to be amongst family and old friends. I remember it now as it represents
the last such day before the war began.

We had returned to England after the sudden pull-out from the Zaire
project in March 1976. Now we were back in Suffolk and looking for another job. Sarah had recovered from the cerebral malaria picked up at Club
Makakola on Lake Malawi on our way home. I was recovering too from a broken ankle sustained immediately I took to the ski slopes above Teheran where
on my way home I was staying with my brother Roger and his wife Joy.

One day a letter arrived from Richard. The war had come to Odzi Farm
it said. He described how in the middle of the night, he and Heather had been
woken by the crackle of fire from automatic weapons. It must have been a
horrific moment, yet one that they had been half expecting for some time.
Heather's first thought was baby Philip and as she ran down the corridor to
fetch him, a bullet from an AK passed through her nightdress just beneath
her elbow. I don't know the full details of those terrible moments because
Richard and Heather were always reluctant to talk about them. What is clear
is that the thatched roof was on fire, set alight by a rocket-propelled grenade.
It seems that after returning fire through the farm house windows Richard,
concluding that the attack was not being pressed, climbed onto the roof to try
to put out the fire. Meanwhile Heather was on the 'agricalert' radio talking to
the army rapid response unit. 'Tell your husband to get off the roof', shouted
a voice on the radio. Soon the army arrived by helicopter and by road, but
by then the guerrillas or 'ters', as the farmers called them, were long gone.

When they were attacked, Richard and Heather were still in the manager's house while his father and mother still occupied the main farm house

which Phil Senior had built in the early 1930s. Clearly a drastic review of
security was called for. The manager's house had been protected by a single
security fence which was not electrified. Now it was decided that Richard
and Heather would move into the main house which had overhanging trees
protecting the roof while the parents moved out into the border city Umtali
about 30 miles away. Much work was needed to make the old house more
secure and I was to see exactly what measures were taken when I visited a
few months later. The news from the farm was ominous even though it was
entirely predictable that with the Portuguese losing their guerrilla war and
their sudden departure from Mozambique in 1974, the situation in Rhodesia
was pretty well bound to get worse. I loved Rhodesia though I was not in sympathy with its government. For years since the end of Federation in 1963 it
had been moving to the right. This was a point of contention with several of
our friends whom I accused of betraying the principles of partnership which
we had espoused in our university days. My years in Northern Rhodesia and
Zambia had reinforced me in my certainty that I was on the right side. I still
felt that Britain, which I had felt held the key to a prosperous future for the
region by steering a course between black and white extremes, had let Africa
down badly. She had dressed up an irresponsible scuttle as a noble act. In the
process, she had let down all the moderate people in the countries of the Federation. Though I could never support what I regarded as the racist policy of
the (Southern) Rhodesians, I could understand why they did not trust British
intentions and what had pushed them to declare UDI. Ever since UDI, I had
tried to give Richard and Heather a positive perspective of realities in the
black countries to the north and the inevitability of black nationalist rule.
After the attack, Richard's letters told of his and Heather's determination to
stay on the farm. There were also details of the escalating war and his periods of military and police reserve service. Mainly they were optimistic, as he
gave details of huge successes for the Rhodesian army in Mozambique where
it had set up RENAMO to fight against the UNITA government. Richard
told of how the Rhodesians were welcomed as liberators by ordinary rural
people, sick of the neglect and maladministration of the government they
had inherited.

We stayed in close touch with the Valentines through letters and phone
calls through the summer and into the winter of 1976. With the sad end of
the Zaire mining project, I was looking for another job. The search through
headhunters and speculative letters to companies with overseas connections
was made all the more urgent because our eldest, Juliet, had started at a

little girl's prep school with an excellent reputation but very expensive, in Norfolk. With our number two, Ting, coming along behind, I needed an overseas job which would pay education allowances. In August I was offered what seemed to be the ideal. It was admin/personnel manager of a British led project to build a steelworks in Morocco. Because the Algerians had had one built by the same company, the Moroccans wanted one too. My first trip therefore was to Algeria to talk to the management. Algiers was magnificent with its villas stretching up the hillside and the superb French that everyone spoke, quite a contrast to Zaire. Annaba, formerly Constantine, the site of the steelworks was even more memorable because my bedroom in the hotel was on the mountain behind the city and looked straight over a precipice and I could see eagles circling below me. That night I was taken to a restaurant in the mountain village run by a pair of elderly French ladies. The very excellent meal was accompanied by one of the most delicious wines I have ever tasted. It was Algerian. Soon from the company's base near London, I started to make regular trips to Morocco. The first was to Casablanca, where I made contact with the leading British businessman. He had been in the country for many years and told me that though there was a lot of bribery and corruption, he had never paid a bribe. 'I always tell them that we don't do that sort of thing in Britain', he said.

Our company headquarters was to be in the Moroccan capital Rabat, a short drive along the coast. There I used to stay at the best hotel, the Tour Hassan, while I made contacts, investigated employment law and looked for suitable housing for our management, including myself, due to arrive soon from England to take up residence. I enjoyed more than a taste of the magnificent golf courses near Rabat built by the King and carved out of the cork forest. It is true that a golf ball hit into the woods there makes soundless contact with the trees. At the Tour Hassan in what seemed to be permanent residence was an old gentleman in flowing robes who said he was the chief of the Tuareg tribe of the Sahara. He said that he was enjoying the temporary hospitality of the Moroccan government but he did not explain why. One evening he invited me to his table to eat a special meal. When I told him that my career had started in the colonial service he told me how much he had admired the British administration in West Africa. He said he had met several administrators in northern Ghana 20 years before. He went on to give me his opinion that Ian Smith's stance in Rhodesia was the right one. Any weakness shown towards the nationalists would be his undoing.

On trips to Morocco I twice drove to the site of the proposed steelworks at Nador along the Mediterranean coast. Nador was a one-horse town with a moderate hotel. Just down the road was one of Africa's anachronisms, the Spanish enclave of Melilla. This bit of Spain in Africa had been Spanish for 500 years and now lived mainly off the duty-free trade. I had barely heard of Melilla and the other enclave along the coast towards Tangiers, Ceuta. I was amazed that Spain was running these colonies in Africa while claiming that their status was fundamentally different to Gibraltar. Once I drove from Nador along the inland road to Tangiers, over the magnificent Rif Mountains covered in massive cedar forests. We kept being offered marijuana by roadside sellers who, I was informed, were in league with police ready to stop and search unwary travellers further down the road. Back in Rabat it became clear to me that the funding for our project was still far from being secured. Therefore, there was no immediate prospect of moving to Morocco and receiving education allowances. At about the same time my boss revealed himself as being someone for whom I would never be happy to work. I said nothing, but resigned from the company immediately on my return to England.

Now I was back, looking for a job in mid-1977. One day I had a phone call from a headhunter. Would I consider a post in Mauritius as a consultant to advise a leading company on modern training and personnel management? I would be on expatriate terms so there would be education allowances. Once again my fluency in French was considered a vital factor. Would I? Mauritius had been a sort of Mecca for me since I had travelled there by boat from Durban in early 1957 while I was at University in South Africa. My French had improved immensely during the three weeks I was there and the two-week-long voyages. I loved the empty beaches, the gin-clear water and the superb coral. There were indigenous forests too, full of hundreds of species of unique native trees. There were unique bird species in these forests, though sadly most were on the verge of extinction. I did not hesitate and with Sarah as enthusiastic as me, within a few weeks I was on my way leaving Sarah to put both girls into Juliet's delightfully up-market boarding school in Norfolk. In London, after being interviewed and accepted by Blyth Greene Jourdain Ltd, the parent company of Ireland Blyth in Mauritius, I had arranged to travel to Mauritius via Rhodesia and South Africa. I remained as concerned as ever about the poor Valentines now living in a real war zone. I had already written to the British Foreign Secretary Dr David Owen urging British intervention which I saw as the only way that the country could be saved. On the flight out to Salisbury, my seat on the aeroplane was just in front of one occupied by the ex-prime minister of Southern Rhodesia, Garfield Todd. I had met Mr Todd briefly when I was at Cambridge and he came to give a talk. I had always admired him as the only white Rhodesian politician who truly understood what was meant by partnership between the races and had tried to put it into practice nationally. Tragically for the country's future, he had been ousted by people representing white privilege whose attitude and policies were bound to lead to conflict. I saw Todd as farsighted where others were blind and as honest and straightforward where others deceived themselves and the electorate. We talked a lot on that plane journey. I was out of date with realities on the ground as the war had raged on and it was more than 18 months since our family visit to Odzi Farm and Peplow. Now he said the war was everywhere and I ought to take the very greatest care. The way the country had changed was soon to be brought home to me. Richard was at the airport to meet me and was accompanied by a farmer friend. They both had guns in the car, FNs I think. We set straight off for Odzi along the main road which goes to Umtali and the East and on to Beira. As we passed through little places like Ruwa, Bromley and Marandellas, all seemed normal to me. It was after Macheke that we started passing burned-out cars and lorries. There were several along a stretch of road passing through some wooded hills as the road climbs towards headlands. Apparently a band of 'ters' regularly operated there and due to the nature and extent of the terrain was proving extremely difficult to flush out. In another hour and a half we turned off the main tarred road on to the dirt road to the farm and the Makoni Tribal Trust Land (TTL). At the farm, the other farmer picked up his car and drove on to his farm further down the road. As always, Heather gave me the warmest of welcomes. She had lost a lot of weight and was looking strained. She was smoking non-stop. We had arrived well before sunset, which was essential under the circumstances of the war. The first thing to do was to lock the gate leading through the outer barbed wire fence surrounding the farm house and garden. It was electrified as was an inner chain link fence topped with razor wire. Amongst the trees in the garden and spaced regularly on the lawns were what looked like giant matchsticks with a sort of oval mould like a small rugby ball. These were scatter bombs which could be set off individually from inside the house. Outside all the windows of the main part of the house were walls about two foot into the garden and varying in length and heights according to the size of the particular window. The whole scene was brightly lit with arc lights positioned on the inner fence. It was an eerie frightening scene. Inside, all the curtains were heavy and tightly drawn. To complete the defences was an 'agricalert' radio to call for help in the event of attack. Richard told me that the main house was much safer than the manager's house because all the big trees both in the garden and beyond the security fences formed a very effective shield against mortar bombs. As we settled down to talk and talk, I began to appreciate the sort of tension under which my hosts, in common with most other Rhodesian farmers, were living. In our telephone conversations Richard had made light of the dangers, but I could appreciate how real they were when he told me about the farmers whom I had met on previous visits, who had been killed in night attacks or by land mines planted on the dirt roads.

We went to bed early that night and as Richard led me down the passage to the spare room he handed me a repeater shotgun. He told me to fire indiscriminately out of the windows if we were attacked. It was the quantity not the quality of the fire that would put off the attackers. Needless to say, despite having hardly slept the previous night on the plane I hardly slept a wink. Perhaps I slept a little as it started to get light and the dawn chorus began, but then as usual at 5.30 am the maid arrived with the tea. Accompanying Richard on rounds that day was like all the others over the many years and I was struck by the easy relationship he had with his labour and with his two senior lieutenants or 'boss boys'. It was as it had always been and though I looked for differences arising from the war or from the attack, I found none. On Richard's side this was perhaps surprising as I was aware that he knew of elements in his labour force which had been collaborating with the ters; perhaps even helping them the night of the attack. He was also aware of the immense pressure they were under, both from the ters who threatened them and from their families and alternately from the security forces. The labour was in a dreadful position with no arms or anything else with which to defend itself. Already I sensed their most earnest desire was to see an end to the war. Meanwhile they continued to earn money and feed their families and a sort of unwritten contract of co-operation between employer and labour continued. As we continued our tour round the farm it struck me that Richard carried no weapon and I asked him why. He said it would be pointless. 'If they want to kill me they can do so any time they like. In any case, I think openly carrying a gun is a sort of provocation. Most of the other farmers think I'm mad.'

I had got to know a good number of local farmers over the years mainly at the Odzi Club for Saturday afternoon tennis. That morning nearly all of them were at the club for a meeting with the Minister of Agriculture Mark

Partridge. Because of my connection with Richard over the years and more recently with Heather, they regarded me as a friend. Sentiments towards Britain, however, were hostile. Virtually everyone held Britain responsible for the war because of our refusal to grant independence to Rhodesia and our support for international sanctions. The prevailing sentiment, however, was to win the war and return to the state of peace and productive co-operation between the races which had prevailed before it started. I was very lucky to be attending this meeting. The minister spoke well and was listened to with rapt attention. What he said and what interested the farmers only concerned the security situation. I sensed that he felt that the overall situation in the country was worrying but not desperate. He expressed concern at a new trend amongst farmers to group together and to go into the TTLs on horseback in search of stolen cattle. He warned farmers that taking the law into their own hands would not serve their cause. He said that winning the battle of hearts and minds was essential if the war was to be won. Richard's hand went up immediately, 'Minister, that battle has already been lost', he said. I remember nobody could gainsay him.

Before leaving the farm the next day I told Richard and Heather that they must bring the family to stay with us in Mauritius as soon as possible. More than anything else they needed a good holiday and change of scene after the huge and constant pressures they were under. Having seen them, I was more worried than ever about their situation. I could see that come what may, they were determined to stay on the farm and resist what they saw as the forces of destruction and national disaster.

Mauritius was as delightful as I had imagined it would be. We had been given a large house with a vast garden standing in three acres and staff paid for by the company. Until recently, it had been the managing director's house while he was still British. The extraordinary thing was that the very same Managing Director Bob Shilling occupied the same block of flats on Putney Hill in London as my parents. He talked of Mauritius with great love and nostalgia, as he and my parents became great friends. He tended a large bed of roses in the spacious gardens using only compost in competition with a retired admiral who used only fertiliser on his rival bed. It was only when we got to Mauritius that we found we had been allocated Bob Shilling's house. It was like living in Buckingham Palace, as the houses around us beyond the thick hedge and wall pressed in on ours. The island was much as I had remembered it from 20 years before. This time what inspired me more than anything was the wherewithal for a genuine democracy, virtually unknown in Africa at the time. There was free speech, a free and diverse press and mutual tolerance between the different communities, the Hindus, the Muslims, the Creoles, the Chinese and the Franco-Mauritians. It struck me that the African continent had everything to learn from this tolerance of diversity. At that stage, Mauritians, not long independent, did not yet appreciate the strengths they gained from their different cultures. There were as yet only potential advantages in Rhodesia and South Africa.

My job was consultant to the leading company on the island Ireland Blyth Limited known as IBL. As a traditional trading company, it had diverse interests including in hotels, pharmaceuticals and insurance. My job boiled down to helping the company appreciate its strengths and fulfil its true potential. I had been told by the parent company in London which recruited me that IBL in Mauritius had two main problems. First its management systems were antiquated and in that respect it needed to modernise and catch up with the rest of the world. There were no personnel policies to speak of and almost no training either. There were communication problems too, and these were made worse by the company being involved in so many different activities so that a uniform approach and consistent policies were difficult to sustain. The second main problem which was closely allied to the first was that there was a general lack of confidence in the company's Personnel Manager Maurice d'Arifat. He did not have the experience or the authority to bring in the new policies which were sorely needed in the teeth of all the opposition he would surely encounter. My job would be to take a good look at the whole company and then propose and gain acceptance for new personnel and training policies to meet the situation and help Maurice implement them. Obviously I needed to befriend and strengthen Maurice. If I could get him promoted to personnel director, I was told, my two-year consultancy would have succeeded.

I found a fascinating company with some very strong characters who headed up the various divisions which included engineering, hotel management, insurance, tuna canning and pharmaceutical retailing. Most were very friendly, but I detected strong undercurrents of suspicion of me, the outsider, trying to understand their problems. Of these they had plenty, including the fact that few of them believed that it would be a good idea to tell employees anything very much. If they knew too much this would give them ideas above their station and by implication detract from the divisional directors' own power and authority. As was to be expected, the latter tended to be defensive about their own management style and would not have admitted that they were part of the problem. They preferred to put all the blame on poor Maurice who had become the all-round general scapegoat. The Managing Director Toy Dalais, the first non-Briton to hold the position, was not very forthcoming either. He too lacked experience and confidence. The two directors with whom I had by far the best communications were a former senior civil servant Beroit Arouf, the only ethnic Creole on the board, and Maurice's brother Constant who was immensely fat and jovial and was much loved across the island for his great kindness to everybody. He would treat me to long sumptuous lunches at his club when we would discuss how IBL's problems could be solved and how Maurice could be helped. These problems it seemed to me arose not so much from Maurice's failings but from the general low morale caused by employees feeling that they were not valued enough to be told what was going on, much less being consulted on the decisions that affected them. I persuaded Toy that it was of key importance that a system of communications should be instituted across the company. He took the message on board straight away but instead of putting the onus on his divisional directors and managers to support his policies by briefing on them themselves, he insisted on big meetings when he himself did all the talking. This gave the directors the chance to stand back and say that they were not consulted on this or that and would have done things differently.

After a few months I produced a report for the management of IBL which I tried to make constructive, but inevitably it contained some criticism of the way the personnel department operated. My regret now is that I did not involve Maurice more in the way it was drawn up. I think I had been told that it would go only to the board. In the event Maurice somehow acquired a copy and he proceeded to produce an alternative report which of course did nobody any good particularly as he now began to see me as a potential rival rather than an ally. I regret that I never really gained his confidence. I think in retrospect that he may have got wind of whisperings of which I was unaware at the time that I should get myself appointed personnel director. I would have regarded this as a betrayal.

Other work I did was to produce a management handbook and I instituted sales training which was badly needed in IBL's retail outlets. I was also able to arrange a seminar for senior management at a hotel at the seaside where I was assisted by a contact at the Industrial Society in London, Clive Peacock, who came out to Mauritius for a few days. In those days senior management was overwhelmingly Franco-Mauritian. They were the minority race but remained the main power in the Mauritian economy. Despite being hospitable and friendly, rather like white Zimbabweans, they were sure deep down that the rest of the world did not really appreciate or understand them. Looking back I can see that I was in Mauritius at a vital time in its history and that I was able to bring in some modern policies and practices over the management of people. I think I helped the company and perhaps the country as a whole appreciate their strengths and to appreciate that they had things to learn from other cultures and countries. In 1990 Jim Jourdain, who had recruited me, wrote to say that the management handbook that I had drawn up and introduced was still in use. Overall since the late 1970s, the growth of the Mauritian economy has been phenomenal, so that the island came to be known as 'the new little tiger of the Indian Ocean'. Like the Seychelles and Malta, I got the feeling that the country would have preferred to have remained British rather than be granted independence. The national mood in the United Kingdom in the 1950s and 1960s would not have catered for that.

Outside work Sarah and I became members of the Mauritius (Naval and Military) Gymkhana Club where we played golf, tennis and squash. In the 1860s the young Gordon, later General Gordon of Khartoum, had been a member of what is one of the oldest golf clubs in the Commonwealth. Our other main leisure activity was involvement with the programme to breed and re-introduce the very rare Mauritian kestrel into the wild. It was re-garded at the time as the rarest bird in the world. The area of breeding and re-introduction was the Black River Gorges area, covered with native for-est and descending in cliffs from the plateau of the McCabe Forest and Black River Mountain, the highest on the island. As a family we spent many a week-end in this wild area akin to lush African bush country, with literally hundreds of species of native trees found nowhere else in the world. During nearly two years in Mauritius, Rhodesia was seldom far from my thoughts. I was con-vinced from what I knew and had seen that it was only the British government that could save the country. After all, the country remained legally a British colony. If Britain did not intervene to preserve all that had been built up over a hundred years, it risked being destroyed by communism or by inter-tribal or racial conflict. In my opinion, the Rhodesians had thrown away their main chance of a multi-racial future through their failure to make partner-ship a reality in Federal days. Nevertheless, they had demonstrated bravery and initiative of the highest order in what they had built up since UDI in 1965 and it was now 1978. I worried about the physical safety of the Valentines and my second cousin Chris Cunliffe and his family farming near Beitbridge in the South. I decided to write another letter to the Foreign Secretary David Owen saying that my insights into the Rhodesian problem due to my southern African past qualified me uniquely to help. I was concerned, however, that Dr Owen's style was not one likely to achieve a great deal. He came over to me as aggressively and patronisingly certain of the rightness of his viewpoint (a common mistake amongst British politicians dealing with Africa). This would be bound to put up the backs of the white Rhodesians who would need more convincing than anyone else of British bona fide. Unfortunately the record of British governments of all persuasions as they manoeuvred to extract themselves from their African responsibilities meant that there was an enormous credibility gap which would have to be bridged.

The Valentine family came to stay with us. They desperately needed a rest. Heather put on a whole stone while they were with us and Richard drove a car at night for the first time in two years and he and I played many games of golf and tennis. Another highlight of our sojourn in the Indian Ocean was a voyage on the old cargo ship the *MV Mauritius* to collect phosphate from Assumption Atoll just 19 miles across the Indian Ocean from the biggest atoll in the world, Aldabra, a world heritage site with its hundreds of thousands of giant tortoises and no people. I produced a paper on the birds of assumption for the Smithsonian Institute's Atoll Research Bulletin. From there we carried on to Agalega Atoll, a dependency of Mauritius to collect copra. The voyage was our Mauritian swansong and led to my abiding interest in Indian Ocean birds and atolls.

11

A Chance to Help

B ack in England in 1979, at the end of my Mauritian contract, the Rhodesian war seemed to have reached a sort of stalemate. The Valentines continued to write cheerfully and optimistically, but I continued to dread that their bravery and commitment would be wasted and that they would be killed. The election of the Conservative government seemed to lend hope for a settlement of the long-running Rhodesian crisis. The new British Prime Minister Margaret Thatcher did not seem to be carrying too much baggage from the past and gave the impression of being willing to tackle even the most difficult and complicated issues. She appointed Lord Boyd of Merton the former Colonial Secretary Sir Alan Lennox-Boyd, to a post which gave him an input into the Rhodesian question. To me, he had been the last colonial secretary with positive and constructive attitudes. This was all lost under the likes of Macmillan, MacLeod and Duncan-Sandys. I wrote to Lord Boyd in the same vein as I had to David Owen. I received an encouraging reply.

Meanwhile, that autumn, things started to happen. Lord Carrington was obviously calling the shots and there was the Thatcher determination behind him. The way Thatcher hit it off with Kenneth Kaunda at the Commonwealth Conference in Lusaka seemed to unlock more doors and very soon there was real hope. Out in Rhodesia (still legally Southern Rhodesia), the Prime Minister Ian Smith had formed an alliance with the nationalist leader Bishop Abel Muzorewa. This accommodation was obviously of immense importance. The country became known as Zimbabwe-Rhodesia and elections were to be held. These were new steps forward and there was now a real prospect of black majority rule where Ian Smith had said 'not in a thousand years'.

The Smith–Muzorewa elections were peaceful and seemed to have been free and fair. The problem was that the war continued. It became clear that however much white Rhodesians wanted to believe that they had a genuine accommodation with the black nationalists, this was not necessarily so. The question was whether Rhodesian blacks felt that Muzorewa represented them or whether their real support was for the outside nationalist leaders Robert Mugabe of ZANU and Joshua Nkomo of ZAPU, who were still fighting.

I knew nothing of the diplomacy which led up to the talks involving the existing government of Smith and Muzorewa and the outside nationalists at Lancaster House in London. But I found the whole thing immensely exciting and I longed to be involved. As the talks got going, the main point at issue must have been whether Smith and Muzorewa really represented the Rhodesian Zimbabwe people as a whole and whether the recent elections had been free and fair. I think that Mrs Thatcher would have liked the answers to both questions to have been yes. My old friend Chris Andersen, who was now Mr Smith's minister of justice, arrived to take part in the negotiations. Obviously there was great pressure on the Rhodesians to settle. This came particularly from Carrington and his deputy Ian Gilmour. Chris told me he particularly resented the latter's methods and style. Chris was staying at a top London hotel and was soon joined there by his wife, Anne. They did not know the UK at all. Sarah and I were able to invite them up to Suffolk for a couple of weekends and return a little of the great hospitality we had enjoyed from them over the years in Rhodesia when we came down from Zambia and Zaire. I was spending most weekdays in London, based in my parents' vacant flat and working temporarily at the Industrial Society. Back in Suffolk one October evening, I was having a shower when Sarah shouted that the Foreign Office was on the line. I rushed dripping to pick up the phone in my study. The official on the line was friendly and businesslike and asked me if I was interested in helping with the elections, which it was hoped would be part of a settlement in Rhodesia. Was I interested? There had been few things closer to my heart for the past three years. I arranged to go and see a man called John Cumber at the Foreign Office the following week.

John Cumber turned out to be very tall and slightly stooped. He was currently head of the Save the Children Fund, but he had been in the colonial service and had risen to provincial commissioner in Kenya. I found him charming and well briefed on the whole Rhodesian issue. We talked for some time in his office and then walked across Whitehall to a small pub where we continued to talk over a beer and a sandwich. This was the first of two meetings I had with John. He made it clear that he was looking for suitable people to help with Rhodesian elections. He produced a list of names of people I had never heard of. They were ex-bankers, businessmen, missionaries etc.

who had experience of Southern Rhodesia. It seemed likely that he was consulting me because of my letter to Lord Boyd. The people on his list had apparently written at some time or another perhaps to a minister or to the Foreign Office itself. I was not impressed by John's list and told him so. I gave him my opinion that the people best suited to help were ex-colonial administrative officers, particularly those who had served in the provincial administration in Northern Rhodesia or Nyasaland. These people would be familiar with the region. The way people thought and behaved in the northern territories of the old federation was not very different from Southern Rhodesia. Sensitivities involving race were similar as were many of the problems arising from the application of democracy to people for whom it was a totally new concept. Prevailing and historic attitudes, including the fears and prejudices of southern African whites, would be familiar to them as would all the intimidation arising from a culture in which tolerance of the other man's viewpoint had little or no priority. Most importantly, they would be seen by all as people who knew and cared about the region. Bringing in people without this sort of background would leave them with too much to learn. John agreed with me. The next time I saw him he showed me a list made up mainly of people who had been in the administration in Northern Rhodesia. This time all that was required was a yea or nay as to their suitability. I said yea to almost everyone. Nearly all had been senior to me and some better qualified for a headquarters or provincial role. I made it clear that I thought my particular value would be my fluency in Tonga, the language spoken in the Rhodesian part of the Zambezi Valley. I told of my contact with Binga on the southern side of Lake Kariba when I had been DC at Gwembe from 1964 to 1966. I said I was extremely keen to be sent to Binga, and John Cumber understood and indicated he would do his best for me.

Back in London, Chris Andersen and I let off steam with a pub crawl in Wimbledon down the road from my parents' flat on Putney Hill. We were both able to communicate and enjoy ourselves without revealing the precise nature of our respective preoccupations. On another occasion he asked if he could use the phone in the flat as he feared that his hotel phone would be tapped. I agreed and then made myself scarce for a time. I did not however tell Chris about the approach I had had from the Foreign Office as in a sense we were on opposite sides. One evening however, I was most surprised when he told me that he gathered that I was coming out to Rhodesia to 'help us' with the elections. He said the Foreign Office had consulted the Rhodesians over a list of names. Chris told me this time how impressed he had been with the intellectual quality of the top ZANU and ZAPU leaders with whom he was negotiating. He wished that the Muzorewa men in his team could match them. He also told me how the British were clearly trying to split Muzorewa from Smith and how they seemed to be close to succeeding.

About this time, John Cumber and a senior ex-PA man from Northern Rhodesia, Mike North, went off to Rhodesia and made news as they travelled around the country talking to senior members of the administration. Things were really moving. Meanwhile, I had been offered a senior personnel and training job in Saudi Arabia with British Aerospace. I was allowed by the company to accept the post on the understanding that I would join after returning from Rhodesia. This was ideal. Soon agreement at Lancaster House was announced and things started to move very fast. Broadly, the agreement meant that Britain would reassert sovereignty by sending a governor into the colony of Southern Rhodesia and supervise new elections to include all parties, prior to granting independence. First though there was to be a ceasefire, and guerrilla forces would move to predetermined areas called assembly points where they would be under the protection of a monitoring force consisting of troops from Britain and other Commonwealth countries. The whole exercise would depend on high levels of trust on all sides. Both the guerrillas and the Rhodesian army would have to trust that the other would not take advantage of the ceasefire to improve its position on the ground. The guerrillas, if they all moved into the assembly points, would be sitting ducks for attack by the Rhodesians. In the event of such attacks, would the British troops be willing to protect them or even be in a position to contemplate doing so? Both sides according to past experience had reasons for not trusting the British. Yet here was a life-and-death situation which, if success was to be achieved, would depend on their doing just that.

Back in England, the prospect of going to Rhodesia became more exciting as the days passed. There was intense media interest and the ceasefire seemed to be holding. I did not yet know for certain where I would be going, but soon a date was fixed for our departure in early January 1980. There was not much information forthcoming from the Foreign Office, but I remember one circular saying that as we would be arriving in the middle of the rainy season, it would be advisable to take a pair of Wellington boots. The only time I had seen those worn in central and southern Africa was underground in the Zambian mines.

When the hundred or so British election supervisors congregated at RAF Brize Norton in Oxfordshire on a dark January evening, I was delighted to see

Arrival of Election Supervisors in Salisbury

that by far the biggest group was ex-Northern Rhodesia/Zambia. We ranged in seniority from an ex-provincial commissioner, the remarkably fit-looking John St John Sugg aged 74, to the two or three PA types of my generation, in our mid-40s. There was also a sprinkling of officers ex Kenya, Tanganyika, Nyasaland and Swaziland. Besides them were people from county and borough councils around the country. They were due to supervise the elections in urban constituencies. Few of the latter had ever been to Africa before, but clearly they held senior positions in the UK. As we waited in the departure lounge talking, a man I knew came up to me chortling with laughter. He pointed across the room to the object of his mirth which was an upstanding looking gentleman wearing a pair of green wellies no doubt in response to the Foreign Office briefing paper.

Before boarding the aeroplane, we were collected together and given what everyone agreed was an excellent and professional update on the situation on the ground, by a young Foreign Office official. He was thoroughly upbeat about the ceasefire taking hold and the prospects for a peaceful election.

The journey itself was uneventful. We flew overnight to Salisbury via Larnaca in Cyprus in an RAF VC10. In the RAF mode the seats all faced backwards which made me feel queasy.

On our arrival in Salisbury next morning, the airport was buzzing with activity with lots of RAF C130 Hercules aircraft on the tarmac and lots of helicopters. They all had a white cross painted on their undersides to show neutrality, hopefully to deter anybody from taking a pot shot with a missile. Also on the runway were a couple of massive USAF transport aeroplanes which I gathered had brought in the helicopters. It reminded us that though this was essentially a British exercise, for anything really big, the Americans were needed to provide logistical support.

Having settled into the very excellent Jameson Hotel, I phoned my cousins who lived in Mount Pleasant near the university and was invited to dinner that evening. I also arranged to go to the Andersens the following evening and then spend the weekend down on the farm with the Valentines. At my cousins were three generations of adults including my mother's first cousin, two of her children and their children. Although the family was generally politically and racially liberal by Rhodesian standards, I was in for a bit of a shock as I had assumed that everyone would be supportive of the new British role being played in their country. I was cheerfully optimistic about the future and no doubt came over as pleased with myself over being able to help at this crucial time. I now know too that I was ignorant and lacking in sensitivity. I learned a lot that evening, much arising from the fact that my hostess's youngest son had been killed during the war. Somebody reminded me that there were few white Rhodesian families who had not lost family or close friends during what had been a terrible war. Now, whatever their view of the future, there was the prospect of all they had fought for being lost. It was not as if the British were looked on in a favourable light. There was deep cynicism about the British, who were seen not just as not understanding, but also as not caring either. Amongst the views expressed that evening were those of the grandmother who was in her 80s and definitely a 'one off' in the Rhodesia of those days. She despised Mr Smith and looked forward to 'dear Mr Nkomo and dear Mr Mugabe coming to power'.

I had not learned enough that evening. At the Andersens next day, finding the British government under attack for supposed duplicity, I blurted out that surely Rhodesians should be grateful to the British for the peace that had broken out and for giving the country new hope. Chris just about hit the roof and said that Rhodesians owed Britain nothing. He was articulating the view commonly held by whites. I did not agree, but I held my tongue and was doubly chastened. Like virtually all whites, he was worried at the prospect of intimidation by the Patriotic Front comprising ZANU and ZAPU. He felt that truly democratic and intimidation-free elections would certainly result in victory for the Smith–Muzorewa alliance.

Those first few days in Salisbury were taken up by some really excellent briefings for us British election supervisors. We heard first from our chief, Sir John Boynton. He gave us his opinion that the Rhodesians were more than capable of running the whole election on their own. The problem was acceptability of the result to the world. He also spoke of Rhodesian sensitivity and profound suspicion and the measures we could take to allay these. He wondered whether there was anything we could do about the problem of underlying intimidation and implied threats. Very little, was his conclusion, apart from continually trying to get across to all parties that their vote was secret. He suggested that there was a lot we could do to take the pressure off DCs in the districts to which we would be going as well as some of the flak. Much would depend on personal relations and the trust we could build up. In the last resort we had the power of direction, but meanwhile the co-operation with the Rhodesians through the Election Council was excellent.

Then came the briefings from the senior officers who had recruited us in London before coming out to Rhodesia to set things up on the ground. First there was Malcolm Carruthers, a Foreign Office man with a great deal of African experience. He said our role was to supervise but not to take over and to avoid getting in hair or under skin. He said that local DCs were mostly young and dedicated but sometimes testy and difficult. There was the need for great care and much diplomacy. He said that we should be in on all planning so that local actions could be justified to the press and media. At the same time we should make contact with all party agents and sit in on the periphery of political meetings. He said that regular reporting both on district planning as well as on political activity was essential so that the election commissioner could answer adequately at ministerial level. Carruthers laid emphasis on the need to get around the district as much as possible and to be seen by all sides. He warned though that it was not safe to travel on country roads in a vehicle which was not mine-proofed, that is a one-inch-thick steel plate under the floor of the vehicle. I could not help thinking that the dangers would be particularly acute in the Zambezi Valley with its remoteness and its thousands of miles of dirt road. A large proportion of ZAPU fighters based in Zambia would have to come through the Binga district where I was going. I gained some comfort from Carruthers' assurance that DCs had promised that a mine-proofed vehicle and an escort vehicle would be made available for our travels. As regards relations with the DC, Carruthers warned of the danger of being seen to be too much in his pocket. He said that we should try and get an office some distance away from his. Finally, on personal relations he advised against all contentious argument but added that the local resentment was not as bad as might have been expected. On the Patriotic Front side, he warned that many people would be looking for points on which to criticise us. There was a general feeling that we were in league with the Bishop.

The next briefing was from John Cumber on the details of the voting and how it would be supervised and monitored. Voting would take place over three days at polling stations in local schools etc. There was also provision for mobile polling stations. There was no voters' role, but people voting would be required to dip their thumb into an indelible dye to prevent them from voting more than once. There would be no candidates' names on the ballot paper, only the names of political parties and their symbols. For instance, the PF symbol was a soldier carrying a child. Cumber said that during the poll, security would be the responsibility of the Rhodesians, with police in close proximity and an outer ring of army discreetly out of sight. It had not yet been decided whether the count would be at district or at provincial level.

Then it was the turn of Mike North, an ex-Northern Rhodesia man with a lot of experience of elections to talk about the legalities and the organisational hierarchy. At the top of the pile was the Governor Sir Christopher Soames. Reporting to him was the Election Commission and staff, all British, led by the Election Commissioner Sir John Boynton. From the commission a dotted line extended to the National Election Directorate, all Rhodesian. The directorate which was not constituted in terms of law, directed the work of eight provincial commissioners and through them 55 district commissioners responsible for nearly 700 presiding officers.

Rhodesian civil servants and policemen who briefed us included a Mr Plowden who informed us on the country's tribes and languages and the tribal provenance of the main politicians. I noticed that no mention was made of the Batonga in the Zambezi Valley where I was going. I knew that like their brothers across the water in Zambia, they had no time for politics, preferring to be left alone. One briefing was of particular interest to all of us. It was given by a particularly military-looking monocled British officer, a Brigadier Adam Gurdon. The brigadier gave us a rundown of the Rhodesian organisation set up to fight the nationalist armies. The whole country was divided into five joint operational commands known as JOCS, named Hurricane, Thrasher, Repulse, Tangent and Grapple – all suitably bellicose names I thought. Beneath them were sub-JOCS coinciding with district boundaries. He said that under present circumstances, the Rhodesian planning and attitudes were more important than what they were actually doing. The PF military organisation which now had its headquarters in Salisbury, mirrored the command chain of the Rhodesian security forces. He painted a picture of a steady build-up of trust on all sides.

It transpired that at first the Rhodesians could not believe that the monitoring force soldiers could be so stupid as to go into the bush to make contact with the guerrillas on the ground and to establish the assembly points. In the event, once the assembly points were established, the guerrilla fighters poured into them. Contacts with small bandit groups continued to persuade them all to come in. Now the problem was the future of the PF army and a programme was urgently needed. It would need to be explained to the soldiers by their own generals. He said that the PF was not the mob that might have been expected. However its trust of the Rhodesian military was very limited and time was running out. Despite this, a situation was approaching whereby the PF forces could be actively involved in putting the ceasefire into effect. He said that the monitoring force was getting increasing co-operation from villagers over security. At the same time, the British South Africa Police was being steadily re-introduced into the rural areas. He added that the BSAP was way ahead of the military in its attitudes. Overall and steadily, almost miraculously, peace was descending on Rhodesia. Another part of the briefing concerned arrangements for Commonwealth and other observers as well as journalists to visit the rural areas. It was hoped that there would be adequate arrangements for these visitors to meet the people. It was stressed that in dealing with visitors, we should try to stand four-square with the DC.

On one sunny evening in Salisbury, we election supervisors were asked to drinks at the beautiful Government House where Sir Humphrey Gibbs had stubbornly stayed on for years trying to represent continuing legality after UDI. The house on the corner of North Avenue and the Borrowdale Road has impressive Dutch gables and stands amongst beautiful lawns and rose gardens. We queued up on the veranda to meet the newly appointed Sir Christopher Soames and his wife, the delightful Mary, daughter of Sir Winston Churchill. For me the occasion was memorable because of what it symbolised. Sir Christopher came over as a big man in every way. Most importantly, he seemed to be getting on with everybody, not least the nationalist politicians and their main African backers, Presidents Julius Nyerere of Tanzania and Samora Machel of Mozambique. I think now that if only successive governments had continued to deal with the Zimbabweans through people of Sir Christopher's status and stature, the major problems that subsequently came to blight relations between Britain and Zimbabwe would not have been allowed to fester and then blow up. That evening was an all-British affair and the governor made a speech to encourage us. In those days it was all goodwill, sweetness and light between the Soames and the white Rhodesian hierarchy too, with Lady Soames visiting Churchill School and entertaining General Walls to tea.

Finally, on the Friday we were told of the arrangements to deploy us into the rural areas. Those of us going to Matabeleland North Province which included the Binga district, would go first to Bulawayo in a Hercules C130 transport aeroplane on Monday morning. So I had the weekend off. I had been lent a motor car by my cousins in Salisbury, so on Friday afternoon I headed off to Odzi and the farm. Driving through Salisbury there were few signs that the whole country had been, and in a way still was, in the grip of a dreadful civil war. The war had been fought almost entirely in the rural areas, leaving the towns and cities virtually untouched. So driving through the industrial area leading east, it was plain that the country's industrial base remained untouched. One incident reminded me not just of the divisions in Zimbabwe Rhodesian society, but also of the fact that the vast majority of the Rhodesian military personnel were black. I found myself at the traffic lights where two open-topped lorries both full of young men and coming from opposite directions had stopped. That they were carrying supporters of rival political parties was apparent from the shouting and jeering and the different political salutes. After this release of steam, the lorries carried on peacefully on their ways.

Down on the farm, Richard and Heather looked vastly more relaxed than when I had seen them there two and a half years before. There was still a security fence, but only one now and the scatter bombs had gone from the garden. I gathered that the workforce was similarly much more relaxed.

We had a great weekend with golf, tennis at the club and a great deal of talk. Both Heather and Richard were worried about intimidation, but nevertheless were confident that the Smith–Muzorewa alliance would win the election. Richard was less sure, but felt that it was the rural African women who would be the key factor. They were sick of the war and through their votes would reject the outside politicians. However, were the PF to win, both

Richard and Heather felt there could be no future for them in their country. Richard mentioned becoming a car salesman in South Africa. I said this was ridiculous and that whoever won, the country would need its experienced and productive farmers as much as ever. Knowing the Valentines as well as I did, I am sure I added something about the future attitude of farmers being appropriate to the new realities.

Driving back to Salisbury on Sunday morning, there were literally tens of thousands of people all along the road walking westwards. They were obviously desperate for lifts, but there was little traffic on the road. I stopped the car next to a group and almost immediately six or seven people piled in. Too many. I had to literally push one large lady out of the back door before starting off again. Once under way, my five passengers started punching clenched fists salutes out of the windows in the direction of the groups of people along the road. They were responded to enthusiastically by similar salutes. Opening the conversation I thought it best that I play completely dumb. I explained that I had just arrived from the UK to help supervise the elections and I asked where everyone was going. I had guessed that the great movement of people had to be something to do with politics, but I was genuinely surprised by the answer. It was that Mr Mugabe himself was due to arrive by plane from Mozambique that evening and that everyone was going to meet him. I ventured a question: 'Who is going to win the election?' 'Can't you see?' was the reply, adding 'Nearly all black people in Mashonaland will vote for ZANU PF.' I had had an idea that supporters of the outside nationalists had kept their heads down and that support for the Bishop was only temporary, pending the arrival of the real thing. But this looked overwhelming. It looked to me as if all the predictions of a Smith–Muzorewa victory could be completely wrong. If I was right, I did not think this would please Carrington/Thatcher or the British government, who it seemed had been persuaded by the Rhodesians that this new multiracial alliance would win any election that was free and fair. I was to learn over the next few weeks that nearly all whites had persuaded themselves of this. A Mugabe/Nkomo victory was unthinkable for them. I had already met people at the Odzi Club who had told me that if this happened, they would head for the South African border immediately. Back in Salisbury, I called in on the Andersens briefly before dropping the car with my cousins. When I told Chris of what I had seen and heard on the road and my impression of the overwhelming support for Mugabe, he dismissed it as intimidation. He was after all a minister and this was the government line.

The next morning we were out of the Jameson and the Monomatapa early and shortly after dawn were taken by bus to the airport where we stood around on the runway with our luggage. The great C130s were open at the back providing a ramp for us to walk up. Those of us going to Matabeleland were flying to Bulawayo via Grand Reef near Umtali and Fort Victoria. It was like the poem 'The day we went to Birmingham by way of Beachy Head'. The RAF had kindly provided mattresses and cushions on the floor of the aircraft and 30 or so of us climbed up the ramp and sat along the sides where we were strapped in. I noticed my ex-provincial commissioner from the Southern Province in Northern Rhodesia days, John Sugg aged 74. I was proud to be in such company and very excited. The excitement moderated and then drained away over the next half hour as we flew to Grand Reef between Odzi and Umtali at treetop height. Apparently we flew directly over the Valentines' farm house, but I was in no condition to notice. I have never been a good traveller, but this was a type of discomfort of a totally new order. As the floor bucked and reared beneath me, I needed a constant supply of paper bags. Most of my colleagues were in the same state. Having dropped off the Manicaland contingent, we carried on in the same way to Fort Victoria. I have never felt so ill. Blissfully, for the last leg of the journey, we started climbing and flew at a very high altitude before spiralling down to Bulawayo. It was blessed relief. It had all been about avoiding being attacked by missiles.

At the airport, to meet the team for Matabeleland was an old friend Charles Chadwick, an ex-DO from Northern Rhodesia whom I had met in Livingstone before joining the PA. Charles, who had lost a leg in the Korean War, was well known for his fluency in the Tonga language spoken in the Zambezi Valley in both Zambia and Rhodesia. He had made a name for himself in the early 1960s as the DO in charge at Lusitu, where he was said to dance with the locals on one leg. Now he was doing a senior job for the British Council, but like the majority of us, he had been released temporarily by his employers for this job. He was the provincial election supervisor for the Matabeleland North Province and I could think of no one better qualified. The other provincial officer who was also at the airport to meet us was Robin Beechy whom I had met in Suffolk. He was a high flyer from the Suffolk County Council and would have the difficult task of supervising the election in the city of Bulawayo. As Charles drove us into the city, we were stopped on some suburban avenue by a black BSAP policeman, for speeding. Charles explained who we were and what we were doing in the country and expressed regret. If any of us thought any of this was going to impress the policeman, we were wrong, and Charles got a thorough but polite dressing down.

We arrived at the Victoria Hotel next to the municipal park and the swimming pool. The hotel was built in 1953 to accommodate visitors to the Rhodes Centenary Exhibition held that year in the park. My parents lived in the city then and I was 17 and home for the holidays and got mildly drunk with friends from boarding school on delicious Portuguese wine at the Mozambique Restaurant. Now the group of six going to districts in rural Matabeleland North Province decided to spend the afternoon at the magnificent municipal swimming bath where I had been many times as a boy. First though we had to check into the hotel, and immediately I encountered my bedroom attendant a man of about 40. I explained to him what I was doing in the country and asked him who was going to win the election. Before replying, he walked to the door and made sure it was locked. He said that there were two sorts of people in his country. 'Blacks and Whites?' I asked. 'No', he said, 'amongst the blacks'. There are those, he said, who have and those who have not. He went on to explain with much emphasis and feeling that everybody, everybody, was sick of the war and would give anything to see it end. He added that if the 'haves' win, the 'have nots' will simply continue the fight. All black people, he said, knew this and for this reason all would vote for the PF as the only side capable of stopping the war. I left the hotel with my swimming costume and walked the 100 yards down Wilson Street to the swimming bath.

We had three good briefing sessions at the hotel the next day. The first was from the returning officer for Matabeleland North who spoke mainly about co-operation with the DCs, the BSAP and the military. He said that there were no assembly points in the Binga district, mainly because, though guerrillas came into the district from the north, they nearly all wanted to move on south. A big assembly at St Paul's Mission just outside the district border had opened and then closed down for lack of takers. Robin Beechy, who had travelled extensively around the province with Charles Chadwick, gave us a useful picture of what was happening in the province as a whole. He said that while the DCs were not being uncooperative, the urgency of getting on with detailed arrangements for the elections had yet to come home to them. For instance there was a vagueness about arrangements for mobile polling stations, and we would have to chase to get them to go firm soon. He also gave us the first real picture of how things were on the ground. In Binga for instance, all mission stations had been closed as well as all schools.

Four chiefs had been murdered. He gave the impression of a tired DC of the old school who was right out of touch. He would take a bit of getting to know. His predecessor had, in a tragic accident, been shot by the Rhodesian security forces as he steered his speedboat into Binga harbour. I wondered how ordinary Tonga villagers were reacting to the war. I could not believe that there would be too many militants amongst them. Things would not be as they were amongst the Matabele in Nkai where ZAPU virtually ran the district.

The last briefing came from the British colonel who was the chief monitor at the Rhodesian JOC. He said that ZAPU's Zipra fighters were making a big effort to abide by the ceasefire, which on the whole was holding. Dialogue with ZANU's Zanla fighters was more difficult. The Rhodesians were acting very responsibly and certainly wanted the ceasefire arrangements to work. It was what he said about arrangements after the election that sent a chill down my spine. At that time, the monitoring force would no longer be obliged to provide security for the guerrilla fighters gathered in the assembly points. Theoretically, this would leave them exposed to attack by the Rhodesians. This point was left hanging in the air and I feared the worst if things went wrong.

12

The Choice

Next morning I was driven to Bulawayo Airport to meet up with the small Cessna plane which would fly me the 300 miles to Binga, at the upper end of Lake Kariba down in the Zambezi Valley. I had been there first in 1962 with Bruce Rodwell flying from Kalomo and calling in for respite during our search the other side of the lake for the elusive Amazon women. Afterwards in 1964 and 1965 there had been the liaison with the DC Binga before UDI when I was his counterpart on the other side of the lake. I knew Binga had been built at the same time as the new dam to be the government headquarters for upper part of the lake. I had even met leading citizens Angus and Hazel Van Jaarsveld, who owned trading stores and had been starting a business to breed crocodiles for their skins. Though the government outpost which we would have called a boma in Zambia, stood on high ground about 500 feet above the lake, it was going to be extremely hot.

Now on a January morning I arrived at Bulawayo Airport travelling very light. Most importantly in my luggage was my little Hitachi shortwave radio with good length of wire for an aerial. I have always put a priority on having a good radio in the bush so as to be able to get the BBC. It was all the more important now because I knew that Rhodesian radio was highly biased, unreliable and still full of war propaganda. The other important items in my luggage were a tiny pair of Leica binoculars which I had bought specially in Bury St Edmunds. I also had a copy of *Roberts Birds of Southern Africa*. The manager of Kingston's Bookshop in Salisbury had very kindly sold me his last copy. As a backup to my excellent Minolta SLR camera, I had a tiny little camera of the sort I imagined was used by spies. This would fit neatly into one pocket of my shorts leaving room for the binoculars in the other. The pilot of my aeroplane, painted military khaki, was a very pleasant young man dressed in shorts and a camouflage shirt. He had lost a leg when his car drove over a land mine, but operated cheerfully and competently with an artificial one. As we flew north on a wonderfully clear day we could see literally a hundred miles or more and the pilot pointed out St Pauls mission a long way down and ten miles or so to our right. He said he was unwilling to go any closer as there still were many ters around there and he feared an attack from a ground-to-air missile.

We were met at the airstrip at Binga by a young man Mike Hughes, barely out of his teens, wearing the seemingly obligatory military khaki, long stockings and so-called *vellies* (short for veldskoen), locally made safari boots. I said goodbye to the pilot, and Mike drove me the mile or so to the government offices. The offices were as I remembered them from 16 years before. I was struck straight away however by the number of young male Europeans, presumably clerical staff. They were all wearing the same khaki camouflage, though a few wore shirts with no sleeves. Several carried handguns. There were two or three young European women. One wore camouflage hot pants. Apart from a lone clerk called Paul, the only blacks I saw were the so-called messengers. They too wore military uniform. These people seemed down in the mouth. They certainly failed to demonstrate any keenness at all. In fact as I was to discover they were of little significance in the scheme of things. They were not consulted on anything and certainly did not play the vital intermediary role between the DC and the people like district messengers used to in Northern Rhodesia. They looked to me like a thoroughly demoralised bunch.

The first person I met at the office was the Senior DO Dave Brink who came over to me as being a pretty sparky character. He was in his mid-30s and a bachelor. It was he who introduced me to the DC Mike Yates. Mike was in his 50s and looked tired, but he was friendly and welcoming and assured me of his full co-operation. I gave him reciprocal assurances and he said we should have a talk later. I sensed that it was Dave who got things done. Indeed it was he who offered to show me the office earmarked for me, a little building standing on its own behind the main offices. After that he drove me to my accommodation at the Binga rest camp down a winding road where it stood amongst the trees near the lake shore. We drove down in an ancient Land Rover, which was the vehicle which had been earmarked for me. Although pretty clapped out, it seemed adequate for the two-mile journey up the hill two or three times a day. The rest camp itself consisted of half a dozen thatched huts built of concrete blocks with mosquito gauze instead of windows, surrounding a spacious bedroom and a bathroom at the back. Sited conveniently next to the camp entrance was a restaurant doing basic meals. Completing the complex was the Van Jaarsveld's store, a delightful well-furnished cocktail bar and a garage and filling station. There were boats and outboard engines evident around the garage, and the mechanic there had a sparkling antique Jaguar motor car. Just down the road towards the Binga township was a clearly visible swimming bath from which steam could be seen rising. This I was told was a hot spring. It was geologically similar to the one I had seen 20 years before on the other side of the lake in the remote hills near the Mulola River. There was a T-junction near the hot springs. There you turned left to go up the hill to the township and right to the harbour, the croc farm and the houses along the lake shore. Those belonged to the three Van Jaarsveld brothers and one or two others and were magnificent with lawns to the clifftop, swimming pools and magnificent views. The immediate view was of a bay with big trees on the other side. In these nested magnificent fish eagles. That afternoon Dave helped me settle into my chalet and introduced me to my manservant or batman. He was a cheerful young man called Sandy, whose English was more or less non-existent. This gave me the chance to use my Tonga straight away. This was very important. I was sure that my knowledge of the language would be a major advantage. I had been running the language through my head for weeks, reading old agricultural department booklets from Northern Rhodesia days and looking up words that I had half forgotten in my little green Tonga dictionary. Sandy would clean my room and wash my clothes and hopefully be a source of news and gossip. He was absolutely delighted to hear that I used to live on the other side of the lake with his fellow tribesmen in Zambia. We hit it off immediately.

After I had put my belongings in my chalet, Dave and I had a beer and light lunch at the restaurant. He asked me what I would like to do and I said that I would like to go and visit an ordinary village. He said he could arrange that though I think my request surprised him and I gained the impression that arrangements would present a few more difficulties that I would have anticipated. It certainly proved to be the case. We drove up the steep bumpy road to the offices and immediately Dave started organising. There would have to be at least one more Land Rover he said and it would be necessary to take a lorry load of soldiers with us. These turned up in what I think was called a 'hippo'. This was a flat-backed lorry which had been fitted with protective armour and was used to transport armed men. There were slits in the armour plating from which they could fire their guns. I was to learn that there were animal names for all the various vehicles once they had been armoured. An armoured Land Rover for instance was a 'kudu'. All the black soldiers in the hippo carried guns as did the four or five European district officers and other officials from the office who would be coming. I was taken aback by all this though I knew for them the country was still supposed to be at war. I had asked to go to a nearby village, so I was not surprised when our convoy turned off the main road only a few miles out of Binga and headed up a well-worn path to a small village at the top of the slope. There were only about ten huts in the village but no people. That the village was inhabited however was clear from the cowed dogs which ran off on our approach and the chickens which scratched in the sandy soil between the huts. I was taken aback by what happened next. The men in the hippo leapt out of steel doors cut in the back and with guns in hand ran to the huts. There they proceeded to poke their guns in through the entrances to the huts telling people to come out. Out they then came, two or three young men and larger numbers of women and children, all looking terrified. My plan was to ask everyone to sit down while I started a dialogue about the forthcoming elections. I wanted to talk about peace and to assure them that their vote was secret. I got no response at all. Surrounded as they were by all these people with guns, the villagers remained too terrified even to ask simple questions. As we drove away I reflected on the fact that as far as rural Binga was concerned, for the government and for the rural people, the war was still on. It suddenly dawned on me that the gap between the administration and the people was total. It looked as if there was no trust at all on either side. As we drove back to Binga Dave asked me how I thought it had been. I told him of my shock at what I had seen. He took this in good part, giving me the impression that he appreciated the chance to see things from a fresh perspective.

Back at the rest camp that evening I decided to go for a walk up the old road to the township. I took my little pair of binoculars and my *Roberts Birds* book. Soon I was in the woods surrounded by a great variety of lowveld trees and other vegetation. It was not thick bush, more like an old English wood with shady paces and a lot of sunshine too. As I walked I became more aware of the great variety of bird song. Soon I started to see them in all their varied magnificence. Birds like golden orioles, African hoopoes and paradise flycatchers. Having been a late convert to birdwatching, I had never before appreciated the wealth of beauty and variety of African birds. There in the remote Zambezi Valley there must be more species than almost anywhere else on earth. In just half an hour that evening I identified 20 species. On subsequent evenings I saw similar numbers and many more species. It was a glorious and stimulating experience. Buoyed up by my walk and refreshed by a shower, I made for the cocktail bar before dinner. The only other customer was a very smartly dressed young African male. I engaged him in conversation imagining him to be a businessman or perhaps a politician. I asked him what he did for a living and he told me that he was a domestic servant. Whatever he was, he was good company and he told me a great deal about life and work in Binga. Shortly after dinner in the restaurant, I listened to the eight o'clock news from the BBC. The ceasefire seemed to be holding. That was the main thing. It had been a long day and I went straight to bed.

Over the next few days I spent the time getting around and meeting people. Early on I met no less than five chiefs, all either refugees in Binga or in town for their pay. They were all elderly and pretty much uneducated; they were in an unenviable position between the people, the nationalists and the government on whom they were dependent. As several of them had been murdered, others had fled to the relative safety of Binga. At the top of my visiting list was the so-called 'member in charge' of the police, known since the days of British South Africa Company rule as the BSAP. He turned out to be a delightful man called Denbeigh Hopkins, who told me he was born in Northern Rhodesia. This somehow got us off to a good start, which continued when I met his superior officer who was visiting from Wankie. He asked me whether I had ever been to Africa before and he was clearly highly impressed when I replied in the affirmative and added that I had even visited Binga in the 1960s. Denbeigh gave me a good run-down of the political and security situation in the district. Whereas few of his colleagues were prepared to admit that the war was coming to an end, he said that his informants had told him that the security situation was improving almost by the day. He said that any day now he was hoping to send out police patrols wearing their normal peace-time uniform of grey shirt and khaki shorts to carry out ordinary policing. He added that the people of the district desperately wanted that.

Though I continued from time to time to make use of the surprisingly sophisticated little bar between the rest camp and Van Jaarsveld's store, it was at the police club up the hill in Binga proper where it was all happening at night. Though I never saw the DC and his wife nor the Van Jaarsveld families from down the hill at the bar, all the other white residents foregathered there every night. There was music, good friendly company and the beer flowed. I got to know the man who ran the hospital, Wally Laudon, and his wife; the government mechanic Keith Taylor; the Deputy Police Chief Kevin Lawless and a number of young men who were always around the government offices doing what I am not quite sure. At least one was involved in developing and training some sort of government paramilitary organisation set up to counter the political parties. They had greenish-yellow uniforms and a similar coloured truck for transport. Apart from Mike Hughes, who had met me at the airfield, there was another cadet of similar age. For years these young men had lived with war and killing. This norm had somehow affected him and led to some rather strange behaviour, which I found difficult to define. Later I was told that there were literally hundreds, if not thousands, of such disturbed young white Rhodesians all over the country. Of course conversation at the police club revolved around the war. The people I met there, all white, were invariably friendly. They were all determined that their beloved Rhodesia would be saved from the ters. Even if things looked bleak at times, they were sure that they would win through in the end. The idea of a Patriotic Front (PF) victory in the forthcoming election was unthinkable. At about 9 pm in the middle of the bonhomie of the police club, the hubbub would suddenly cease and there would be total silence as the latest news came over the radio from Salisbury. It detailed various security incidents around the country and the way the security services were dealing with them. It struck me that these people confronting the whole world were very brave and that the prevailing atmosphere must have been similar to that in the UK during the dark days of the Second World War. I did a lot of listening during those evenings. I had learned from many years in southern Africa how important it was for outsiders to be sparing with their opinions. In this case there seemed to be a serious skewing of what was going on in the country. The reality was that the war was coming to an end. Yet the Rhodesians were for the moment taking the line that the arrival of the monitoring force had made little difference to the situation. To maintain a realistic perspective I relied on the BBC and my little shortwave radio when I got back to my chalet in the evening to go to bed.

During this time I had some real conversations with Belle, who was the DC's secretary and lived in another chalet at the rest camp. Her boyfriend was the mechanic at the garage opposite the store where, when he was not tinkering with his own Jaguar, he repaired both marine and motor vehicle engines. Belle had a degree from my university, Rhodes, and argued persuasively that giving way to the PF would mean the end of European civilisation in Rhodesia. Another interesting member of the community was an American evangelistic missionary married to a Tonga woman. He certainly managed to view the situation with a degree of objectivity. He was cautious though about being seen to be sympathising with one side or another, so was regarded by the whites with suspicion. He was the only white man I have ever met living south of the Zambezi who spoke Tonga. He told me that he regularly listened to the Tonga service of Radio Zambia. He said the radio spoke of Zipra forces continuing the war whatever the outcome of the elections.

Down the hill and between the rest camp and the harbour and the croc farm was a line of smart houses along the right of the road. I had met the owners of one of the houses, Angus and Hazel Van Jaarsveld, on my previous visits to Binga in 1964 and 1965 and in due course they provided a wonderful friendly haven where I could go for a good meal and a relaxed chat. Angus's brother, the famous 'bald eagle' Des, had played rugby for Rhodesia and Hazel's brother Fred worked as a government development officer. Angus could see that like their brothers on the northern side of the lake, the Tonga mainly just wanted to be left alone. Though they were fed up with being dominated by the Ndebele through ZAPU and Zipra, they were realistic enough to appreciate that there was no future in support of the Smith Muzorewa alliance. Though the Van Jaarsvelds, like all whites, were anxious about the prospect of ZANU/PF victory, they were confident that they would be able to stay on and run their croc farm as well as the store and the newly established business fishing for *kapenta*. These are little whitebait-sized fish, native to Lake Tanganyika, which were introduced to Lake Kariba in 1964 by the Northern Rhodesian fisheries department in my day. Now they had spread throughout the Lake and could be caught at night in small mesh nets suspended under water beneath bright lights which attracted massive shoals. Already dried *kapenta* formed an important part of indigenous African diets in the big towns of the region.

After I had been in Binga for about two weeks, Charles Chadwick flew in from Bulawayo to visit me. I went out with him, Dave and Mike and the usual truckload of armed men. Since my first visit to talk to the terrified villagers, I had been allowed to call on Chief Siabuwa, who happened to have gathered together the headmen from his area. I persuaded Dave that he and the armed men should stay in the background while I walked into the middle of the chief's village and introduced myself. I supposed I was distinguished by my Union Jack election supervisor badge. I had greeted the assembled people in Tonga, which seemed to have an almost magical effect. Soon I was able to sit down and talk about the agreement between Smith and the Bishop on the one hand and Nkomo and Mugabe on the other with the British government. I said I was from Britain, and I talked about peace and peaceful elections and asked the chief and headmen to pass on the message to their people that everybody should vote and be confident that their vote would be secret. This was because the elections would be supervised by Britain, which had resumed her constitutional responsibility for Zimbabwe/Rhodesia. All this went down incredibly well.

Dave and company had been impressed by the way I was received. So, when on the afternoon we went out with Charles and we drove to a rural school serving a number of villages, Dave said that as I seemed to get on much better on my own, I should go ahead. He and the others stayed in the background. As I walked past the school there was nobody to be seen except two women up the hill about 100 yards away. As I approached them I could see they were picking berries off a bush. '*Zilaligwa?*' (are they edible?) I asked in Tonga; '*E zilaligwa*' was the reply. Then I greeted the women, explained who I was and asked them to go to the neighbouring villages and tell everyone to come to the school because I wanted to talk to them about peace. They did a good imitation of a casual departure over the crest of the hill. It was not more than a few minutes before people started to arrive in increasingly large groups. Soon there must have been about 150 people and so I started speaking. Again I talked of the end of the war, of lasting peace and of the forthcoming elections. As I spoke the people kept on arriving until by the time I had finished ten minutes later there must have been 300 people there. I was delighted and touched by their reaction to what I had to say. Like the hotel bedroom attendant in Bulawayo had told me, everyone in the rural areas longed for an end to the war. Charles too was impressed by what he had seen. He told me that night over dinner at the rest camp that he had found the experience very moving. He subsequently described it in an article for *The Observer*.

Apart from getting accepted and involved, it was very important to make contact with the local politicians. The Smith/Muzorewa people really only operated in Binga township, where civil servants, their families and others with a vested interest in the status quo were supporters. I saw no sign of them operating anywhere else in the district. I met the PF candidate one afternoon along the road west towards Milibizi. I found him aggressive and bombastic, but as soon as he realised he was not going to get a rise out of me that way, he turned much more affable and we were able to have a conversation about working together to ensure that the election was free and fair. In the following weeks I saw him several times moving about the district with his entourage in their brand new 4×4 provided, I was sure, by some international agency. I doubted whether his electioneering consisted of much more than threats or implied threats of what would happen if he was not elected. That the power of the nationalist politicians over the people was a reality was shown by the fact that village people to whom the government started distributing desperately needed famine relief mealie meal obeyed the party's order to throw it all over the road.

Meanwhile I started to travel further afield around the district. Dave had his own mine-proofed Land Rover without doors. It was important I was told that the doors be removed so one could get out of a vehicle quickly and take cover in the event of an attack or following the triggering of a landmine. We went on one particularly long and fascinating tour which took us away from Binga for four days. On the first day we travelled up the main valley road going westwards past Siabuwa towards Kariba 150 miles away. There had been a lot of rain and we came across a number of lorries stuck in the middle of the road in deep glutinous brown red valley mud. While our convoy negotiated the obstacle, Dave and I spotted a number of knob-nosed ducks on a small lake formed by the rains. We managed to shoot a couple before moving on. The main road runs along the valley bottom across flat lands and then some low hills. Every now and then there are views of the mighty lake to the north, with the line of mountains of the Zambian escarpment rising to over 5000 feet behind. On our right but only a few miles away and towering above us was the Rhodesian escarpment. We passed the road leading up to the very remote Chizarira National Park set in 2000 square miles of pristine, wild, mid-escarpment country, about 2000 feet above the valley bottom. I made a mental note to visit it if the opportunity arose in the future. Later on we passed beneath Tundazi Mountain, which at more than 5000 feet is the highest point in Matabeleland. After good rains the countryside was stunningly beautiful and we saw a lot of game, particularly impala and kudu, and signs of elephant. The bird life was magnificent too. One benefit of the war was that because the bush was a dangerous place in which to venture, wildlife had been undisturbed for years and numbers everywhere were soaring.

We stopped for the night at Nabusenga dam at the foot of Tundazi. There was a small boat which we rowed out in and I particularly remember the wonderful sightings we had of white-fronted bee-eaters. We spent the night in a fortified camp beside the dam. It was a bit tense as we slept in a trench with guns at the ready and ate Rhodesian army 'ratpack' food which was not very exciting. The next day we drove on through mopani woodland and on to the site of the remotest polling station in the district at Chunga. Work on it had yet to start, indicating again that preparations for the elections were lagging. After Chunga I was taken to a safari camp where we were entertained

British Election Supervisors, Matabeleland North

by the owners, Rupert and Verity van der Riet, to a delicious lunch in their lovely house beside the lake. I quote from my diary:

> He is very well set up with a lovely house beside the lake, fishing boat (for *kapenta*), aeroplane etc. Very hospitable. His wife is the heroine of an incident involving a gang who lined up every European including various guests and visitors, up against the wall intending to shoot them. She broke and ran crouching low, the story goes. She was fired on from outside. The ters inside thought they were being fired at and there was almost total confusion. Then she returned with a gun which jammed. She ran back to get another and opened fire. The gang fled but firing over their shoulders killed one of the guests. Our hosts showed us a baby buffalo, rescued when its mother was caught in a snare. They also had a fully grown tame lioness which apparently had once jumped on to the dining room table to the consternation of the overseas dinner guests who had not seen her coming into the room.

They were delightful people but conversation indicated an attitude which was typical at the time. Again I quote from my diary:

> When I told him I had worked in NR/Zambia for nine years he said, 'Oh well you certainly know them', in a tone which invited a mutually morale boosting condemnation of blacks. The attitude was so negative but perhaps

understandable. The gulf is still stupendous. No attempt on the part of whites to take stock and really try to understand and then to think positively about the future.' I went on to say that 'Dave leaves the others in the shade re attitude.'

Back in Binga there was a message to say that Charles had arranged for the Matabeleland North supervisors to meet in Bulawayo to review the situation and compare notes. A small plane collected me and we flew via the districts en route to pick up colleagues. At Lupani there was a meeting taking place near the airfield. There was a small gathering of about 40 strong all black and all civil servants and their families sitting on the ground. There was an impressive-looking white helicopter in the background which had obviously brought the speaker. It was Bishop Muzorewa himself.

It was great to see colleagues but we were all worried by what Charles had to say about developments in Salisbury and what seemed to be a serious rift between the commission and the directorate. Colleagues all said they were receiving good co-operation from the Rhodesians at district level but all talked of a continual preoccupation with security. The Rhodesians continued to carry guns they said and there was little positive talk about the future. On a practical level, we all felt that the Rhodesians if not dragging their feet were not giving arrangements for the election the urgent priority that was required. Another matter of great concern was the intelligence received that government officials had been given some pretty strong and scurrilous anti-PF propaganda leaflets to distribute. To do so would of course be illegal and seriously compromise their supposedly non-political position. We were asked to make discreet enquiries and report back.

At this time we were also told of plans to send out a number of British policemen from the UK, up to a dozen to each district. The idea was that their presence in uniform at polling stations would reassure voters. There was no question of them having any sort of security role and they would be unarmed. I thought the idea was a brilliant one. Before we all dispersed back to our districts Charles told me that I would be receiving visits at Binga both from Commonwealth observers and from the world's press. The prospect of the latter visitation was particularly exciting for me as I knew it would give me the chance to put myself and the British role in a very favourable light by being able, unlike the Rhodesians, to communicate with the indigenous people of Binga in their own language.

The night before flying back to Binga I was in the lounge of the Victoria Hotel waiting to meet colleagues for a pre-dinner drink and I got into conversation with a young South African policeman from Natal. He said he had

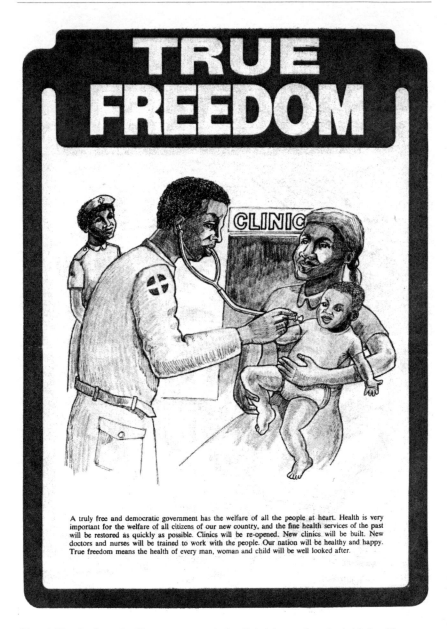

Illegal Rhodesian election propaganda leaflet (above, front; right, back)

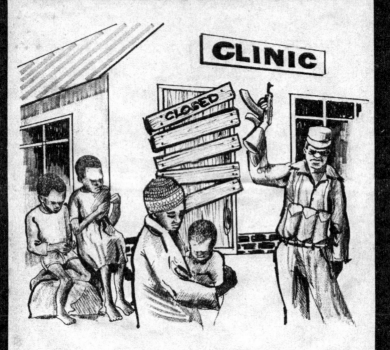

Those who are supported by Communist Russia claim they will look after the health of the people. But it was the so called "freedom fighters" who forced your clinics to close. They forced your families to live without health services that were already there. How can you trust these men? They do not care about the health of your children and wives.

originally come to Rhodesia 'to fight kaffirs'. In fact through getting to know his comrades in war, he had for the first time gained some understanding of the feelings and aspirations of ordinary Africans. In particular he thought that the attitude of young whites, especially the all-white Rhodesian Light Infantry, was crazy in the extreme and boded ill for the future of the country. In rural Natal, he said, whites all knew how important courtesy and mutual respect was for race relations. I was surprised because from my university days I remembered how many South Africans never spoke to a black man without denigrating him. Whatever might be wrong in Rhodesia, it seemed to me that blacks and whites had in the main been able to talk to each other man-to-man. Perhaps the war and the bitterness and hatred it created had turned things around for young Rhodesian whites.

One of the first things I did on my return to Binga was to go and see Denbeigh to ask him if he knew of any propaganda leaflets in circulation. He said without any hesitation that he did. In fact he could show me some. He said he had been sent bundles of leaflets which he was supposed to dis-tribute discreetly around the district. He said he had taken one look at them and decided that they were illegal and that to pass them on would seriously compromise his position. He had therefore decided to put them in his strong room. He showed some of them to me. They were certainly strong stuff, illustrating scenes such as the burning of schools and clinics. The caption suggested that to vote PF was to support such actions. I noticed that the leaflets were printed on the low-quality, yellowish paper used by the govern-ment printer. Clearly these leaflets came from the government printer but the usual indication in small letters at the bottom of the page was missing. Denbeigh assured me that he would let me know if he came across any more of such propaganda.

The announcement of the arrival of Commonwealth observers in the country said they were particularly interested in intimidation. I quote the comment from my diary:

> I have not heard of any in Binga. In a sense everybody in this country is subject to some sort of intimidation or the threat or fear of it. Who is intimidating who?

Before the Commonwealth observers visit, I had a meeting with the DC and Dave from which it emerged that the Rhodesian Election Directorate was at last asserting itself and putting pressure on the districts to get on with the detailed arrangements for the election. I agreed that time was short. I did not say that in Binga at least the delays reflected a lack of enthusiasm for the election and that if there were cock-ups due to a last-minute pile-up causing a hiatus, as sure as eggs were eggs, we the British would get the blame!

The Commonwealth observers turned out to be a party of four, a Jamaican politician called Princess (I thought at first that she was a genuine princess), the Nigerian head of his country's Africa department, a Nigerian colonel and a Sierra Leonean. They had very little time, but after a rather weak briefing from the DC, I gave them some of background to Tonga history in the Zambezi Valley as well as Kariba and resettlement. Denbeigh was away and his deputy had little to contribute. I observe in my diary that he might have talked about new moves for the police to tour villages in their peace-time uniforms. It was interesting how the observers after the briefings made a beeline for the trading stores in the township where I could see them engaging in earnest conversation with the storekeepers, the nearest thing to a black Binga professional class. A very sensible move I thought, particularly as I saw a couple of teachers join the group. They would certainly have got a realistic line on black opinion before leaving. They indicated concern at the distances some people would have to walk to get to polling stations. It also worried them that the count would take place in Bulawayo rather than in Binga. They said they would raise these issues in Bulawayo. I had planned to take them to a village, but there was no time.

Again over the next couple of weeks I travelled extensively around the district by Land Rover and by plane. I went first to Kariangwe, set in the hills to the south. There in the mission school I addressed a meeting of school teachers and their wives and was questioned about how far they could go in advising village people who to vote for. I advised them to take care as they were civil servants and that what they said could not be capable of being construed as political bias. Then it was off with the DC westwards to Milibizi up near the top of the lake where there was a delightful little fishing hotel. We met a party of white fishermen from the Kamativi Tin Mine up the road towards Wankie, where I had played cricket in my youth. We dined that night on delicious eland steaks cooked on the barbecue and we partied into the early hours. The next day before leaving I addressed a meeting of hotel employees, tsetse department workers, their wives, etc. on the lawn. Unlike in the villages there was little response. As I observed in my diary, 'No doubt all watching each other very carefully and perhaps mindful of whatever the boys from the bush might have told them.' Back in Binga later that day I attended a meeting of the Sitole version of ZANU. There was a national organiser there whom I found impressive. Meanwhile, Denbeigh told me of various PF meetings being held around the district. He did not seem partic-ularly worried that PF had in no case asked permission to hold the meetings. He discounted reports of threats to kill people who failed to vote for PF, but he had had reports from school teachers that what was said was that people would die of starvation if they did not vote for the party.

Another trip that I made with the DC was a flight to very remote Lusulu, inland from the lake and beyond the Chizarira National Park. Soon after take-off we saw the steep wall of the Zambezi escarpment rising 2500 feet in front of us. Then we were over the park with a single road snaking south through the empty savannah. Twice the pilot came down low to look at herds of buf-falo and elephant. Lusulu is in the middle of an area settled by people who used to live right on the banks of the Zambezi before the lake formed. I wondered if they were doing any better than their Tonga brothers on the north in adapting to new forms of agriculture and animal husbandry. Along the river they had planted their giant sorghum in the soft fertile alluvial soil after the Zambezi flood had receded. Could these people, barely touched by so-called civilisation, survive by growing unfamiliar crops on the dry sandy soil, utterly dependent on the unreliable rainfall? Now in this remote place, virtually all the women, young and old, went bare-breasted, had small sticks through the lower part of their noses and had knocked out their front teeth. They also smoked large gourd hubble-bubble pipes. This traditional female behaviour may have had its origins in women deliberately making themselves less attractive to Arab and Portuguese slavers. Now they were regarded as a sign of beauty. But were they now beginning to abandon these customs? I thought they probably were.

Lusulu had a tsetse department presence and a small police outpost which seemed to have been abandoned. There was anti-British graffiti on the walls including a picture of a bulldog and under it 'bullshit'. We had a good meet-ing with the tsetse department workers and their wives and some women from nearby villages. There were some wistful looks when I talked of my past in Zambia and mentioned names like Kalomo, Sinazongwe and Chipepo. The DC spoke excellent Ndebele. He was clearly a very experienced man but had told me that he missed working with the urban Matabele in Bulawayo. We flew back to Binga very low over the Chizarira. Suddenly as we reached the escarpment, there was the valley floor way below us.

As time went on I was really getting to know Angus and Hazel. They were two of the most hospitable people in the world and a sign of this was that their dining room table was permanently laid with silver and cut-glass

as if prepared for a sumptuous dinner party. They were as close as I had to
an unbiased sounding board. I learned a lot from them about local attitudes
and I enjoyed their company. I was lucky enough to have an open invitation
to drop in and see them. I quote from one day's entry in my diary:

> Got back late and went down to Angus and Hazel for a swim and a beer. She
> said she had hardly been able to control her feelings when the PF candidate and
> aides came into her shop. Luckily she had and they were civil. The candidate
> had met Angus too and said he had heard of him. Our conversation moved on
> to considering what it would be like living under an African government. I said I
> thought such a government would be pragmatic and there were great advantages
> in a strong leader. Angus went on to tell me that he loathed the business of
> carrying a gun all the time. In fact he no longer took his FN everywhere. He
> agreed some white youngsters were far too fond of their guns and he told me the
> story of a farmer friend from West Nicholson whose house servants were forced
> by ters to bring them beer and food. This became a regular thing until there was
> an attempted ambush of the farmer. When beer and food was next demanded,
> the servant gave the ters a dressing down. The commander apologised and said
> the people concerned were new and his unit had promised to discipline them.
> When the farmer went off to do his army service this was considered to be his
> duty, as a soldier on the other side.

A day or two later I learned by telephone that the visit of 20 journalists
from the world press was being cancelled for lack of interest. It transpired
that they had decided they would rather go to the Victoria Falls, where of
course there was nothing of particular interest regarding the election. I was
very disappointed as was the DC as we had made careful preparations for
the visit. Apart from anything else it seemed to me that the story of some of
Africa's most 'backward' people voting for the first time should have been
very newsworthy. I suppose there was a lack of appreciation in journalistic
circles of just how cut off the valley Tonga had been from so-called civilisation
and how different they were from all other indigenous people in the country.
I would have liked to have shown off the rapport I had established with the
DC, the people and the politicians.

Now all of a sudden preparations for the elections started to accelerate.
I flew up the lake to Chunga with the DC to see how the two fat boys Mark
and Fred were getting on with building the polling station, made of long
grass for the roof and walls. Chief Chunga and his headmen and elders were
waiting to talk to me and afterwards they all came up to me and shook my
hand. Afterwards we flew on to the Sengwa River mouth for lunch with
Rupert and Verity van der Riet. On the way back to the plane we stopped to

Rhodesians building polling station with DC

photograph a sacred ibis. We flew back to Binga along the coast at low level and spotted a herd of 200 buffalo and lots of small groups of elephants. What a wonderful environment. Once again my diary records 'dinner with Angus and Hazel'.

Arising from a meeting with a senior Rhodesian military man in Denbeigh Hopkins's office, I was invited to visit the headquarters of the Matabeleland North Joint Operational Command (JOC) in the mining town of Wankie, up on the plateau about 60 miles from Victoria Falls. I was to go by air with the DC Wankie piloting the plane. We flew westwards along the flat valley bottom over dense bush looking very green as a result of all the recent rain. Suddenly in front of us, only a couple of hundred feet below, was the tiniest Rhodesian army outpost consisting of a square low-walled structure topped by a flat roof all on top of a rocky outcrop. This little fortress was manned by a single white Rhodesian soldier who gave us a cheery wave as we flew right over him. He and others like him were very brave men. I supposed that from their vantage point giving views of several miles in every direction, it should have been possible to see or hear the approach of hostile soldiers. He must have had some superb views of animals and birds. Near him we spotted a family party of magnificent kudu. Soon however, we were gaining height over rising ground. It was rough country but not as rough

Author addressing Binga headmen

as the wild hills and mountains across the Zambezi just to the north in the Kalomo district where I had toured 20 years before.

In Wankie at the JOC I got the impression of relaxed efficiency. I met a lot of friendly people who were genuinely keen that I should talk to everybody and see everything. It seemed that the Rhodesian military were rather enjoying the presence of some New Zealand soldiers who were monitoring their activities. I was introduced to a very young and attractive white Rhodesian girl in military uniform. It transpired that she and a New Zealand officer had fallen in love and decided to marry.

Back at Binga we were preparing for the arrival of the British bobbies. I thought the idea was a brilliant one. The men coming out from all over the UK would be unarmed and not play a security role at all. However, their presence in uniform, particularly with their distinctive helmets, would underline the British supervisory role to the population as a whole. Before their arrival, political activity was hotting up. Denbeigh told me that permission for a PF meeting at the airfield had been refused as it was a security area and two busloads of Nkomo advance guards had had to be sent back to Bulawayo. Then a UANC (Muzorewa/Smith party) man accompanied by a national women's organiser came to see me to say that amongst those who had come in the buses were two known guerrillas who had obviously come out of an assembly point. I thanked them for the information and sent them on to see Denbeigh. Later on that day the DC said he thought he should mention that in his conversations with newly arrived army officers they had given him the impression that their instructions were to deploy at polling stations without any attempt to remain out of sight. I went straight to see Denbeigh who said all this was news to him. In our conversations thus far, the assumption had always been that the police would handle all security. He did not anticipate any security problem. Charles had told us that the army had been instructed to remain well out of sight. So I arranged a meeting with the DC, Denbeigh and the army commander. The latter's attitude was conciliatory though he emphasised that his job, which could not be compromised, was to protect the polling station and the public. He said though that he was prepared to accept my point that the population was terrified of the army and he promised that its presence would be as discreet as possible. I was amazed that the army had not been given a detailed briefing on this sensitive issue at the JOC.

A few days later I was at the airstrip to meet the bobbies. They arrived with a roar in a massive low-flying Hercules. The aeroplane circled the little strip, did a perfect landing and came to a stop very quickly. The bobbies, all 11 of them, were sergeants or constables from the West Yorkshire police. They were all wearing uniform and looked very pale compared to local Europeans. Though slightly apprehensive, they were delighted to be in Africa, all for the first time. Accommodation had been fixed for them at the police mess, though they would eat at the rest camp before being deployed to the polling stations around the district. The first thing I did with them was to give them a broad outline of the historical background to the election and the general situation in the Binga district. I put most emphasis on the sensitivity of white Rhodesians vis-a-vis Britain and the British. I was nervous about the possibility that the bobbies would get into serious arguments with whites in Binga or with Rhodesian soldiers who were beginning to arrive. I needn't have worried. Perhaps there is a sort of world-wide understanding between policemen but immediately the Binga police officers took over the bobbies and heaped hospitality on them. It was the same story the next day after six had deployed and the remaining five were down at the rest camp bar. There was a party on at the rest camp pub and I took the five remaining bobbies with me. Soon an aggressive white reservist challenged the bobbies to a darts match and the two ended as friends. It was an excellent evening. Somewhere along the line I remember a very strongly built Yorkshireman lifting and cradling the wife of the hospital administrator with one arm.

Afterwards I congratulated my little team on the way they had joined in the party spirit and diffused any hint of confrontation. The response was that any hostility they might encounter in Binga was nothing compared to the hate that was directed towards them in Bradford. In short, they were very used to swimming in antipathetic water.

The next night it was the same story but this time in the police club. I remember a local fascination with the bobbies' helmets which they wore as part of their uniform during the day. One managed to exchange his helmet for a leopard skin. The same evening I was confronted by a reservist who said he thought we British were utterly crazy being in an operational area without carrying a weapon. Once again here was evidence of an inability to accept that the war was over.

As the election approached, the rain got heavier by the day. Serious doubts began to arise about the deployment of polling station staff by road. The day before the great day it was still raining, but all the separate polling staff accompanied by bobbies managed to get to their stations. Last minute instructions from Charles in Bulawayo arrived together with my special metal seals and string for tying up the ballot boxes. That day the PF candidate came to see me and butter wouldn't melt in his mouth. Though I had had no particular difficulty with him, he had certainly acquired a reputation in Binga for being difficult. Now it seemed that he had been instructed to mend fences all round.

As the great day dawned and as I waited for a lift up to the offices, I heard from the two bobbies based in Binga that they had had a lift up to Chunga and had seen elephants and other game on the way. As one of them told me how he had been totally captivated by Africa, I was on tender hooks. My particular concern was about the arrival of a helicopter which on this first day of the three-day election was due to ferry me to the polling stations in the most remote parts of the district. The weather seemed to be settling down and it was still dry by the time my lift arrived to take me up the hill to the helicopter-landing pad next to the police station. The DC was already there and we did not have long to wait. The helicopter was brand new and had the words 'Election Supervisor' emblazoned on its side. There was also an indication that it had been hired from a firm in Perth. The pilot was new to Africa. He supervised the fill up with aviation spirit and soon we were on our way carrying a third passenger, a senior police officer from Scotland.

I had never before travelled by helicopter and it was a revelation. It struck me forcibly that this was certainly the way to travel in Africa. As we rose and headed along the main road towards Siabuwa there were superb views of the vast lake stretching east and west, the mountains of Zambia and the nearer Rhodesian escarpment. Soon, as we approached Siabuwa we could see long lines of people stretching away from the grass polling station, all waiting for their turn to vote. We landed nearby and found the station incredibly busy. All was in order with the party representatives sitting in a line in the polling station watching the voting. I asked them if all was well and they said yes. The bobby had placed himself inside the station and was looking important. The Rhodesian police were in evidence outside the station wearing peace-time uniforms and clearly had nothing to do except be there. There was no sign at all of the army. It was a very encouraging scene.

That day in the helicopter was one of the most stimulating of my life. Of course there was a serious job to be done, but the ability to reach all the remote polling stations in an area half the size of Wales was exhilarating. This was certainly the way to travel in Africa. Flying west towards Chunga for a few minutes we were lost. The pilot was ex-Royal Navy and though young was very experienced. We gained height so we could see the road to Chunga and the branch to the Sengwa mouth and van der Riet's camp. I was pleased that I knew the area well enough to be able to point the pilot in the right direction.

At Chunga the crowds waiting to vote were massive. There the bobby dressed in a sky blue shirt and wearing his helmet was shepherding bare-breasted old Tonga women with their front teeth knocked out and smoking hubble-bubble gourd pipes to collect their ballot papers, and dip their thumbs into the indelible ink to show that they had voted and could not vote again. He was a large gentle man and as he showed them where to go he called them 'love' and 'duckie'.

The polling staff were frantically busy but maintaining their good humour. The agents of political parties sat quietly observing the proceedings and chatting to each other. I noticed there were some UANC posters on trees close to the polling station and I got the presiding officer to remove them. The party agents all seemed happy. I was talking to the PF man when an old man with one leg approached the polling booth with his ballot paper. Clearly he did not know what to do. He hovered around the entrance before putting the still unmarked ballot paper into the ballot box. The PF man and I agreed that as he had not asked for help, under the rules, the polling staff could do nothing for him.

From Chunga our trusty helicopter took us back to Binga to refuel and then off we set again to Lusulu. The rain had stopped, and as we flew up over

Election day, January 1980

the escarpment there were stunning views of Tundazi and as far as the eye could see over the undisturbed bush and vlei of the Chizarira National Park. Touching down at Lusulu we were immediately aware of immense crowds of people waiting to vote. Many of them were elderly and had been walking since before dawn. The old women seemed to be from the pre-resettlement era and they sat legs stretched out under the trees, bare-breasted and smoking their gourd pipes. I took a number of photographs, one of an old girl with a child, presumably a grandchild or great grandchild, sucking away at her big toe.

Back into the helicopter and we headed due west to Kariangwe where it was the same story of massive crowds, overworked polling staff but peaceful, orderly voting. Again there was no sign or report of anybody being told or pressured to vote in any particular way. As had become my habit, I struck up conversations with people well away from the polling station. Usually I talked to individuals to whom I explained who I was. When I had the opportunity to ask them who they intended to vote for, to a man or a woman, they replied without hesitation, 'soja u jisi mwana' (soldier carrying a child), the PF symbol on the ballot paper.

I only had the helicopter for a single day but had managed to visit all the remote polling stations away from the main valley road. It had been

Polling station with bobby and Baobab

an exhilarating day and it was with some reluctance that Mike Yates and I bid farewell to the pilot and the Scottish policeman as they headed back to Bulawayo in the late afternoon.

There were two days of polling to go and now I went with Dave Brink to the more accessible polling stations along the main valley road and found everything in excellent order. On the last day it was time to catch up with the mobile polling stations which had done very good work getting as close as possible to the far-flung communities or those cut off by the floods. Now on the last day, Dave and I drove along the main road westwards to rendezvous with the mobile station at a rural school with its thatched roof supported by pillars on a low wall which surrounded the classroom area. Thus the sides of the building were open. The mobile station had yet to arrive and everyone was waiting. The police, the army and of course the voters. It was all very relaxed as we sat around on the grass outside the school. By now the presence of the security forces did not seem to be disturbing anyone and I sat and chatted to voters as well as white soldiers. Eventually in the later afternoon the polling station arrived and quickly set itself up in the school. I sat on the low wall near the ballot box which in this case was in the open on a table, not in a polling booth. As people placed their ballot papers in the ballot box, Dave was on hand with a little stick to help push them into the slot. An old

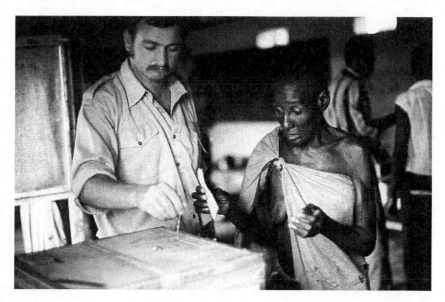

Binga voter

woman, bare from the waist up but no stick through her nose, caught my attention. As she held her ballot paper ready to place in the box, the pure terror and tension of the moment showing on her face and the sinews of her neck painted a vivid picture of her thoughts. Though it was probably illegal I could not resist taking the photo of her contrasting with the bored-looking Dave with his little stick.

That evening back at the government offices I witnessed the Binga district count. The ballot boxes had been escorted in for the count by local staff and witnessed by party agents, bobbies and myself. Now after the count, I had to re-seal the boxes with my own seal and they were placed under guard for the night. The next day the bobbies and I were packed up and ready at the airstrip for our transport to take us and the boxes to Bulawayo for the main count. The plane, when it arrived, turned out to be an old Dakota of Air Botswana. A number of Binga residents had come to say goodbye including the Hopkins. I was sure that we had done a good job. For me it had all been a highly stimulating and fulfilling experience and the culmination of many years' frustration and disappointment over Rhodesia. Now at last a British government had acted decisively. I was sure of the result; so were the blacks. By now it seemed local whites were beginning to think the same way. Now thoughts turned to local reactions.

Down in Bulawayo the evening of my arrival from Binga, I was debriefed by Charles and was in my room at the hotel when I received a phone call from the provincial commissioner for the Matabeleland North Province. He said he had had reports from the presiding officer for Kariangwe that there had been instances of intimidation of voters by PF activists. I told him that I had been to Kariangwe and nobody had complained to me. Moreover, the presiding officer who had been present at the count in Binga had said nothing to me either. I said I had to be very doubtful about the claim. The PC did not disagree. This was the only complaint I received from anybody over possible malpractice during the elections.

The following days are a bit of a blur and I can't remember the precise sequence of events. One of the major worries was how the whites would react in the event of a PF victory. I knew that for many this outcome would be traumatic. Many had told me that if this happened they would drive straight to the South African border at Beitbridge. From top to bottom, whites were convinced and had convinced themselves that Smith and Muzorewa would win a free and fair election. A PF victory would mean that there had been massive intimidation. I think that the Rhodesian police special branch had played the main role in convincing the government to believe what it wanted to believe. This was despite the fact that to an outsider like me, the indications staring them in the face were pointing in the other direction. It also seemed to me that the Rhodesians had convinced the British government too. I got the impression that it would have preferred a Smith/Muzorewa victory.

The election result when announced was a massive PF victory. Two things then happened that saved the country. The first was Robert Mugabe's speech which was a model of good sense and reconciliation. It praised the whites, assured them of their future role in independent Zimbabwe and spoke of 'beating swords into plough shares'. I could imagine people who had re-solved to head for the South African border hesitating. The second event which came shortly after was a speech by the Army Commander General Walls accepting the result and assuring the newly elected government of the army's loyalty. This speech too was of enormous importance as one of the very big worries was the reaction of white troops and white reservists, vir-tually all of whom had been mobilised for the election. Besides, with the PF fighters concentrated in assembly points, and with doubts about a monitor-ing force commitment to protect them, there was undoubted temptation for the white Rhodesian army to move in and clean up.

Very soon after the result I was down on the farm again with the Valentines and did all I could to try to talk Richard out of any thoughts he might have had of leaving the country. I tried to persuade him that the new Zimbabwe would need competent productive commercial farmers. Besides, I reminded him, he had always been an excellent manager of people and got on very well with the employees. As if to back me up, *The Herald* newspaper was trumpeting the line that the farmers were heroes. Most of them had come through all the difficulties and terrors of the war and there were more than 4000 of them still farming and more than capable of continuing to be the country's major foreign exchange earners. There was every reason too as to why they should continue to produce the food needed to feed the country and great swathes of the rest of Africa. While I was on the farm I had some moments of real anxiety when it seemed that all that had been achieved through the election might be lost. One morning I heard on the radio that the Rhodesian Light Infantry (RLI), the battalion made up entirely of white troops, was being allowed to parade with colours through the streets of Salisbury. Could this start a counter coup? I need not have worried. The parade passed off without incident.

I stayed on in Rhodesia (as yet to become the new Zimbabwe) for a few days and witnessed the change of atmosphere from fear and trepidation mixed with determination, to near euphoria. I remember one open-minded and intelligent white woman in Umtali telling me that she knew nothing at all about Mr Mugabe because the press had always presented him only as a terrorist. Now she said she was more than happy to give him a chance.

Of course Robert Mugabe and to a lesser extent Joshua Nkomo, were the new heroes of the moment. I was hoping that the governor of what was still legally the colony of Southern Rhodesia was exercising a moderating influence. Clearly influence was coming from very experienced and respected African leaders such as Julius Nyerere of Tanzania and Samora Machel of Mozambique. I was reliably informed that both had earnestly advised Mugabe not to do anything which would risk alienating or losing his white population.

I left the country a few weeks before the official independence celebrations attended by Prince Charles. I was immensely proud to have been involved in an exercise which gave the country the chance of a new start in the world. Though not my country, it contained some very dear friends and now having been in on its birth, I felt I had a renewed right to identify with it. I had been very disappointed by the failure of the Central African

Federation because of what I considered to be the short-sightedness of the whites. I had been more than depressed by the slide to the right under Ian Smith after 1963, followed by UDI. Though I could not support UDI, I could understand it because it seemed to me that the Rhodesian whites had every reason to mistrust British intentions over Southern Rhodesia. It looked sometimes as if there were no intentions at all and pure unguided expediency prevailed. Moreover, for years Britain had failed to assert itself with the Southern Rhodesian and federal governments and damagingly short-sighted and racist policies were allowed to continue. I had long felt that as the legal power Britain had a continuing responsibility for the country and needed to act before it fell into total chaos and ruin as a result of the war. I had felt that my background gave me special insights which would be of use in putting together a settlement. It had been immensely stimulating and fulfilling to have been able to play the part which I had foreseen for myself.

Looking back on the peaceful elections leading to the transition, I don't think that anyone other than the retired colonial service officers, particularly those ex-Northern Rhodesia, could have pulled it off. There were complexities and sensitivities that nobody else could have been able to understand and relate to. I don't think this was ever really understood by the British government. It was Sir John Boynton who got most of the credit, but it seemed to me that the main players were John Cumber and Mike North. Nevertheless, it was a great British achievement arising mainly from Margaret Thatcher's courage in deciding to stick her neck out and tackle the running sore that the Rhodesian problem had become. She provided the political weight and Peter Carrington the realism and professionalism. They could not have done it without each other. Though at the time she, in common with Rhodesian whites, would have liked to have seen a Smith/Muzorewa alliance carry the country, there was no way that such a result could have stuck.

As I had discovered, most of the black talent and commitment was on the side of the PF. Whites had been desperate to convince themselves that it was otherwise, but this would never be. Now there were new realities to be faced by both sides. The black nationalists, despite the Marxism on which they had been nurtured, needed to recognise not only the scale of their inheritance, but that it had been built up through hard work and entrepreneurial spirit. The black complaint that rang most true was that over the years they had not been allowed to share in the success story. Partnership had turned from being a sham into outright white political and economic domination under Ian Smith. Though blacks had contributed to it, it had been in the capacity of the 'horse' in Sir Godfrey Huggins' infamous 'rider and horse' analogy to describe the federation. This could never be compatible with black dignity and this was why they had in the end to fight. Whites, with all their endless talk of building a country, would now look for signs that the black nationalists were genuinely prepared to share what they had sought to keep for themselves. There were realities to face too. Despite all that the old Rhodesia had meant to them, they had to move on. Surely they could see that their country had come back from the very brink of total disaster and that they were extremely lucky to have the chance for a new sort of partnership with blacks. Harking back to a past which could never return would do them no good at all. They had come close to losing everything. Now there it all was to be saved and built upon in new ways with new attitudes reflecting respect for the aspirations and dignity on both sides. Surely all sides could not possibly fail to see this and together build the new Great Zimbabwe.

13

A Multinational's Foresight

I had to move on. From my new job in Saudi Arabia, I could not stop thinking about the new Zimbabwe and wondering how things were going. So after just over a year, Sarah and Tom aged 4 and I decided to swap our first-class return tickets to the United Kingdom for an economy class trip to Zimbabwe and back via South Africa, Mauritius and the Seychelles.

Zimbabwe in September 1981 before the rains, was marvellous. We hired a car at an amazingly low cost and travelled 3000 miles all over the country including to the Van Jaarsvelds in the Zambezi Valley, to my cousins Chris and Cynthia Cunliffe on their farm near Beitbridge, to the Andersens in Harare and to the Valentines in Odzi. The country seemed to be in wonderfully good heart. Everyone was happy and grateful for the peace and for the fact that the new government continued to be conciliatory. There was no anti-white rhetoric and everywhere we went, blacks could not have been friendlier. There were almost no tourists however, not even from South Africa, and it felt as if we had the country to ourselves. The nearest thing I came to a sign of previous conflict was from a black policeman of the old school to whom we gave a lift, who boasted of how with his FN he could better the new boys with their AKs. The question of arms was one that preoccupied a lot of people. There was the fear that former guerrilla fighters would retain their arms and use them for a life of robbery and extortion. These fears had so far proved groundless as the government put the highest priority on clearing the country of unauthorised weapons. There was much agitation amongst white farmers as they hurried to destroy their armouries dating from the war and threw guns into dams and rivers. Despite the worry, everyone agreed that getting rid of the arms was one of the best things Mugabe did.

We found that a significant number of whites had left the country shortly after independence mainly for South Africa. Of those that remained, many

were strongly anti-Mugabe and against the Patriotic Front. Several prominent members of the old regime remained in parliament including Ian Smith,
PK Van der Byl and my friend Chris Andersen. They were frequently vocif-
erous in their opposition to Mugabe's policies. I saw this merely as a stage in
the country's evolution. I was amazed to witness a ding-dong televised debate
between PK Van der Byl, certainly no moderate, and a group of young PF
supporters. With my experience of other African countries, I found it amazing that such an exchange should take place. It was surely a healthy thing
that white doubts and fears, even if expressed stridently by the likes of PK,
should find expression. It was surely less healthy that there were so many
'Rhodesia is Super' stickers and tee-shirts on sale at hotels for instance. Even
so, I thought of it as part of the transition towards an acceptance of the new
realities rather than a dream of hanging on to the past. Perhaps more worrying was that many whites were not prepared to give Mugabe the recognition he deserved for his policy of reconciliation. Such people included
some I knew to have been sympathetic to the black nationalist cause pre-
independence. One was a relation who had been an outspoken supporter of
Nkomo and Mugabe and who turned against them merely because of aspects
of pensions policy. Other old friends who had supported the black nationalist
cause left for South Africa despite the fact that Mugabe's policy could hardly
have been more moderate or accommodating for whites. After two weeks
in the country, despite a few doubts, I moved on feeling that Zimbabwe was
well launched in harnessing the skills and ambitions of blacks and whites in
building a genuine African success story.

I continued to work in Saudi Arabia until mid-1982. From the point of
view of finances, it was worthwhile as I was able to save for children's education. The job, personnel manager on Britain's biggest ever overseas contract,
training the Royal Saudi Airforce, however, was non-pensionable and I was
well into my 40s. My work was concerned with the company's 2500 British
employees who thought of little else but their pay and conditions. There were
continual disputes over a multitude of material benefits and I had to try to
hold the line with little support from our managers around the kingdom,
whose military culture decreed support for their men in all circumstances.
All this was tedious and I had little sympathy for what seemed like a culture of popular greed. Contact with local people was positively discouraged,
even forbidden. All this was a far cry from a career in which relating to indigenous people was the main part of the job. In Saudi Arabia people were
there just for the money. Motivation at work hardly came into it. Yet I had a

marvellous boss, Don McClen, who consulted me on everything. Sarah and I enjoyed the comfortable house with servants and swimming pool, frequent leaves and first-class air fares. We enjoyed alternate weekends camping in the desert and playing desert golf off plastic bottle tops at the Riyadh Golf Club. Nevertheless, I longed for Africa.

In mid-1982 an advertisement appeared in a British newspaper for a director of a trust, to be funded by the Rio Tinto company (RTZ), to develop indigenous technical managers for southern Africa's mining industry. I jumped at it. The trust was to be called the Zimbabwe Technical Management Training Trust (ZTMTT) and was to be based in London, but the job would involve frequent travel to southern Africa. I was invited first to see RTZ Personnel Manager Terry Ball and later to meet the then mining director – the charismatic Ronnie Walker whose idea the trust was. I remember at the first interview he asked me whether I liked Africans. Of course I answered in the affirmative. I was pretty confident after that interview that I would get an offer, but there must have been a number of other candidates and it was a fortnight before I heard again. This time I was invited to meet Sir Donald Tebbit, another RTZ director and chairman designate of the trust. Before the interview in the early afternoon, I lunched at the old Royal Commonwealth Society Club in Northumberland Avenue, where I saw an ex-boss and mentor from Northern Rhodesia days, Peter Burles. When I told Peter about the interview, he immediately showed me a letter from Sir Donald in that day's *Times* which he happened to be reading. What luck. I can't remember the subject, but I agreed with his viewpoint and as it was relevant to what we were discussing at some point in the interview, I was able to raise it. I was offered the job.

For many years I had wanted to work for RTZ. Here was an offer which would take me into the company at a good level with a pensionable salary. More importantly, it would give me maximum scope for individual initiative and involvement in a part of the world I knew well and still identified with. I soon learned more about my new boss Ronnie Walker and his fervent commitment to the company and to Africa. I learned too what a very special company RTZ was. I would be reporting direct to Ronnie who was metals director. ZTMTT would essentially be my show, but I was to keep Ronnie aware of all significant developments. He made clear the importance he attached to the scheme and the strong support I could count on from him. I had a taste of his vision and foresight very early on. I learned that he had been the executive chairman of Rio Tinto in Southern Rhodesia during the time of the Central African Federation and later after the unilateral declaration of independence (UDI) by Ian Smith. I gathered that he was one of a minority of Southern Rhodesian whites who had wanted to see a genuine partnership between the races. Now following the terrible war and a new start under black majority rule, he saw that one of the major problems would be the shortage, even total lack, of competent indigenous technical management. This could have a catastrophic effect on the whole mining industry, resulting particularly from the departure of many whites.

Ronnie had another important and looming African problem on his mind. It was South-West Africa now increasingly being called Namibia. There the company's Rossing Uranium Mine was of great strategic importance to Britain and the West. However, the company was operating in contravention of UN sanctions and of necessity in co-operation with the de facto authority, South Africa. I had never been to Namibia, but I was aware that it was run as if it was a province of South Africa. There were therefore, next to no black Namibians qualified to run anything at all, much less a sophisticated mine. The South African policy under apartheid was to deny higher level education in maths and science to blacks. On the face of it, it would be impossible for RTZ to do anything about this. The clear scenario was that when independence came, and in terms of UN resolutions this could be very soon, power would go to the SWAPO nationalist party currently in exile. As RTZ was in contravention of UN sanctions and co-operating with the de facto authority, SWAPO would almost certainly be unwilling to co-operate with any Rio Tinto scheme to train people who were getting technical qualifications abroad with SWAPO's help. At the same time, the South Africans would not look kindly on any RTZ co-operation with what it considered to be a terrorist organisation. So it would be a ZTMTT function to take on SWAPO Namibians. SWAPO would be able to support the scheme because it had the backing of its newly liberated Zimbabwean friends. Before I did anything else, I was told that I needed to go out to Zimbabwe and Namibia to get a good feel for the way things were on the ground. Within ten days I was on my way.

It was great to be back in Salisbury now called Harare. Friends like the Valentines and the Andersens seemed pleased that I would be spending part of the time in Zimbabwe and working on an important scheme to help the country. Chris Andersen, who I learned had given Ronnie Walker the thumbs up over my appointment, was now minister for the civil service in the Mugabe government. I booked into the marvellously friendly and

Richard and Phil, on an Odzi kopje

efficient Meikles Hotel overlooking Cecil Square with stunningly beautiful jacarandas in full purple bloom. There was a welcoming message from Chris with a request to come and see him in his office right away. Having sat me down with a cup of tea, he explained how and why he had become a minister in the Mugabe government. He said he had become increasingly worried by the negative stance taken by Ian Smith towards Mugabe and his government. He felt that this was not good for the country nor for the country's whites. He went on to tell me how Mugabe had frequently tried to consult Smith on policy matters but in view of the negative reaction he was getting, was doing so less and less. When Mugabe's offer had come, it was made clear to Chris that he would not be expected to join the ruling ZANU/PF party. Now Chris said, he was back in politics and in a position to make a really important contribution. Moreover, he said he was enjoying the work and had received the friendliest of welcomes from cabinet colleagues. He explained too that he saw it as his role to explain the whites' point of view to the government and the government's view to the whites. He saw no prospect of being required to do or say anything he did not believe in. I told Chris that I fully understood and supported what he had done. I was to learn that though he had no problem with black colleagues in the cabinet nor indeed with the majority of whites still in the country (about 150,000 at that time), a few whites regarded him as betraying their cause. Though in the minority, such views were strongly held even if in the context of the new Zimbabwe; in my opinion they made no sense at all.

The minority of whites who held negative views were of the sort which would find it nigh impossible to accept black rule under any circumstances. They were determined to ignore successes and spurned the chance of a new beginning. It was as if they wanted to see the new Zimbabwe fail so as to justify their prejudices. In the early days of my new association with Zimbabwe, I came to regard such views and attitudes as insignificant and to be expected, particularly among older generation whites. The people with whom I had dealings such as Chris and the head of Rio Tinto Zimbabwe Don Bailey, were totally constructive and positive in their attitudes and committed to the new Zimbabwe. The Valentines too, after their fears and doubts in the weeks after Mugabe came to power, were now reconciled. Richard was getting on with making the most of his talents as an excellent farmer and a great leader of men. He and Heather had always enjoyed the respect of local people. There were still doubts however; for instance over the Odzi Club, which members were afraid could be swamped by new black members more interested in its bar than in playing tennis, squash and cricket. They feared that it would no longer be a haven where whites could meet, play sport and socialise and so reinforce their community. It was obvious to me that any measures to keep out blacks would immediately be seen as racism and be totally unacceptable. But how could the club prevent an influx of new members who might ruin the club? Chris was with me staying at the Valentines one weekend and when the conversation turned to the club, he said that the whole thing was very simple. The club should invite the local administrator, party secretary and chief of police to become members, thus dispelling any suggestion that it was trying to keep blacks out. The issue would then cease to be contentious and would probably go away. And so it proved. Over the following 23 years, I never saw a single black man at the club.

14

African Self-Discovery

I became aware of just how many thousands of black Zimbabweans had returned home to take up jobs in the civil service, in commerce and industry and throughout the economy. Many of these people had degrees, recently achieved from UK universities. Some of these graduates had done their A levels in the UK too. There were other people who had been working in significant jobs in various parts of the world. Now they were back in strength, most of them in Harare and constituted a new black professional class. Not all of this new class had been educated outside the country. There was a high proportion of people who, having done their A levels at one of Rhodesia's excellent all-black schools such as St Augustine's Penhalonga or Goromonzi Secondary, had gone on to do a degree at the University of Rhodesia, which had maintained high standards of excellence throughout the UDI years. The new professional class, though it usually supported ZANU PF, was not specially political. Returnees also included educated people who had been involved or in one way or another committed to the struggle for majority rule. One such was Bernard Mutuma.

I met Bernard on a visit to Zimbabwe soon after taking up my new position as the director of the Zimbabwe Technical Training Trust but based at RTZ headquarters in London. He had left Southern Rhodesia as a young man in the early 1970s and had trained and then worked as a chemical engineer in Cairo. Back in Harare he was deputy secretary at the Ministry of Mines and one of the two Zimbabwe government—nominated trustees on the board of ZTMTT. It was my job on my visits to get to know him and gain his trust. The Mugabe government was socialist and RTZ was a multinational company, so I expected that it might take time to convince him and the government of our bona fide. Of course what we were doing with ZTMTT could not be separated from RTZ's activities in Zimbabwe at the time. For instance, the company needed to close the large Empress Nickel Mine because the ore reserves had run out. Sadly this meant making many hundreds of people redundant. I had nothing to do with the run-down of Empress, but I gathered that Bernard and the government came to show total appreciation of the company's position. It also saw that much as it wanted to see blacks promoted to senior positions in the company and in the industry as a whole, this could not realistically come about too quickly. This of course was where my trust came in, so there were high hopes and expectations from the start for its success. I got the impression though that for the government as a whole, the expectation was of a sort of training school with 'Zimbabwe Technical Management Training Trust' emblazoned over the entrance. I kept being told that eventually the trust would be based in Zimbabwe. Of course this was in contrast to our view that the programme needed to be based out of Africa to enable trainees to escape from all the cultural and race-based attitudes which could inhibit change away from the old attitudes of subordination and dependency. Meanwhile Bernard with his huge optimism and enthusiasm was easy to get on with. We soon became partners in an endeavour to provide Zimbabwe with the technical managers it would need to become a truly modern African country. I saw a lot of him and his charming wife Olivia. As a couple, they embodied the best of what could be expected of the new Zimbabwe. Bernard's passions, which were there for all to see, included a huge pride in his new country and in his Shona culture. It was as if the years he had spent away had given him perspectives that he would not have been able to gain had he stayed at home. This was a factor I came to appreciate more fully amongst the trainees in later years. The other quality, which I came to appreciate very early on, was his ability to sum up a situation quickly and take a decision. This was not supposed to be an African strength, but with Bernard it was characteristic and was very useful too as we made mistakes and needed to put things right. The other Zimbabwean trustee, who also became a personal friend and a very effective colleague, was Robson Muringi who had gone to the USA as a young man, worked and trained with IBM and married an American, Lorraine who was a boxing promoter. Robson tended towards caution and thorough consideration, which was the perfect balance to the Bernard style. The Muringis brought their international perspectives as well as their charm to the party. Bernard and Robson were typical of the new black professional class in Zimbabwe. They were experienced, educated and delighted and proud to be back in their country. They had virtually everything in common with their white colleagues except for the colour of their skin. Increasingly I found it worrying that despite all the reasons for a coming together there was very little the whites as a whole did to seek a common cause to which the new black middle class was totally open. Things were different in the circles in which I was now moving. My family accompanied me to Zimbabwe on several visits and I remember a marvellous evening which Bernard and Olivia hosted at the night club in the Monomatapa Hotel, which included Sarah and our children. We were lavishly entertained and Tom aged ten was monopolised on the dance floor by an admiring middle-aged white female.

Looking back on those early days of the trust, virtually everything we saw and heard about Zimbabwe was reassuring. Amongst many whites the formally hated Robert Mugabe was becoming 'good old Bob' as they saw that in most ways life carried on much as before. There was however the worry that the vital help which we were giving might be taken for granted. It worried Ronnie, Sir Donald and me that we did not seem to be receiving the sort of official recognition as reflected in the media, that we deserved. Even minor help or news of mutual visitations involving communist countries such as North Korea or Cuba always seemed to be big news. I supposed the government felt that it would be betraying the socialism which theoretically it espoused, if it gave us a multinational company, the recognition we felt we deserved. We contented ourselves with the practical co-operation we received. I was tempted to think that Zimbabwean Marxism was mainly for show, but I well remember early on what the white University of Zimbabwe professor said when we sought his opinion over the future. Referring to the national flag he said 'watch the red star'. To me concerns over political affiliations seemed to be misplaced, even niggardly in view of how well the country was doing on all fronts. My experience told me that the concept of right and left in politics was taken much less seriously in Africa than in the West.

Indeed on those visits to Zimbabwe while we were setting up the trust from August 1982 through 1983 and after, I could not help marvelling at the wonderful friendly and peaceful country Zimbabwe had become. I took periods of leave tagged on to work visits and travelled to many parts with my family. The message though, had not got through to the rest of the world, even, perhaps especially, South Africa. On one visit we had the wonderful Great Zimbabwe ruins virtually to ourselves. There was a young white South African couple we met there who told us that they found Zimbabwe completely different from the image projected by South African media. This situation was to persist until 1993.

We stayed regularly with the Andersens in Harare, climbed in the Chimanimani Mountains with the Valentines, camped with the Cunliffes on their game ranch in the wilds near the Limpopo River and hired lodges at Sinamatela in the Wankie Game Park at the Victoria Falls for £5 a night. However, we became conscious when we visited in 1986 that though most of the country remained relaxed and peaceful there was trouble in rural Matabeleland. There we gathered, there was some sort of security clamp-down involving so-called dissidents. When we got to cousin Chris's farm we learned he was worried because two of his teachers, both of the Venda tribe, had been arrested for breaking the newly imposed curfew. The police were apologetic because the two men were only a few minutes late getting back to the farm. However, their instructions were very clear. The men had to be handed over to the army. They were never seen again despite continu-ous and strenuous efforts by Chris to find out from the government what had happened to them. It appeared in retrospect that there were other even more sinister things happening in other parts of Matabeleland at the hands of the army's North Korean trained fifth brigade. Whatever was happening did not attract a lot of media attention and I was barely aware of it. Again in retrospect it seems that the public as a whole and the media avoided digging too far to find out what was going on. This was because of the overwhelm-ing desire on all sides to see peace and prosperity maintained in Zimbabwe and to avoid sinister interpretations of what was happening in Matabeleland. Over that period I visited mines and smelters and saw a lot of people in government departments and stayed with friends. To the ordinary man or woman in the street or in the countryside I was of course indistinguishable from white Zimbabweans. So the attitudes I encountered were the attitudes they encountered. I met nothing but friendliness and a palpable desire to be helpful at every turn. Race relations seemed to be as near perfect as could be imagined. It worried me a bit that there seemed to be a lack of appre-ciation amongst some whites of the overwhelmingly good things that were happening in the country including the arrival of more members of the new educated black middle class with whom they should have had a great deal in common. I found it strange that some whites who a few years before were in the middle of a horrific war which they were lucky to survive, were now tak-ing a negative view of their country. In contrast to attitudes of people I saw in Riozim and amongst friends like the Valentines and the Andersens, several whites I met would assure me that the country was going very rapidly to the dogs. I would point out that Zimbabwe was in my experience more sophis-ticated and a better place to live than anywhere else in Africa. Had they, I asked, recently been to Zambia, Malawi, Kenya, Uganda or the Congo? The reply would come, 'but this country is going downhill more rapidly than anywhere else'. I could not understand this attitude which I saw as betraying ignorance, prejudice and even a desire to believe a deeply ingrained and distorted perception of black rule, which did not reflect reality. Such people did not explain why they were unhappy. It was clear to me that they simply did not accept the reality of majority rule. The way I saw it these people simply did not appreciate how lucky they were. Their attitudes were a strange phenomenon, which though they were frequent enough to be a worry, I preferred to dismiss as part of the new nation settling down. Of course it was worrying that Mugabe and his ministers would frequently rail in public about the wickedness of exploitative policies of the multinational companies without mentioning RTZ or ZTMTT. However, again one had to remember where he came from politically. In fact, pragmatism was predominant and as a result the economy was doing very well. I kept on hearing around the country that Mugabe, apparently concerned that some of what he and his ministers were saying might worry businessmen or farmers, would reassure them by saying 'pay attention to what we do, not what we say.'

I imagined that all the war veterans would not be happy that their desire for land was not being fulfilled, but it seemed that the government had managed to persuade most of them that they could not expect too much too soon by way of the fruits of victory. That was the price of stability and prosperity. An agricultural industry which made up half the country's export earnings. The government's priorities over national prosperity and the land were surely signalled by the early appointment of a white farmer Denis Norman as Minister of Agriculture. The reality was of course that there were not enough war veterans for them to be able to exercise significant political power. Their wants and needs could be put 'on the back burner' and a higher priority given to keeping the hundreds of thousands of urban Zimbabweans in the teeming townships of Harare and Bulawayo happy with jobs and a rising standard of living.

In the early 1980s, the extent of the Zimbabwe African National Union (ZANU) party and Mugabe's determination to brook no opposition was simply not generally appreciated due to a compliant media. There was also the fact that people simply did not want to think that things might be going wrong. Yet the army's fifth brigade's actions in Matabeleland were a sign of that determination and the government's dictatorial leanings. I was barely aware of anything untoward despite the disappearance of cousin Chris's teachers after they were taken away by the army on the first evening of the first general curfew. This should in retrospect have signalled that even more sinister things were afoot. Nevertheless I took my family to his farm about that time after he had written to say there was little to worry about. Again in retrospect it is clear that anyone who stood up to what was going on was subject to every tactic of intimidation that it is possible to imagine. Only in 2007 with the publication of Judith Todd's book *Through the Darkness: A Life in Zimbabwe* is it possible to get an idea of what was really going on and the lengths to which Mugabe and ZANU were prepared to go to retain absolute power. Bear in mind that Judith knew everybody and as a nationalist supporter exiled by Ian Smith, had only returned home the year of independence. Had the world as a whole been more aware and taken more notice of the ruthlessness she was prepared to confront so bravely, it would not have been so surprised by the apparent moves towards economic suicide manifested by the farm takeovers from 2000. That was the year of the last genuine test of Mugabe's popularity when his recommendations on changing the constitution were overwhelmingly rejected by the electorate at a referendum. For those who wonder why the war veterans did not make a fuss earlier about the land issue, the answer is surely that Mugabe would not have tolerated it until it suited him.

To return to 1982 and the setting up of ZTMTT, it was important for me to have a good idea of what was going on at the Rossing Uranium Mine in South-West Africa, Namibia. First though I wanted to know how the copper mines of Zambia were dealing with the need for competent and confident indigenous technical managers, so I went to Kitwe to see mama training herself, my friend Petal O'Brien. She acknowledged that ZCCM still had a problem in this area but had never had and still did not have a special programme to tackle it. She added that in the days of Anglo American there had never been special measures either. When I moved on to Namibia I found Rossing highly stimulating. The mine had started operations barely five years before and as a result of the South African government's policies, there was a grave shortage of black people with any education at all, much less secondary education or any sort of formal training. The only way black people could get a full education was to leave the country. To counter these difficulties, the mine instituted the most vigorous policy towards on-the-job training that I have seen anywhere, before or since. Every single employee at any level above the bottom had to regard the training and therefore the effectiveness of his subordinates as his main priority. It was truly extraordinary to find low-level white employees, either Afrikaners or so-called South Westers (Namibians of German origin), totally committed to the training of their black subordinates. The policy had an amazing effect in boosting morale, raising the level of skills and getting the most out of the workforce. The supervisors felt fulfilled as well. One or two Rossing managers, recognising how the mine might benefit from ZTMTT trainees, seemed to think that they could join the mine as soon as the training was over. It was sometimes difficult to get these people to understand that the benefit to the mine would come after Namibia had become independent. This was because any Namibian with the minimum qualifications for the programme would be bound to be a supporter of South West Africa People's Organisation (SWAPO), which was currently waging war against South Africa, and he would lose all credibility by breaking ranks and returning home before SWAPO came to power.

So how were we to get hold of suitably qualified Namibian candidates? This was where co-operation with Zimbabwe kicked in. I was asked to go to Lusaka, and there in the plush office of the Zimbabwean High Commissioner himself, I interviewed two Namibian geologists who having qualified recently in Russia were now working in Angola. They came over as intelligent and keen, and though their English was a bit weak, I took them on. The business of finding suitable Zimbabweans was much easier. We put advertisements in the Zimbabwean press calling for applications from technical graduates only. We were inundated. I remember getting help from Richard Valentine and going through the forms in his dining room on the farm and piling up the applications, which seemed worthy of serious consideration. Then came the interviews at Meikles Hotel in Harare. I supposed that the Zimbabwean government might be suspicious of the criteria for selection or some other aspect of the process. I was keen that everything should be seen to be above board. So we settled on a procedure involving me in the chair assisted by one officer each from the Ministries of Mines and Labour. I was nervous that there might be pressure to take on this or that individual or give some sort of tribal or political preference. I need not have worried. In fact the panel worked very well together though it was an exhausting business interviewing up to twelve people per day for several days. It was very useful getting insights from my colleagues, which my cultural perspective would never have picked up. We settled on a final selection of six excellent high potential people conscious that there were many more very strong candidates in reserve. There was one female candidate, a recently qualified metallurgist called Demetria Chidyausiku whom I reluctantly turned down. This was because Bernard said she could not be released from her vital job with the

Ministry of Mines. I was keen too to demonstrate to everyone in government and Riozim that the exercise was not all about benefit to Rio Tinto but was for the benefit of the mining industry as a whole. In this way we risked alienating Riozim, particularly when I turned down an apparently strong candidate who came from one of their mines. Though he was undoubtedly very bright and had qualified at the Camborne School of Mines in Cornwall, he came over as lacking the necessary strength of character.

By the end of the recruitment exercise we had a big party at Meikles Hotel for the selected trainees, the government and the industry. The Ministries of Mines and Labour attended the ceremony, but as happened so often subsequently, we were kept on tenterhooks not knowing until the last moment whether this or that minister was going to turn up. I felt that considering what Zimbabwe stood to gain from this scheme as well as what it was costing, the government was being very casual. When it came to recognition and publicity it seemed that some gift of books from North Korea, for instance, was more important to the government.

Meanwhile back in the UK, I had been working to prepare for the first intake of trainees. I had been working on terms and conditions for trainees, preparing for their accommodation and planning how work experience was going to be alternated with business skills training during the 20 months they were going to be in the UK. On the business skills front, early on Ronnie Walker asked me to talk to an academic Professor John Donaldson of City University London, where he headed the Department of Industrial Chemistry. Ronnie had met him at a dinner in London where he had told John that in his opinion the academic world did not co-operate sufficiently with industry. He challenged John to come up with the academic part of a scheme he was planning, to train technical managers for the mining industry in southern Africa. John indicated that he would be willing to try and help and I had to meet with him to decide whether this was indeed the way ahead. A meeting with John convinced me that it was. Most importantly he was very flexible. He could muster a good deal of expertise on subjects such as accounting, finance, economics and planning from within his department. Other expertise could come from the university as a whole, including the City University Business School during part of its MBA programme. In addition to this, I would myself give a number of lectures on things like leadership skills, communication, motivation and appraisal interviewing. On top of all this, I would arrange for a good level of practical input from friends and contacts in RTZ and other companies and associations.

In the months that followed I worked with John and his assistant Dr Sue Grimes on the programme. It would last for two academic years and would lead to a postgraduate MSc degree in Industrial and Administrative Science. The qualification was important for several reasons including the priority placed in Africa on degrees. It was also an important part of the whole business of building trainees' self-confidence. Not least it would provide them with business skills training and insights which would take them away from the concentration on mainly technical considerations and link them with all the other factors a manager or leader needs to think of. Of course at the university it would be mainly about theory. More important was how we hoped trainees would gain confidence and come to see themselves and relate to the management function as a result of their practical work experience. I well remember the main considerations while we were doing the planning. Trainees we assumed, would need to get as wide a view of the various aspects of running an enterprise as possible. Thus on a mine for instance, they would need to gain an appreciation of what went on in the various administrative as well as technical functions and departments. Though our idea was that they would make themselves as useful as possible, inevitably they would spend time looking over peoples' shoulders and having things explained to them. Another priority I thought was to send them to the companies in groups for mutual support. I also thought it is better that they should go to the same company for their three- to four-month attachments. I felt that too much moving around would be unsettling. How little did we understand at that stage how misguided was much of our thinking.

For work experience we settled on three RTZ enterprises: the Wheal Jane mine in Cornwall, the Anglesey Aluminium smelter in North Wales and the Capper Pass metal refinery on Humberside. I had long discussions with the managements of all three and we identified local monitors who would take special responsibility for trainees' progress. All three managements were keen to co-operate with a scheme that had full backing from the very top of RTZ. I received all the help and co-operation I needed. All these things were put to and discussed by the ZTMTT trustees at their regular meetings, which alternated between London and Harare. In the chair was Sir Donald Tebbit, a retired senior diplomat who was also an RTZ main board director. His commitment was total; he got on with everyone and he and the Zimbabwean trustees took to each other immediately.

A worry was accommodation for trainees while they were in London. The plan was that they would all arrive on single status. Only after the initial term at the university would those who were married have the option to bring over their wives. We had settled on levels of allowances that made it possible for wives to join their husbands in the UK. Those who did, normally settled at a single location where they could look after children and/or perhaps get a job rather than attempt to move backwards and forwards in and out of London with their husbands.

For trainees' accomodation we were lucky to have contacts with London House for Commonwealth Students. This was high-level accommodation with potential friends and contacts and an academic atmosphere. We always had marvellous help and co-operation from London House. Another consideration was so-called culture shock. Although about half the trainees had taken their degrees in the UK, for others the new environment would be very strange and different, so I arranged a four-day induction course at Farnham Castle Centre for International Briefing. This became a regular feature of the programme and was always a success. When the first intake of ZTMTT trainees arrived in September 1983 planning had been going on for a year. I met the group of eight at London House for a talk and then led them to a nearby bank to open accounts for their monthly allowances. We went on to meet John and Sue at the Department of Chemistry at City University.

From the first, trainees were encouraged to question anything and everything. They soon gelled into a powerful group which did not hesitate to express its opinion or wants. This was natural and understandable if at times it all seemed like a series of negotiations. Generally all was going pretty well and it was easy to imagine all of these highly intelligent people in senior positions. I did wonder however, exactly how they would get there and whether what we were doing for them would really produce the goods. What we were doing for them was perhaps the vital question. Certainly that was the way we had started out. They and we clearly assumed that there was a gap created by past discrimination and disadvantage, which we would help them to bridge. We were assuming that they needed help of all sorts and we were providing them with this. At the same time we were urging them to think management at every stage both on attachments and at the university. Not unnaturally I was continually being asked, 'What level will I be prepared for when I get back home?' Even in the early stages I began to wonder where these preoccupations were leading. It was worrying that after three or four rounds of work attachments there were distinct signs of fatigue amongst the three companies providing them. Looking after trainees was time consuming for the companies and they received nothing for their trouble. When the trainees had problems or complaints they became a potential irritant. I tried to pre-empt some of the latter during my rounds getting to know the trainees and the managements and heading off problems. One factor was that there were a limited number of RTZ companies where we could send trainees. With the high price of tin, however, more possibilities were arising in Cornwall.

It was at one of these mines that our first serious problem arose after just over a year and the second intake had arrived and their first work attachments had started. We had anticipated trouble and it was John Donaldson who had observed that we would really have to watch out when the two intakes got together and became a single pressure group. It was a Monday morning when I arrived at my office to be told that the general manager of the Cornish mine wanted to speak to me. When I got through on the phone he told me that the recently arrived trainee had gone right over the top with a string of complaints and demands. The tone and language had been totally unacceptable. The GM told me he was sending the offender straight back to London and did not want to see him again. Later that day he was in my office clearly aware that he was in deep trouble and very contrite. I heard his version of what had happened, asked a number of questions and told him to come back the next day. What had happened was the culmination of a trend that had been steadily worsening since the beginning. In a distorted way trainees had come to see us, particularly me, as standing in the way of their being given all sorts of mainly material benefits to which they had convinced themselves they were entitled. It was a classical 'them and us' situation. Anyway it was making things difficult for everybody. Immediately I consulted Ronnie Walker and managed to get the other trustees on the phone. I was sure that we needed to take firm action. Even if the British trustees were on side, would the Zimbabweans see things my way? I need not have worried. I explained the situation to Bernard Mutuma and without hesitating he agreed with my view that the errant trainee should be sent straight back home. Robson Muringi followed suit. All the trustees agreed that despite the temptation to give the man another chance it had become essential to act firmly and immediately. The unanimity was important not just for the trust but for Riozim in Zimbabwe. The trainee was sent straight back home.

The incident turned out to be transformational as it was the spur to a rethink of our whole policy and approach. Clearly we had been mollycoddling trainees and thus encouraging them to make yet more demands. Though the academic programme was going well, work attachments were

Author with trainee and trustees

clearly becoming a burden on the companies. Another consideration was that we were effectively encouraging trainees to band together by sending them in groups for their attachments. Surely we could expect them to be self-sufficient. Besides the problem of a shortage of companies to take trainees, would they not be more acceptable if they did useful work? The question really was whether you learned anything very much merely by looking over somebody's shoulder? Surely real lessons came only from real experience. Even if this experience was to come only in a single field of activity, it was surely better than flitting between departments and functions. Most impor-tant of all was the fact that hitherto it had been a matter of what could we do for trainees. It surely needed to be a matter of what they could do for themselves or for their hosts. It also occurred to me that there was no reason why these needed to be Rio Tinto companies. After all we were doing this for the industry and southern Africa as a whole. Several companies in the UK and elsewhere might participate.

The trustees accepted all these arguments and we embarked on a new beginning. One of the first things I did was to telephone Tara Mines in Ireland and spoke to the general manager. I asked him if he would be happy to have a single African trainee on attachment for three or four months. I said that the trainee would be an intelligent technical graduate who would be happy to do any work at all that he was given. I said that the trainee would put himself forward in his work and in making friends. He would take an interest in anything and everything that came his way. I asked that the trainee should be treated as nearly as possible as if he were an ordinary employee. Finally I said there would be no cost at all to Tara. The GM to my surprise agreed immediately. He asked only that I should go over to Tara and discuss details. It was a similar story with Union Carbide Sheffield, British Steel at Ravenscraig, Caterpillar at Darlington, English China Clays, Geevor Tin and many others. Meanwhile the trainees were told to accept that they would have to do any and all work that host companies might require. The judgment as to what this might be was for the company to make. I made it clear that besides treating them as one of their own, I had asked that wherever possible the company should provide the greatest possible work challenges including the scope to take initiatives and gain supervisory experience. I told the companies that the onus was on the trainees to get the most out of the attachments. Only if they put themselves forward and showed how keen they were to contribute and to learn, would they really be accepted. I told them too that in order to provide them with an additional incentive to make local friends, in future trainees would always go on attachments on their own. Finally I told them if they were not happy with the new approach they should tell me and I would send them home.

Change was virtually instantaneous. Most importantly this could be seen in the changed attitudes of the trainees. As I did my rounds of the companies I could see that without exception they were challenged and fulfilled by the challenges they were being given. Now the emphasis was on what they could do for the company and not what the company could do for them. The companies themselves were delighted and as promised gave them challenges which would test their abilities. Thus were they able to start contributing and because they contributed, they were truly accepted. Thus they became part of teams, made friends and were able to share in success and failure. All the while they were learning. Now they could see that they were just as good as or better than their British or European counterparts. The resulting boost to their self-confidence was massive. At first this might not have been articulated, but I could see what was happening. The move to bring in a wide variety of companies turned out to be a huge success in itself. We brought them in steadily and so over the years built a great variety of experience we could offer. We needed them all. Apart from the mines in Cornwall and at Tara,

I persuaded the new RTZ mine in Portugal, Neves Corvo, to take trainees. Union Carbide in Sheffield came on board with one of the senior managers Peter Townsend, providing some of the most testing work challenges which the trainees were delighted to accept. He wrote in the company magazine how ZTMTT trainees were saving the company large sums of money. There were the cement works at Pitstone and Stanford and Ribblesdale and Rugby, mechanical engineering at Caterpillar, electrical engineering at a small company near Preston and chemical engineering at Rhone Poulenc Chemicals. There was British Coal and the smelter at Avonmouth where the company always seemed to be able to achieve significant supervisory experience for trainees once they had proved themselves. In all there were 32 companies which provided work experience. After the attachments the reaction was nearly always 'when can we have another trainee?'

At all the companies the key to success was a supportive top management backed by a special mentor whose job was to take a special interest in the trainee. This was the person who judged the level of challenge a trainee could cope with, who was the sounding board and who nearly always became a friend. To a man the mentors understood what they were about and were enthusiastic about what was being achieved. I came to see that we were pioneering a highly successful approach which was really achieving change. On many occasions it was remarked to me how trainees brought in new ways of looking at problems arising from their African experience and culture. All this time I became ever more conscious of the importance of culture factors in management and how all cultures have things to learn from each other.

As time went on, I also came to appreciate more fully that in management there are few definite rights and wrongs. It is mainly what works for you that is important. We certainly did not try to tell trainees that this or that was right. We merely provided the environment in which they could reach their own conclusions. People who were sceptical about our methodology, mainly people within the industry in Africa, would say that it was all very well for trainees to come to conclusions in a UK or European environment but would they be applicable back in Africa? Surely, the argument went on; in Africa the new managers would be dragged into local political or other distortions which would render useless their outside training or experience. I never found this to be the case. It became a matter of feeling and being managerial. After that you managed within the context of local realities. I came to recognise from all my conversations with trainees over the years, as well as their achievements, the extent to which being managerial is an attitude of mind. The key factor it seemed to me was gaining genuine self-confidence. I had seen how local attitudes to race and what was expected of them had affected the attitude of black people in southern Africa towards taking responsibility particularly for other people. The inevitable self-stereotyping produced in this environment had to be escaped from if there was to be progress. A crucial question was whether any escape achieved would be permanent. I was sure that it would. It was a matter of understanding and facing up to whatever challenges confronted them when they returned home.

The academic modules at City University were a vital part of the whole process of learning and changing. They gave trainees the chance to link practice with theory and make sense of both. They had the chance to compare notes and learn from each other's experiences and they learned skills such as accounting and financial management, which would be essential for them in senior management. Above all, the academic qualification, an MSc in Industrial and Administrative Sciences was a boost to their self-confidence and a measure of a new status in their own eyes. It was confirmation to themselves and to the world that they were as good as anybody. Over the years several distinctions were achieved. The deep commitment of both John Donaldson and Sue Grimes was maintained right to the end of the programme.

Of course the changes within the overall ZTMTT programme came too late for the first intake of trainees. They returned home with thoughts of the elevated status for which they assumed they were now qualified on the basis of a new academic qualification, uppermost in their minds. Where they returned to their former companies this was exactly what the managements had anticipated and the cynics were proved right. It was sad that the trainees themselves, all of them high-potential people, would have to come down to earth with such a bump. Our initial formula to help them discover themselves had not been quite right. They had also been handicapped by the fact that though their academic qualifications might have matched their potential, they were a bit too young and simply had not had enough work experience to relate to before coming on our programme. We on the trust came to see this as a minimum of two years.

Now with the second intake going full steam ahead, the new third intake arrived and did very well from the start even though it included two Namibians who, though the best we could find, were handicapped by not having full technical degrees. We were bending over backwards to find suitable Namibians to match the high-quality Zimbabweans but this proved almost impossible though SWAPO found us a teacher from Cuba and two relatively

Author with trainees

low-level technicians from Rumania. We were, however, supposed to be a trust for the region as a whole and so the trustees accepted my recommendation to include Botswana and Zambia in the programme. Suitable candidates from Botswana (the people are known as Batswana) tended to have obtained their degrees in Canada. For the fourth intake, I found four excellent Batswana candidates. I could not take them all on that year, so I decided to take the two from De Beers Botswana first and leave the others, from the government and from Selibe Phikwe mine, for the following years. De Beers was not at all pleased and tended to think that it was a matter of RTZ pinching its high-potential people. I managed to reassure the De Beers technical director in Gaborone, Ken Trueman, that this was not the case and that the two men had assured me that they intended to return to the company after the programme. I also promised to keep Ken up to date on their progress.

By the time the fifth intake started in October 1988, members of the second intake were back home and starting to prove themselves. Even the first intake was making progress after first falling flat on their faces. It was part of my job to keep track of all the trainees who had returned home and visit them regularly as well as the managements of the companies of where they were working. Meanwhile the trustees stayed in close touch with those currently on attachments and at the university. I travelled down to Cornwall several times with Bernard and Robson. Bernard's personal style went down very well with the managing director of the Wheal Jane and South Crofty Mines, Brian Calver, and we were entertained royally. I took our trustees to see our trainee at Ravenscraig Steel at Motherwell, Leonard Makwinja, later to become technical director of De Beers Botswana. We found a photograph of him on the MD's desk. He was wearing a kilt. We also took in a visit to David Livingstone's house at nearby Blantyre with all the slavery memorabilia. The Zimbabweans were much moved.

Bernard's personal interest in trainees and his commitment to the programme was a great incentive to them. I was delighted when my pressure on him over taking the outstanding female candidate Demetria Chidyausiku finally paid off. Demetria had some very successful attachments, particularly at Union Carbide Sheffield with Peter Townsend. The whole scheme was going swimmingly and within a few years all of us involved with the trust had become personal friends. We had shared experiences in Europe and Africa and together had overcome the various problems that were bound to arise. It came as a dreadful bolt from the blue when Don Bailey who had followed Ronnie Walker on to the trust, following the latter's retirement, rang me at home over the weekend to tell me that Bernard was dead. Apparently he had had a bad toothache and had been taken to hospital in Harare where he had died. The speculation was that he had been allergic to antibiotics. It was a dreadful shock and my heart went out to his widow Olivia. Bernard with all his experience, expertise, enthusiasm and commitment would we knew, be almost impossible to replace. However, we did pretty well in persuading David Murangari who had recently taken over as secretary or head of the Ministry of Mines to be a trustee. David, a delightful open character, had gained his experience as a geologist in the same part of Zambia where I had worked as a young district officer. We sometimes spoke the Tonga language to each other and to our amusement, discovered Tonga words which had rude meanings in his native Shona. He saw ZTMTT in the same light as Bernard and gave his full commitment to the programme.

About the same time Chris Andersen who had been minister for the civil service was appointed minister for mines. This was wonderful news. It was great to have support and help from Chris's level. He already knew Don Bailey well. Now it was important that our Chairman Sir Donald Tebbit should get to know him. In the event they became firm friends. Chris was immensely supportive and in combination with David Murangari, we had

Sir Donald Tebbit with Alec Gumbie at Rio Tinto

all the encouragement and help we needed. It was still a bit disappointing though that the local media did not seem to be able to understand or catch on to the significance or importance of what we were doing. It was as if there was a sort of political correctness operating which failed to recognise the significance of this close co-operation between the government and a leading multinational. In retrospect perhaps there was writing on the wall. The press still referred to black Zimbabweans as 'comrade'. Despite this it seemed to me that overall the country was making great progress.

Meanwhile as a politician and the country's leading white, Chris played his cards to perfection, always being the height of discretion, playing devil's advocate where need be and never being in any way disloyal or telling us things we were not meant to know. Many were the times that I heard him explaining or defending government policies to sometimes sceptical whites. In this role I felt he was achieving wonders through bringing genuine understanding to both sides. I mentioned to the British High Commissioner Ramsey Melluish my opinion of the importance of what Chris was doing. I mentioned that though he was not pro-British nor ever had been, he was a loyal Zimbabwean doing great things for his country. I was delighted that shortly after this Chris was invited on an official ministerial visit to the UK. Within a few years we were to see a turnaround in the mining industry in Zimbabwe as trainees proved the value of the programme by what they achieved back home and by their rapid career progress. The government-owned Zimbabwe Mining Development Corporation quite rightly was in the forefront by taking on a good number of trainees and taking risks with them. The technical director an outstanding Zimbabwean Greg Phimister who had been chief government mining engineer for the former Rhodesian government, was at the forefront of the seismic shift towards black management throughout the industry. It was a matter of taking calculated risks with people. He told me that without exception my trainees were doing well. At the same time the industry as a whole became more supportive and encouraged its most promising people to come on the programme. It was most encouraging to see the remarkable difference that so few people could make. The strengths and potential of the new Zimbabwe were coming to the fore.

I received letters from ex-trainees expressing in almost ecstatic language how they now felt 'The supersonic burst of new-found self-confidence' or 'a fifty-yard start in a hundred-yard race'. I also received some wonderful letters from companies to which ex-trainees returned and where they were now delivering the goods. Miners in southern Africa are not given to being effusive about their staff, but I received many letters which I see now reflected delight and perhaps astonishment at what they saw as transformation of their employees. Though it was gratifying to see rapid career progress it was also encouraging to find that trainees were very well aware that promotion might not come immediately or automatically. In fact several found when they got back home that in order to make career progress they might first have to accept a demotion (for instance a geologist wanting to transfer to mining, needing to do a mining leadership course which included going back to doing labouring jobs).

As I did the rounds in Africa visiting and staying at places like Orapa or Jwaneng in Botswana or the Kamativi tin mine in Zimbabwe, I tried to get a better understanding of what it meant to feel managerial. How did it come about and what were the barriers to be overcome? By now I was fully aware of the need to understand the part played by the genuine and the contrived in self-confidence and therefore of being genuinely managerial. The contrived is often seen in Africa as a sign of over-confidence, whereas in my experience it is the very opposite. A conversation I had with an ex-trainee in Zimbabwe, now general manager of a mine, was particularly enlightening. He is a shy man, even self-effacing. He came on the programme as a very clever chemical engineer with a good technical record. At that stage he did not feel managerial, but achievement and comparison of himself with peers in the UK had helped him to relate to the management function. Back at home his initial challenge was to convince the workforce that he was the genuine article that they needed and demanded. In their experience he could not be the genuine article. The older workers in particular were sceptical. He said he convinced everybody by what he was able to achieve. Now that things had settled down he said, he felt he was a better manager than the average white man ever could be because he understood the culture of the people he was managing and could relate to what motivated and inhibited them. He also understood better when they were taking him for a ride. I had many such conversations. Race was always a major factor. Another was the need to overcome a reluctance arising from African culture, to stick your neck out. African cultures are communal as opposed to being individualistic. The need for the new African manager to embrace a degree of individualism was inevitable and important and most easily achieved with the help of a period away from home influences.

Overall and partly thanks to the trust, Zimbabwe of the 1980s and 90s was a country where race counted for less and less. ZTMTT played a big part in this. Workers came to appreciate that a boss was not necessarily a white man. An unspecified barrier had to be crossed to get to this point. In the case of one mine in the Zimbabwean lowveld, Renco, it was when the trade unions were marching with banners flying to make some demand and a mining engineer, whom I happen to have turned down for ZTMTT, marched with them. It was pointed out to him strongly by the general manager that as a manager he had to be on the management side. One way and another the transition in Zimbabwe came remarkably quickly. Whereas in 1980 there had been no black managers in Zimbabwe's mining industry, by the end of the decade the majority was black. All this reflected massive progress; but were the government and the people aware of it? Most importantly too, was what we had learned having an impact on South Africa? Sadly I think not. Their attitude in those days tended to be that they had nothing to learn from the rest of Africa.

While the mining industry was the pacemaker in Zimbabwe, progress was being made elsewhere in the economy. In banking for instance, cousin Chris on his farm near Beitbridge on the border with South Africa, used to speak of the very good service he used to get from his black Zimbabwean bank manager in the town. This was in sharp contrast to his experience of a white manager he used to deal with at a bank across the border in Messina in South Africa.

As I was spending a lot of time in Zimbabwe I was able to see how commerce and industry as a whole was changing. Now the first-class education system that Mugabe had inherited was kicking in to complement the return home of people who had been at school and university in the UK during the war. More and more in industry, commerce and all branches of the economy, one was now dealing with black people. It seemed to me that considering the time factor, progress had been nigh on miraculous. Not everyone was happy. I met an aspirant black politician who was making political capital out of the fact that the economy was still in mainly white hands. He would not acknowledge that despite Mugabe's socialism and the lack of a black entrepreneurial tradition, there was currently an explosion of enterprise all over the country. Inevitably too I suppose, a few trade unionists were saying that whites were keeping the top jobs for themselves while a few whites stuck doggedly to the line that the country was going down hill. Cousin Chris, a traditional liberal in the locally accepted sense, saw the latter in the same light as those who in the 1950s and early 1960s had killed the supposedly multiracial federation by insisting on keeping black people out of cinemas, restaurants, post offices and hotels and on serving them through hatches at shops. Now despite the horrors of a dreadful war they had another chance. A new partnership was developing which I was sure would now show the way forward to South Africa. Surely those whites for whom government by blacks was unacceptable would eventually come round to appreciate the new realities.

I saw evidence of the new relationships being formed in the schools and therefore leading the way for the country. For instance, in Harare one afternoon I stopped to watch part of a school's rugby festival being held at St Georges College with mixed crowds of children fervently cheering on mixed teams. I found it encouraging too that the government retained the pre-independence names of the schools and the smart uniforms with shorts, long stockings, ties and caps or boaters. Apparently the word had gone out that traditions were to be retained and respected. From the white point of view, I imagined that despite a legacy of bitterness from the war there was surely too much going for the country for it to fail now. The government was doing broadly the right things and many whites who had fled to the south shortly after independence were now returning. The government was

Charles Chadamwiri completes an attachment

magnanimous enough to let most of them in. The well of patriotic love and fervour for the old Rhodesia amongst white Rhodesians was surely worth trying to harness and blend with the patriotism of Bernard Mutuma. I got a taste of this when I saw Zimbabwe playing South Africa in the first-ever cricket match between the two countries after the end of apartheid. I witnessed the atmosphere in business class as top Zimbabweans enjoyed each other's company on the Air Zimbabwe flight to London. I still catch it when I mix with Zimbabweans.

I was motivated and stimulated by the way that over the years Rio Tinto's rival mining companies outside South Africa, such as Anglo American, De Beers, AA Mines and Lonrho, came to recognise that ZTMTT was genuinely for the industry as a whole and more importantly that our approach really worked. They encouraged their best people to apply for places on the programme. However, it confirmed my opinion of Anglo American in Johannesburg when their chairman in Zimbabwe Roy Lander, who was a member of the main Anglo board of directors, told me that in their deliberations on issues related to black advancement, not once was he asked 'what was it like in Zimbabwe?' I found the arrogance coming out of Johannesburg almost breathtaking. They owned a mine called Cleveland Potash in the UK, but despite what the trust was doing for the company as a whole it repeatedly refused to take on a single one of our trainees for work experience. The attitude of De Beers in Botswana came in complete contrast. I was invited to Orapa, the world's largest diamond mine for several days and was royally entertained. One of my ex-trainees there Charles Siwawa was doing incredibly well as was his fellow trainee Leonard Makwinja at the Jwaneng mine. The general manager at Orapa told me that headquarters at 44 Main Street in Johannesburg had little understanding of the issues of black advancement on their mines.

More stimuli came from my visits to the region and not just from perspectives on the mining industry. On one visit to Zimbabwe, Sarah and I were travelling by rail on the overnight sleeper from Bulawayo to the Victoria Falls. Our compartment was between one occupied by two electricians, one white and one black going to do contract work at Victoria Falls, and the other occupied by a white journalist who was fleeing the country. The former two promised to keep an eye on our compartment while we went to the dining car for dinner. We dined well despite the warm white wine. The atmosphere between passengers and railway personnel was almost festive, and when I wanted to return to the compartment to fetch something, the guard handed me the keys of the train amidst general hilarity. The racial mix has always had the potential to make Zimbabwe extra special. It strikes me that neither the British nor the Zimbabweans themselves appreciate just quite how well they get on with each other. This is because despite the racial discrimination, the old pre-independence Southern Rhodesia was settled and run by British people with British culture and standards predominating. My trainees used to tell me that they did not realise how British they were until they came to Britain. More of this than has been generally appreciated has rubbed off on the indigenous population.

My perspectives in the early 1990s were of course mainly of the mining industry where I saw my ex-trainees making huge progress at work. This was matched on the social scene. The then white general manager at the Shabanie Mine Mike Thompson whose family had lived in the country for generations, told me that for the very first time he now had black Zimbabwean friends, several of them ex-ZTMTT trainees. He told me that in common with thousands of his countrymen he had left the country at independence thinking that now the country was in the hands of 'terrorists' there could be no future for the white man. After a few years, however, he had been persuaded to return and found the country happy and prosperous and with race relations on a completely new footing. Looking back now I think how sad it is that there were not more people like him. My ex-trainees would occasionally tell me of whites in their companies with old attitudes to race but even they were steadily being won over by the achievements of the new black professionals. At the headquarters of AA mines in Bulawayo a senior executive told me that he was an old Rhodesian with traditional attitudes to race. He said that in a few years since independence he had seen a total transformation and for him race was no longer an issue in Zimbabwe.

I saw something of the new social scene away from work at the Shabanie and Mashava mines' golf courses where the majority of members were still white. However, it was certainly not a matter of condescending acceptance of black members. Numbers of them were now making an impact not just with their golfing skills but as office holders. Their wives too were not just playing but taking turns with the other ladies to provide teas, cakes and sandwiches on competition days. At Mashava, Florence Gumbie was ladies captain. On one visit to the Mashava Mine and staying at the guest house with my wife Sarah and our two children Tom and Ting there was a dinner party hosted by the white general manager and attended by several ex-trainees with wives. One man Leveson Machiri told us how as a small boy he used to walk several miles every day through the bush to school and back. Now he said his son, attending a well-known boarding school in Bulawayo, was lazy and seemed only to be interested in computer games. 'Welcome to the middle class' I remarked.

At Rio Tinto's Renco Mine I went to visit the first two Namibian trainees who had come out of Russia via Angola and whom I had interviewed in Lusaka. One of them, Kombadeyedu Kapwanga, was doing particularly well. After the end of the ZTMTT programme instead of returning to some SWAPO office he had decided to get work experience to fit him for higher responsibilities when Namibia became independent. This he acquired at Renco where he worked hard and successfully as a mine foreman. Meanwhile the trust was growing in reputation within the mining industry in Africa, within the RTZ group and amongst UK companies. This was entirely due to trainees and their achievements. By the end of the 1980s sufficient progress was being made towards majority rule in South Africa for the ZTMTT trustees to feel it was time to include one or two South African trainees. It was a struggle to find suitable people even though the apartheid policies towards the education of blacks in maths and sciences were being relaxed. As I made contact with the industry in South Africa a story arising from one particular

Alec and Leveson with Ting underground at Mashava

company, Union Carbide, is indicative. The background was the relationship I had built up with Union Carbide in Sheffield, where there had been several very successful attachments. There was also the fact that an ex-trainee had joined the Union Carbide–owned Zamasco metal refinery at Kwe Kwe in Zimbabwe. The message had apparently gone via the parent company to the South African subsidiary that ZTMTT was doing significant work in developing indigenous management. I received a message that the human resources manager there wanted to talk to me. We met over lunch the next time I was in Johannesburg. He told me that his company felt that the time had come to have some senior black executives. So, I was told the company had decided to promote a black accountant to a senior position. He was given a new job title, a big office, a large salary and a company car. The problem I was told was that the company had just discovered that he was robbing them. I said I was not surprised as how could somebody be expected to do a proper job and be trustworthy without adequate training and experience? This case confirmed to me the confusion between promotion on merit and so-called positive discrimination or window dressing appointments. At the time and to this day many South Africans do not seem to appreciate that there is a difference.

Meanwhile news of the trust's achievements had spread to RTZ's newly acquired gold mine at Paracatu in Brazil. The Brazilian company wanted promising potential senior managers to join the African trainees in the UK. It agreed to pay the full costs, which would boost ZTMTT's revenues. I flew to Brazil, saw several promising candidates at the mine and decided on two of them. They started with the next intake of Africans. By now we had had another two Batswana on the programme as well as two Zambians. The Brazilians got on particularly well with the Africans. The programme's international and cross-cultural flavour was completed by the inclusion of two Portuguese on the programme, both from Nerves Corvu mine in Portugal's Alentejo province. Again the two men were strong candidates. One, a mechanical engineer, had been born in Angola and wanted to re-establish his links with Africa which had been cut off in 1974 when he was fourteen and his family moved to Portugal. I tried to reinforce these links by sending him to the Palabora mine in South Africa for one of his attachments. He returned to Europe much stimulated by the experiences he had had at work but depressed by constant insinuation from white South Africans wanting to hear him running down black people in Angola. In terms of the basic issues which he learned in a few weeks, his understanding far outstripped white South African attitudes arising from a lifetime's life with prejudice.

But the effects of apartheid worked the other way too. By now ZTMTT had been going for nine years and with change clearly coming in South Africa, it was certainly time to concentrate more on that country. Why though should it be only RTZ which was organising and funding the development of the indigenous technical management potential which clearly would be so badly needed in the very near future? The trustees decided to organise a conference in London at which the achievements and methodology of ZTMTT would be trumpeted to South African companies and others doing business there. It was 1991 and I shared a platform with the then minister of Overseas Development, Lynda Chalker. Sadly the impact we achieved was not nearly as great as we had hoped. This, I now think, was due to companies not really understanding the significance of what we were achieving and also perhaps not yet being under sufficient pressure to take appropriate steps to change things around. I was hoping for some good publicity, but apart from the *Mining Journal*, which had always been a staunch supporter, this was generally lacking. The *Financial Times* produced a supportive article with a photo of a trainee at work. However its reporting of the event, with its tone seeming to suggest racial condescension, reflected no real appreciation of the barriers faced by southern African blacks in becoming truly and effectively managerial following generations of subjugation and humiliation. There was no appreciation either of the significance and implications of a scheme that had succeeded in helping scores of people face up to these barriers or of how we had found a way to overcome them.

When the ninth intake with two Portuguese and a Brazilian started, it included a South African for whom we had particularly high hopes. I remember when I saw him in Johannesburg, he assured me that he appreciated that he would have to demonstrate his enthusiasm for whatever work he was given on attachment and he was prepared to get his hands dirty. He was obviously highly intelligent, had wonderful academic qualifications, and his record so far showed that he was regarded by the mining industry as having unlimited potential. I could not help thinking of our helping him on the way to being chairman of Anglo American or De Beers. Very soon I was seriously disappointed. I arranged for him to go on attachment to companies where we had had the greatest success. Very soon he was complaining that he had already done this or that. Peter Townsend at Union Carbide said he was very difficult to deal with as he expected everything to be done for him and he was not putting himself forward at work and making friends. We had several talks when I tried to get him to understand how much he stood to learn and to gain by embracing the programme. Luckily his attitude was not shared by fellow trainees. I had not encountered his attitude since our first intake. I was hopeful for his second and third attachments that he would catch on to what it was all about. Sadly it was the same story and he returned home with his prejudices and preconceptions about people and management intact. He was perhaps the highest potential South African it was possible to find at that time. I feared for the future of effective indigenous management in that country if his attitudes were widely shared. Of course I appreciated they arose from a system which was so deeply ingrained that it was hugely difficult for anyone to break out of. It was because of it that we had decided on a method of triggering change which took people away from the stereotypes and preconceptions at home, away from the idea that management is about a job title, a big salary, a big office and giving orders. The move away from this had been so amazingly quick and painless in Zimbabwe and Botswana I suppose we had assumed it would be the same story in South Africa. Effectively this man returned home unchanged by the programme. He had been sponsored on the programme by the Palabora Company and returned home to work there but soon moved on.

Of course we aimed to trigger change through the stimuli of the programme. Thus the ideal was an individual's return home with his culture reinforced by the second culture. For an overwhelming majority of trainees this was the reaction. I was much encouraged by the fact that in these cases it was partly a matter of the individual gaining enhanced perspectives on the strengths of his own culture. Another reaction came from the trainee who arrived on the programme with the idea that he was coming to a country with what he supposed to have a 'superior' culture. He had become disillusioned by experiences of his own country Zimbabwe and thought that in the UK existed a superior value system to which he could relate. What actually happened was that not surprisingly he found things in the UK of which he disapproved strongly. This produced a crisis within him and he returned home a very confused person. He subsequently lost his job. All this helped reinforce my appreciation of the importance of culture in management, which featured strongly in my PhD thesis 'Transcending Culture; Developing Africa's Technical Managers' with which I was making good progress.

By the middle of 1993 the final intake was finishing off writing final exams at the university and returning home. Since the conference at Carlton House Terrace nearly two years before I had spent a lot of time trying to ensure that the successful ZTMTT approach carried on, I met with ODA (now DFID) officials to try to get a meeting of minds on the significance of what we had achieved so that the approach could continue. We failed because officials insisted on comparing the unique ZTMTT approach, which was mainly about self-discovery through work experience, with an MBA course at a university and talked about 'opportunity costs'. Hope flared when Lynda Chalker asked for full details of the trust, its achievements and proposals for the future, to take with her on a visit to Japan; nothing came of this.

I was hopeful of the EU where surely people would relate to issues of culture and the need for local decision makers in the developing world and would be looking for really effective ways of helping; and they had money. It was suggested to me by RTZ, which by now had funded ZTMTT for 11 years, that I could engage a lawyer in Brussels to negotiate through the complexities of a possible secondment there. My reaction, hugely misguided in retrospect, was that our achievements spoke for themselves. Surely all we had to do was to find the department or individual responsible for overseas training aid. In the event it proved impossible to discover who to deal with, much less who could get anything done. The approaches got nowhere. Following an editorial in the *Mining Journal* supporting a continuation, I was invited to the World Bank in Washington. There the Mining Department was enthusiastic and told me that the ZTMTT approach and experience was exactly what it was looking for to help bring about productivity and change in the mining industry of the former Soviet Union. I was asked to produce a budget for a scheme which would cater for Russians coming to Europe, North America, Australia and southern Africa. I put it together as fast as possible only to be told that the Bank had dropped the idea because the Russians were refusing to accept one of the conditions for help: the sacking of a significant number of people from their overmanned coal mines.

There was a last possibility which should have been the most realistic: to set up an organisation for South Africa in which the main companies there would co-operate. John Donaldson and I prepared proposals which we put to companies at meetings in Johannesburg. All were interested but not so convinced that they would co-operate with each other over the scheme. Once again there was a lot of talk about special programmes at the Cape Town University Business School, for instance. I was particularly hopeful that Anglo American and De Beers might set up a programme. I had after all had several high-flying trainees from both companies who were now proving their worth. The managing director of Anglo American in Harare, Roy Lander, who was on the main Anglo board and the technical director of De Beers Botswana, Ken Trueman, who had both witnessed the success of the approach were particularly supportive. However, as forewarned by such people, one was up against the group headquarters in South Africa. There the attitude prevailed that when it came to management in Africa the Anglo group had nothing to learn from anyone. I had seen very differently during the whole time I ran ZTMTT, as well as the ten years I had worked in Zambia and five years working with the Anglo group in the Congo in the 1970s.

Meanwhile the more I saw of the results of the programme, the more I was convinced that the work we had been doing had real significance for Africa and perhaps for the developing world as a whole. As I looked back at my career in Africa and considered the continent's current problems it seemed ever clearer to me that more important than anything were competent local teachers, managers and decision makers. They and not outsiders were needed to decide on priorities according to their countries' needs, cultures and value systems; these people would move the continent away from the dependency culture which still persisted as a hangover from the colonial era. It seemed to me that the whole subject merited closer consideration. For this reason I continued to collect data for my PhD. I was also reading the thoughts of Africanist academics on the general subject including studies on the work being done by international companies such as Shell and

Unilever to develop their managers. They appreciated the positive effects of giving high flyers significant experience of different worlds. Then there was the work of the Dutch social anthropologist Hofstede with his analysis of the various elements of cultures and the differences between countries and how this affected work and management. It seemed to me that there was no lack of theory around on how culture affected the management of people but little or no attempt to make use of these factors in designing programmes to address the practical problems caused by the shortage of local management in developing countries. I was mindful of how in the mid-1970s, I had spent two lengthy periods looking at the massive training programme on Zambia's copper mines. I saw my friend Petal O'Brian, the head of training at ZCCM in Zambia 1982, as I was setting up ZTMTT. She told me that there was no programme and never had been to train local indigenous technical managers. There was certainly nothing in Zimbabwe or South Africa at the time either. It had been the same story with Charter Consolidated's Tenke Fungurume project in Zaire between 1971 and 1976. The only systematic work I ever came across was being done, before ZTMTT, by Belgians working for the state mining company in Zaire, 'Gecamines'.

Though the significance of ZTMTT's success may not have got through to the rest of the world, even, perhaps especially South Africa, increasingly I came to appreciate that we had been doing unique and ground-breaking work of special significance to Africa and to countries and cultures where change was imperative. For several years the mining industry as a whole and the British companies with which we had been involved had come to appreciate the scale of the problem and do something about it. I felt I owed it to posterity and to myself to record our experiences, achievements and conclusions. For eight years altogether I worked on my thesis during weekends in Suffolk. Long train journeys to see trainees in Cornwall, Anglesey or Scotland were also productive as were two week-long stays in a remote shepherd's cottage at the top of Glen Mark on the Dalhousie estate in the Scottish Highlands.

Over the years since 1994 I have been able to stay in touch with the majority of ex-ZTMTT trainees or in other cases continue to get news of them. Most are now in top management though no longer mainly in Zimbabwe. There are several now making a big impact in South Africa which thanks to apartheid has only recently started to develop its own black technical management potential. Perhaps the highest flyers are in Botswana where Leonard Makwinja and Charles Siwawa have been right at the top of De Beers. Also in Botswana Monty Mpathi is general manager of the big Selibe Phikwe mine.

In 2002 I gave a party for several still in Zimbabwe but of these I know several have left the country for South Africa, Botswana or the UK. One, a delightful hardworking, brave and farsighted man, was being persecuted for daring to stand up to war veterans on the mine he was trying to manage. One who turned up in the UK was very proud to have been classified as an immigrant with especially valuable skills to offer the UK. He was a bit hurt when I told him he was needed more in Africa. In Namibia our original geologist on the first intake became the first director of mines and is now running a diamond mining company.

Looking back on ZTMTT, it seems to me that the whole scheme was an example of incredibly far-sighted and public-spirited corporate altruism on the part of Rio Tinto which showed that it was decades ahead in its thinking over Africa, of the likes of Anglo American, De Beers and Lonrho. It was a great tribute to companies in Europe and especially in the UK that so many were able to come together to provide work experience. I believe that it shows the way for the sort of help that commerce and industry more generally could provide to Africa to make a real difference there. It was a tough approach but very many lessons were learned. No money changed hands, no pockets were lined and no bribes were paid. We simply provided the organisation and the funding and hit on a formula to enable 70 or so young people to discover themselves and change their lives. Of course the company had its own interests in mind but it had the wisdom to see that these were bound up with the industry as a whole with which it had the foresight to co-operate.

15

Amos's Age

In the late 1990s I became increasingly aware that things were going wrong in Zimbabwe. One not so happy interlude during this period was a golfing tour to Zimbabwe with members of a UK-based golfing society. Our party included influential, even important people including a Law Lord. Instead of giving these people a good impression of their country, the local white organisers regaled them continually with all sorts of stories of how it was being misled by incompetent blacks. Only I could have, perhaps should have countered some of the racist rubbish being fed to people who in the main had never been to Africa before. Needless to say, we did not meet, much less play golf with, a single black person. Almost bursting with frustration at keeping my mouth shut, I was most relieved and my faith in British impartiality restored when towards the end of the trip, several members of our party told me of the low opinion they had formed of the organisers.

As it was part of my job until 1994 to be a contact with the mining industry and later to monitor the progress of my trainees, I paid several visits over the years to the Zambezi Valley and to Binga where I had been based in 1980 supervising the independence elections and had got to know Angus and Hazel Van Jaarsveld. Now I had several opportunities over the years to visit them, thanks to the close touch I was keeping with the nearby Kamativi Tin Mine from where a trainee Alexander Mukwekwezeke had come and where he returned. Within two years of getting back home from the ZTMTT programme, he was the general manager. We would have long talks about things like the building of self-confidence and how Africans really saw themselves. It was a matter of achieving changes in deeply ingrained perceptions of race and role. There was also the question of dependency and the general association of modernity with whites. Alexander helped me to appreciate fully how difficult it can be for erstwhile dependent blacks to move away from the idea that whites were the decision makers. After lunch, with Alexander

Alexander Mukwekwezeke at Kamativi mine

at the mine, I would drive down to Binga on the new wide tarred road and stay the night with the Van Jaarsvelds. Their magnificent house beside the Kariba Lake with its deep green lawn and wide veranda still had views of the fish eagle's nest across the bay to which the birds always seemed to return. Angus and Hazel had settled very well into the new Zimbabwe. They were hugely hospitable and their dining room table remained resplendently laid out. They were respected by everyone and the croc farm was now doing very well as was the *kapenta* fishing business. The little fish the size of a whitebait, had been introduced into the lake on the Zambian side during my time at Gwembe and had spread everywhere. All you needed was a fine mesh net and a bright light to catch any amount at night. Then you dried them in the sun in a day, bagged them up and sent them to the markets of Bulawayo and Harare.

After a night with the Van Jaarsvelds, I would drive off in the car I had hired at Victoria Falls Airport with Angus's trusted employee from the croc farm Amos Mweende. I had not met Amos in 1980 as he had been a guerrilla fighter, but in the mid-1980s he was Angus's tracker and he knew the bush like the back of his hand as well as all the plants and wildlife. Amos was a Tonga, tough and grizzled from a hard valley life and aged it seemed to me, about 60. One of his merits from my point of view was that he spoke no English at all. This would give me the chance to keep my chitonga going. We would pack a limited quantity of stores, including a kerosene lamp, into the back of the hired car. Amos's luggage was limited to a blanket and his Tonga axe or *keembe*. As we drove along the valley road towards Siabuwa, we talked about our families and the changes to the lives of the valley Tonga. My rusty chitonga would loosen and begin to flow. Once I remember, trying to be conversational, wondering how old he really was, I asked him, *'Mulijisi myaka yongae?'* *'Si yandi kumuambila'* (I don't want to tell you), he replied. I was interested because I was sure that he was a lot younger than he looked. I persisted and he told me he was 45. A sudden thought occurred to me. How old did he think I was? I was rising 50 but kept pretty fit. Perhaps he would think I was 35. So I asked him. He was even more reluctant to give me an answer, but I persisted. 'For god's sake Amos how old do you think I am?' 'Eighty', he said in English. Shocked silence. Of course in a moment I realised he was giving me the answer he thought I wanted to hear based on his own cultural perceptions. For him age meant respect and veneration.

About 40 miles down the valley road, we would turn right towards the looming wall of mountains rising abruptly from the valley floor three or four miles ahead of us. In the distance was Tundazi, the highest point in Matabeleland at over 5000 feet. I had spent a night in its shadow in a trench with Dave Brink and some Rhodesian soldiers in 1980. As we got to the turnoff, we picked up a man who turned out to be the headmaster of the local school which was close by. He took us around the classrooms and again I was enchanted and captivated by the energy and exuberance and sheer charm of the children. It was an experience I had had countless times on tour as a district officer. Another time on that corner we had come across an old Tonga woman, bare-breasted and with the traditional piece of stick stuck through the fleshy part of the nose above the upper lip. She was collecting the fluffy

Author with Sir Donald Tebbit in Zimbabwe

seed heads of a particular type of grass found in the valley even in drought years. Then it was April and there had been no rain. '*Bulaligwa?*' I asked. 'Is it edible?' '*E bulaligwa*', she replied. Amos explained that the grass was harvested for its tiny seeds as a last resort in drought years.

Amos and I carried on up the road which soon started to climb. It was not easy driving for my little hire car. Though the sandy patches and the gradients were negotiable, the two tracks made by four-wheel-drive vehicles with high clearances left a never-ending high point in the middle – the *middel manetjie* as known to local whites. I had to keep either the right or the left wheels on it. It was not easy as we climbed 2000 feet out of the valley. Our objective was to get to the Chizarira National Park, one of the most remote unspoilt areas in the whole of southern Africa. Before you get to the top, the road passes through deep forest with massive trees. This is the home of a remarkably beautiful bird called the Narina Trogon. It was named by the ornithologist who discovered it, after his beautiful voluptuous African mistress called Narina. Up on top of the plateau we headed for the park headquarters where we would pay our fee and discuss where we could camp. This was hardly a problem as visitors were a rarity. We were limited only by where the car could get to.

The car could just about get through the bush to the point on the cliff edge of the escarpment where I could assemble my camp bed and Amos could lay out his blanket. Food was limited to a few tins of baked beans and bullied beef, and drink to two or three bottles of Zimbabwean red wine, all of which we would share. We were then free to take in the scene with the ground falling away immediately beneath us for hundreds of feet and views of the valley and the lake thousands of feet below and with the Zambian mountains in the very far distance across the Kariba Lake. Most stunningly, way below us in the great gorges soared the largest bird of prey in Africa, the black eagle, which specialises in mountain country. The birds are all black, except for great white patches or 'windows' on the upper side of their wings. These of course, could be seen only from above. We spent one night on the cliff face before moving back inland and down the hill via the park headquarters to the Kaswiswi camp in the river valley. There, there were two open-sided grass shelters built on stilts and accessible by ladder. It was late afternoon so Amos and I decided to go for a walk around, me with my camera and binoculars and Amos with his little axe or *keembe*. We were literally 50 yards from the camp, when rounding an anthill, there just in front of us, peacefully grazing was an enormous black rhino. It was the first rhino I had ever seen at close quarters. In the early to mid-1980s, the rhinos were being wiped out in Zambia. The poachers were beginning to cross into Zimbabwe, the world's last stronghold of the black rhino. However, I reasoned the Chizarira population of 300 or so animals would surely be safe as we were some way inland and protected by the formidable escarpment. It was not to be.

Afterwards we walked along the river with clear pools under a steep cliff. We saw several crocodiles, very un-shy, and lots of baboons. We returned to camp to share a bottle of wine and a tin of bullied beef and to enjoy the sounds of the night and the feeling of being at one with nature. It was one of Africa's magical unspoiled places enhanced as the evening progressed by the roar of lions and the eerie call of hyenas. But it was not until just before dawn broke that Kaswiswi really came into its own. I had heard some beautiful dawn choruses before, but the one that was unfolding surpassed anything I could have ever dreamed of. Such was the variety and the beauty of the bird song that I was inspired to try, almost desperately, to record them by turning on my video camera. The next day we went for a very long walk. I remember that we avoided the temptation to follow an insistent honey guide, and then circled a huge herd of buffalo by climbing a hill before running straight into a herd of elephants. I also remember how, as we were following a game path, Amos stopped suddenly, took out his axe and started to dig up a small dried-up-looking plant. He explained that it was much more common here than in the valley and that the roots which were made up of a number of small bulbs were the very best thing for an upset stomach. He gave me a few. I tried chewing one once back in Britain when I was feeling ill and felt much better very quickly.

It is a few years since I have seen Amos. I would have liked him to produce a list of the Tonga names of the valley birds which had so stunned me by their numbers, beauty and variety when I had first taken an interest during the elections in 1980. Sadly his lack of formal education was the main stumbling block. His son has had a go, but the list is woefully incomplete. When I dropped Amos at his house in Angus's compound, he went inside and emerged with a small beautifully made Tonga *mbira*, a musical instrument which produces some beautiful, distinctive African music. I was very touched by the thought behind the gift which is amongst my treasured mementos of Africa. I had four separate trips to the Chizarira with Amos. More recently I was there with Sarah in another more-developed camp where, perhaps attracted by our cooking dinner, the roaring lions approached to the very edge of the camp. We moved our camp beds into the kitchen for the night.

As Zimbabwe showed the way for the future South Africa, I was reminded of how ingrained was the fear and suspicion of anything that went on north of the Limpopo River. So firm was the mindset on the evils of

Mugabe and his socialism. In broad terms the whole of the rest of Africa fell into this bracket. There were, however, a few who travelled north to see friends in Harare for instance. One such person was a friend currently living in Johannesburg whom I bumped into in Harare. I wanted to travel south and she offered me a lift. We decided to spend the night en route at Chris's farm near Beitbridge. It was Easter in the early 1990s, and we were driving south along the main road south of Masvingo. Clearly the woman was nervous about people along the road. She was terrified when we were stopped at a police roadblock. She said she was afraid of being robbed or assaulted or worse and did not want to stop. She then told me that she had a gun which she showed me in the glove compartment. When we stopped, it was to be greeted by a polite policeman who merely wanted to give us a leaflet wishing us a happy Easter and urging us to drive carefully.

It was a year or two later in September 1993 when as part of winding up ZTMTT, I was on a farewell visit to Wankie and Kamativi and other mines all over southern Africa and I stayed at the Elephant Hills Hotel at the Victoria Falls. The hotel was brim full of South African whites who were members of the South African Pharmaceutical Society on their annual conference. This was the first time I had seen such large numbers of South African tourists in Zimbabwe. Elephant Hills is a large hotel and there were a lot of chemists. There was a big party for them in the evening with people spread all over the terraces and down into the gardens. I joined in and spoke to a lot of them. To a man and a woman, they remarked how friendly were the hotel staff and how relaxed race relations seemed to be compared to South Africa. They said that the way they found Zimbabwe was in total contrast with the impressions they had gained about the country from the South African press. It was only about now, in late 1993, more than 13 years after Zimbabwean independence, that South African tourists started to return in good numbers. Since 1980 I had wondered whatever had happened to them.

By the end of the 1990s, Zimbabwe was still set fair even though the issue of land was beginning to arise, with ex-guerrilla fighters claiming that the government had broken its promises to them. The fact was that the issue was a highly sensitive one and had been central to the whole war. Even so in the euphoric atmosphere prevailing in the early 1980s, the government steered clear of the issue as it did not want to upset the farmers who were delivering so magnificently in terms of exports and as major employers. For this reason, the relaxed attitude of the white farmers was understandable. After all, for many years the minister of agriculture himself had been one of their own, Denis Norman. Yet being in the cabinet, he surely must have understood the importance of the issue in the longer term. It seems, however, that neither he nor President Mugabe took any significant steps to address it. It was not surprising therefore that there was a degree of complacency in the attitude of the farmers. The country relied on them and they were citizens. Life carried on much as it had before the war, almost as if there had been no war. This was in stark contrast to what I had seen on the mines. Almost suicidally it seemed to me, some whites even continued to use racist language by referring to *hout kops* (wooden heads) and nannies (any African woman) and made no attempt to learn local languages. This suggested that a minority of them had not come to terms with the reality of black government and the need to move away completely from the racist language and attitudes of the past. I became more aware of these things as time passed and I started to have real worries about the future. Whites were still not making common cause with the new class of professional blacks. I imagined that Mugabe might be feeling that his policies of reconciliation were not being fully appreciated or reciprocated.

On the other hand, though there were now plenty of high-placed blacks in commerce and industry, I saw little sign that the government was doing much to encourage the emergence of more black commercial farmers. There were exceptions including one, Jack, who managed the quasi government agricultural enterprise (ARDA) farm a few miles down the road from Richard and Heather Valentine. He showed a lot of promise and Richard was keen to help him. He did not, however, let the relationship develop into a one-sided affair with the black man feeling he had a right to all sorts of help. Thus, whilst he was happy for Jack to borrow this or that bit of machinery for instance, he would always ensure that he asked reciprocal favours. Richard was just the sort of person Zimbabwe needed. Jack no doubt was too, though I never really knew him.

Many of my perspectives came from the Odzi farming community and Richard. To my mind he showed the way by getting on with everybody. He was totally honest with himself and with others. His wonderful sense of humour got him everywhere. Caring about people and making them laugh is a great recipe for success in any situation. He had a habit of gently mocking the earnestness of outsiders with simplistic views over what was good for Africa. At the same time, he was not afraid to challenge what he considered to be damaging attitudes. I remember him upbraiding a fellow farmer en route to some tennis match in Mutare, who was referring to 'kaffirs'.

Sarah and I paid many a happy visit to Odzi and my positive view of the progress the Valentines were making merged with increasing identification with the way the country was going. It was not perfect. Nowhere is. However, we wanted to put down some roots in Africa for retirement which would be coming up in a few years. The choices were Odzi or the Southern Province of Zambia, perhaps Choma or Kalomo. Perhaps I even harboured the dream that Stephen could come back and work for us. We chose Odzi because we knew so many people. There was golf and trout fishing up in the Nyanga Mountains, and the coast was only 180 miles away at Beira in Mozambique. All was looking pretty good, and a friend agreed to build us a cottage on a hill on his farm. There were lovely views over farmland bush and mountain and the birdlife in the native trees in the totally wild garden was extraordinary. Then a massive blow landed. I was in Suffolk when Richard rang from Cape Town. He was down there, he said, to check on a possible brain tumour. The worst fears were confirmed and he had only a few months to live. He was matter-of-fact as ever and totally lucid. I flew out very soon to see him and Heather on the farm. I brought him some Zeiss binoculars to watch the birds and during a lunch with Sir Donald and other ZTMTT trustees at the Troutbeck Inn, escaped by car with Richard up the mountain road to the Riozim cottage to talk, and promised to stay in close touch with Heather. I continued for several weeks to phone him from England. He was always lively, positive and funny. Then the end came very suddenly. He had been my best friend at school and all my adult life.

By the end of 1990s as the 20th anniversary of independence approached, things were still going pretty well for the country. I still went down to stay on the farm and continued to see the Odzi farmers regularly usually for Saturday tennis and afterwards at the club. They were always interested in anything I had to say about the way I saw how the country was going and welcomed a continuing UK interest even if they were too polite to suggest that we did not understand the situation. One leading farmer Piet de Klerk was interested in what my new employer British Executive Service Overseas (BESO) might be able to do by way of volunteer expertise to train peasant farmers. He suggested that I contact the head of the Commercial Farmers Union (CFU) in Harare. I had in fact talked to the latter a couple of years before but got nowhere with him. Piet suggested I might have got the man wrong, so I went to see him again and received a really offensive rebuff. I could see that here was someone who had still not forgiven the British for perceived wrongs in the past.

The British were however coming back into the equation with increasing signs that land was gradually becoming a major issue. I remember Chris Andersen telling me that he had warned the CFU that it needed to take urgent steps to address the issue with its members. It may have attempted to do so but not to significant effect. When questioned, individual farmers would fall back on the argument that they were citizens and that they were indispensable to the country's prosperity. In the case of farms that had changed hands when they had government certificates saying that there was 'no interest' in their farm, they were surely entitled to feel secure.

After the 2000 referendum on changes to the constitution and its rebuff of Mugabe, he encouraged the so-called 'war veterans' in their illegal occupation of white-owned land. His main motivation was to regenerate popularity by using an issue which he had largely ignored since independence. In his mind, leaving the white farmers alone coupled with his policy of reconciliation had been the tradeoff which allowed the farmers their prosperity and unchanged lifestyle. Though the war vets were aggrieved at the lack of priority given to them, they did not present an immediate problem for Mugabe. Now with whites including farmers joining in the chorus against him, his anger knew no bounds. He turned to the British government which had promised funds for land reform. Understandably, the British had not been impressed by early moves towards land reform involving giving land to party hacks and others favoured by the regime. It was surely at this point that the British government instead of publicly getting on its high horse should have understood how and why Mugabe had got himself into trouble. It should then have bent every sinew to use its considerable power and influence quietly to negotiate a way to get Mugabe off the hook. Instead, moralising outbursts from the likes of Peter Hain and Clare Short suggesting that such matters were no longer Britain's business did huge harm. At the very least, Britain should have put strong pressure on the CFU to come up with some realistic proposals. The disgraceful Peter Tatchell incident when thugs jumped into Mugabe's car outside Harrods in London, upset him mightily and he never received an appropriate apology. In any event, Mugabe decided that the British were to become the bete noir, and he blamed us for the lack of progress on land reform for which in truth, he himself was mainly responsible. Ironically, this is despite the fact that Zimbabwe is the most pro-British country in Africa and that Mugabe himself remains very pro-British in many ways. Britain made a mistake in trying to wash its hands of the land problem which had only been put on the back burner at Lancaster House in the interests of peace. We should have maintained the high-level contacts and all the goodwill established over the independence period. We could surely have prevented relations from sinking to their present depths.

Before 2000 the country's prosperity and stability had priority. The land invasions were a gigantic gamble which opened Pandora's box and the way towards illegality and a complete breakdown of the rule of law coupled with economic ruin. They also gave a good indication of the importance Mugabe gave to retaining personal power. The turn of events shows the major difference with Mandela and his approach in South Africa. There, despite the fact that the law gave sanction to blatant racism and discrimination against black people, it was nevertheless the law. Mandela recognised that maintaining the rule of law had to be an overriding priority.

Mugabe himself has made it easy for people to forget how he had emerged from a dreadful war and had shown a quite extraordinary pragmatism and ability to forgive and forget. He became an African hero and perhaps deserved even greater plaudits than he ever got. Now he was presiding over his country's backwards slide. Having eschewed racism, he now placed his own white citizens in the same category as the British and did not hesitate to try to open up wounds that had already healed. I find the whole thing so incredibly sad when I think of how much had been achieved in terms of building Zimbabwe into a genuine African success story. As I write with possible exception of his ministers, it is very difficult to find anyone in the country who is prepared to support anything that he is doing. After the first land invasions, there were a few whites who felt that the country had to deal with the land issue in its own way. Even if mistakes were made and people were hurt, the country would emerge stronger in the long run. Another viewpoint came from a black Zimbabwean friend in London who told me that after the opposition won a significant number of seats in the 2001 general election, this would encourage Mugabe to pay more attention to the views of people who opposed him. The reverse has happened and the country's problems have worsened. Had it not had inherent strengths built up over many years before he came to power, the deterioration would have been much faster.

Very sadly, events have tended to put a stop to all sorts of progress which was making the country so special. The prospect of any meaningful coming together of the black and white professional classes is one example. On a visit in 2004 I saw more white antagonism towards blacks in general. On the black side, people were beginning to be afraid to be seen consorting with whites. And yet despite all this, Zimbabweans remain delightful people from top to bottom in society and including all races. To the visitor, the courtesy of the young is particularly noticeable. The police we encountered at the occasional roadblock outside towns were invariably smartly turned out and courteous.

On the Valentines farm, one of Heather's Afrikaans neighbours came to tea with four daughters currently visiting from various parts of the world. One, a single teacher, was now working in the Limpopo province of South Africa. When I asked her how she found Zimbabwe compared to where she lives, she said that she felt safe as soon as she crossed the border into Zimbabwe.

Part of the tragedy of Zimbabwe is that the downward plunge has been so unnecessary. Very sadly, it has given ammunition to the racists and sceptics. When such people are white, one wonders whether they would ever be happy to talk to a black man on equal terms. How on earth could so many such people have stayed in Zimbabwe and why were they not won over by reconciliation and 20 years of success? To what extent too did their attitudes affect Mugabe and trigger a matching reaction on his side? Perhaps the depth of his feelings really goes back to the days of old Southern Rhodesia when far too many whites paid no heed to human dignity and went out of their way to humiliate and denigrate blacks to help persuade themselves of their 'superiority' and to justify their privileged status.

16

BESO

A major factor in making my years with ZTMTT and RTZ so enjoyable was the chance they gave me to keep in touch with the Africa I knew, some very special friends and some wonderful wild parts. The then totally unspoilt Zambezi Valley in Zimbabwe is one such example. In Namibia too, during my regular visits to keep in touch with the management at Rossing Uranium and with ex-trainees, I met somebody who as early as 1982 was doing outstanding work for the country. She was a South African-born conservationist called Blythe Loutit, whose husband Rudi worked for the Namibian National Parks Department. They lived in a little house at the entrance to the Skeleton Coast National Park, 50 or so miles north of Swakopmund on the coast road north. I was lucky enough to have a standing invitation to accompany her on visits to some of the wildest, most remote and most beautiful parts of Africa. They were home to the rare desert rhino and desert elephant towards whose salvation she had managed to gain the co-operation of the local Damara people even in the old apartheid days of South African rule. Very sadly, Blythe died five years ago. Africa and Namibia owe her a huge debt of gratitude. In 2007 for a whole week, Sarah and I were uniquely privileged to be able to accompany Rudi on his own into the very wildest part of Namibia. We walked, explored and slept under the stars and saw black rhino and all sorts of wildlife but no human beings.

Elsewhere following my retirement from Rio Tinto and in later years during subsequent retirement jobs, Sarah and I were able to accompany Zambian farmer friends the Deans on camping expeditions to the Selous in Tanzania, the largest game reserve in the world, and to the Liuwa Plains on the Zambia–Angola border to watch the annual migration of wildebeest. I was most impressed by the pride and patriotism of ordinary Tanzanians. We came across no beggars, and when children gathered around our vehicles, it was to practice their English. I sensed the residual influence of Julius

Nyerere. I think he was misguided though, over his insistence on the primacy of Swahili.

Returning to 1994 and my first retirement job after leaving Rio Tinto, by mutual agreement with the company, I was seconded to the British Executive Service Overseas (BESO) for two years. Though working for BESO, I would continue to be paid by Rio Tinto and the years would count towards my pension. BESO was founded in 1972 by a retired businessman Ted Westnedge in collaboration with The Confederation of British Industry, the Institute of Directors and the Ministry of Overseas Development. The aim was to provide high grade training and expertise to the developing world. It was a marvellous institution which made use of volunteers who in the main were retired and keen to help and to keep their skills alive. The so-called clients were mainly small enterprises which under normal circumstances could not possibly have afforded to pay for business consultants or professional trainers. Assignments would last from two weeks to six months and the relationship would be one to one. It was a matter of helping people to help themselves. No money changed hands. BESO paid for the volunteer's air fare and for an accompanying spouse for longer assignments. The fares were the major expense. The staff were all retired semi-volunteers, apart from the Chief Executive Tim Bellers and a handful of people dealing with travel, computers and fund raising. They were divided between the recruiters who recruited the volunteers and the promoters or regional directors like me who generated the assignments. I was the regional director for most of Africa including French and Portuguese-speaking parts, but not at first including South Africa. The first few days were a bit of a shock to the system. I had got Rio Tinto to agree to my taking my beautiful walnut desk and matching furniture including two armchairs, a large table and chairs and a bookcase. As I joined BESO, I discovered that I was to share an office with five other promoters. So my beautiful furniture had to go to Tim Bellers who suddenly had a very well-furnished office. Now my involvement with Africa had a new lease of life and it would cover most of the continent. I was pleased that my French could be put to good use. I could also use my Portuguese acquired in Rio Tinto and used on trips to Portugal and Brazil. It had started in the company's own language school and continued with teachers coming to my office, notably the beautiful, amusing and highly intelligent Brazilian Silvia Costa Kurtz dos Santos, who inspired me to a London Chamber of Commerce advanced level with distinction in Portuguese.

I loved BESO from the start. Life running ZTMTT in London had sometimes been a lonely business. Now in BESO there were like-minded people fiercely loyal to the organisation and though everyone worked very hard, we had a lot of fun. There were six of us promoters, all retired and all with considerable overseas experience, either in business or in the civil service. I was the only person who had been in the colonial service and there were two ex-Foreign Office men. There were an equal number of recruiters who were people of similar background to the promoters, again with their career emphasis on overseas experience. We occupied identical crowded offices on separate floors. I had spent two months with the recruiters and found them a delightful bunch. Their job was to identify volunteers who had capability and potential to take on the assignments identified by the promoters. All had excellent contacts in industry and where they could not identify a suitable person from our database of about 5000 people, they made use of their contacts. Having identified one or more suitable candidates, they would send them details of the assignment before proposing them to the client. I remember it was hugely satisfying when one found a suitable volunteer for an assignment and one could be sure that vital help to a small business in Africa for instance, was as worthwhile as any help it was possible to give.

After two months with the recruiters I moved upstairs and found the promoters an equally friendly and congenial lot. There were seven of us, each with his telephone and computer. We were nearly always very busy and there were a lot of visitors, with volunteers coming in to be briefed or debriefed et cetera. There was a friendly rivalry between recruiters and promoters, but all were passionate about BESO. We promoters all specialised in different parts of the developing world and our main relationships were with the particular recruiters who were handling the recruitment for the assignments we had generated and with our representatives in our individual countries. For there to be a good number of worthwhile assignments in a country, it was essential to have a good representative who knew his or her country well, had good contacts and was committed.

Of course it was essential to visit our countries from time to time. So early on, I made visits to Zimbabwe, Zambia, Malawi and Mozambique, all countries in need of the sort of help we were able to give and ready to make good use of it. I did a lot of travelling. Before leaving the UK it was necessary at the very least to have an outline programme of meetings. The British High Commission or Embassy was usually the first point of contact and mostly carried out a lot of preliminary work setting up meetings with ministers, NGOs, trade associations and the local Rotary Club, for instance. In Zambia BESO was generating very few assignments. Our representative in the country was the man in the British High Commission responsible for trade promotion. Asked why there were not more Zambian assignments, his response was merely that Zambia was different. I spoke to the head of the local Chamber of Commerce who told me that more than anything Zambia needed expertise and training for local people. Now I had to find a good representative. I found the perfect one in the person of John Hudson OBE. John had been a colleague in the provincial administration in Northern Rhodesia in pre-independence days. He had been DC at Mazabuka while I was at Gwembe. He was born in the country and had been educated in South Africa and at Oxford, so he could relate to the blacks and whites and the British. He immediately grasped the importance of the help BESO could give and was soon generating assignments of all sorts. Top of the priority list were small, African-owned enterprises in Zambia which required expertise, and he found plenty of these. Between 1995 and 1999, 42 assignments were carried out. John was assisted by his hugely capable and energetic wife Greta.

A big bonus for Sarah and me was that the Hudsons loved the bush and were particularly keen birdwatchers. BESO paid for Sarah to accompany me once a year on promotional trips and on several occasions the Hudsons asked us to come with them on camping expeditions into the great Kafue National Park where besides enjoying the environment, we fished for bream in favourite secret places. As I had discovered in Kalomo days, the Kafue bream is as good to eat as any other fish anywhere. Another time we drove north and east to the little Kasanka Game Reserve near the Congo border where we watched shy sitatunga antelope in the reeds from a platform high in a giant tree.

In Zimbabwe and Malawi I appointed new BESO representatives and we started to get things going. Zimbabwe was particularly fertile ground for the BESO approach. I managed to find a very good new rep David Vincent, and within three years he had achieved nearly 40 assignments. In Malawi, one of the poorest countries in Africa, Ann Gajda – a British woman married to a Pole, Tony, in Blantyre – was particularly successful, and she knew everybody. She ran an employment agency specialising in the placement of local secretaries. I thought of her as the ideal expatriate, thoroughly in tune with the country and its people. While she was in charge more than 20 assignments were carried out amongst enterprises which really needed us. In contrast, I remember all the NGO 4×4 vehicles buzzing around Blantyre with the organisation's logo emblazoned on the side to draw attention to themselves, it was said. It was in Blantyre that I first heard the term 'aid junkie' and also of the penchant for expensive conferences at expensive hotels which achieved nothing at all. That was not our way in BESO. It seemed to me almost tragic when Ann and Tony had to move to the South African coast because of Tony's health. I called on the Gajdas during a visit to the Eastern Cape in 2002. They said that the saddest thing about living where they were now was that they had absolutely no contact with local black people, except on a master-and-servant basis.

Because of my Portuguese, Tim Bellers asked me early on to get BESO going in Mozambique, Angola and Brazil. In 1994, Mozambique was peaceful at last after 20 years of dreadful civil war. I stayed in the Hotel Embaixador in Beira where Sarah and I had spent part of our honeymoon in 1966. Now all the neon lights were gone and the walls of the taller buildings were pockmarked with bullet holes and curtains flapped from open windows. On the other hand it was still possible to eat the most wonderful giant *piri piri* prawns at local eating houses. I went back and back to Mozambique during my six years with BESO and each time it was a little more normal. BESO's role became a really valuable one, thanks largely to an outstanding local representative Ed Farquharson, who was the country manager of the Commonwealth Development Corporation (CDC), and he spoke fluent Portuguese. I always felt he would have made a good district officer. Two assignments I particularly remember are indicative of BESO's versatility. One was when we found a ballet dancer to teach the teacher at the Maputo ballet school. The other was an accountant to help resuscitate an ailing factory processing cashew nuts, of which Mozambique had been the world prime producer before its civil war. The volunteer not only sorted out the books but also managed to repair most of the machinery in the factory and trained local people to operate it.

Another time in Mozambique I found myself in Quelimane with an Italian girl in her early 20s who was working for CDC. We were staying at a rest house operated by the major local employer Madal, which had fishing, timber and copra interests. The rest house was a good half mile from the city centre. We had no car and had to walk downtown for our evening meals along streets with almost no lighting. We were assured there was no danger, and certainly we did not feel threatened. We ate giant prawns at the hotel where Mugabe had stayed during the Rhodesian war. The whole experience

made me marvel at the speed at which peace had returned after a war which
had ended only very recently.

Angola was a different matter. It was too early to be there. I spent hours
on my own in a windowless office at Luanda Airport before being rescued by
someone from the British Embassy. The experience took me back to Zaire
1971. In the capital I saw Livingstone's tree in the British ambassador's garden
and got an idea of what a magnificent city it must once have been. But the
atmosphere of fear and corruption was palpable and following the current
break in the fighting, the civil war re-started and BESO stayed away.

The other new departures for me, was introducing BESO to French-
speaking West Africa and Madagascar. In Cote d'Ivoire and Senegal, there
was a lot of talk about wanting to get rid of dependence on France and not
being a *chasse gardee*. I met the prime minister in Cote d'Ivoire and the head-
lines in the papers next day trumpeted that 'Les Brittaniques arrivent'. It was
an uphill struggle to get worthwhile assignments. Dependency on France is
hard to shake off. It was a different matter in Cameroon. The local representative there Njoh Litumbe, was a politician and retired accountant who came
from the western and English-speaking part of the Republic of Cameroon,
now a member of the Commonwealth. He visited BESO and I took to him
immediately when he asked me if I would like to 'come and stay with the
natives'. When I arrived, I found a substantial house set in a large garden
which had room for a guest house in the corner. It was set high above the old
capital Buea and just below the imposing German governor's schloss dating
from when Cameroon was a German colony up to 1918 before being man-
dated to Britain. Buea lies 4000 feet up the slopes of Mount Cameroon the
highest mountain in West Africa at 14,000 feet. It towers massively above the
town and supports some unique flora and fauna as well as herds of elephant.
The evening I arrived, Jo (that's what we both came to call each other) took
me to the Buea club. There, Cameroonian doctors, poets and other professional people enjoyed draft beer at a long bar, darts, tennis and snooker. In
the snooker room was the only white man I met that evening. He was introduced to me as 'Froggie' and was one of the very few French living in Buea.
At the bar I got chatting to the chief of police and to a delightful couple who
had just returned from working in Italy. I got the impression in Buea of great
West Cameroonian pride in its British and English-speaking traditions.

I stayed twice with Jo and his delightful wife Sarah. He used to refer
to her jokingly as his 'senior wife'. The third time I came, very sadly, Sarah
had died. By then I was director of the Royal African Society and Jo laid on

Promoting BESO in Cameroon

a special lunch which made me feel very important. The food was brought up from Douala by Jo's daughter-in-law and guests included the governor, the Nigerian consul general, the chief of police and the female vice chancellor of the University of Buea. The latter I thought was one of the most impressive women I have ever met. Conversation during lunch blossomed with the help of some excellent wines and we ended up exchanging amusing African anecdotes. Talking of which, on that visit I was at a lunch with another daughter-in-law in Limbe on the coast. While we were still at the table, the children of various sizes as they returned from school, came in to greet the grown-ups. The last to arrive was a very pretty girl of about 16. Jo said something in the local language and everyone laughed. I asked my neighbour to explain. Jo had said, 'let me know when you grow up so I can sell you'.

In 1996, Tim Bellers decided he no longer wanted me to promote BESO in Brazil and asked me to concentrate on Madagascar. I was a bit put out at first as things were going very well in Brazil. However, as soon as I got to Madagascar, I saw how incredibly poor the country was and how worthwhile BESO help was going to be. One of the vital factors was that the British Ambassador Bob Dewar could not have been more supportive. He told me that BESO was the only help he had to offer the Madagascans or Malgache as they are known. Some excellent publicity helped, but I could see straight

BESO Regional Directors 1999

away that Madagascar was prime BESO country. Without being overtly anti-French, the Malgache were fed up with French attitudes which smacked of keeping them dependent on France and wedded to the French language and culture. The Malgache wanted to break out and to forge closer relations with the British who had originally brought Christianity and education to the country. After independence in 1960, they were persuaded to turn to Marxism. Now with an energetic population, without any special hang-ups, with huge resources and with poverty levels worse than anything I had seen in Africa proper, this was a country on which I felt Britain should concentrate help and investment efforts. One certainly did not get the impression that people felt they had a right to be helped. That was the feeling coming out of relatively rich South Africa at the time. The Malgache desperately wanted and needed us and I don't remember any of the many assignments generated by the embassy or by our very excellent representative Simon Peers which was not a resounding success. Simon, who ran a business making traditional silk fabrics, gave me and BESO a lot of his time. In two years, 18 assignments were generated. Simon and I had some fun together too. In Taomasina, otherwise known as Tamatave, on the east coast, we had volunteers helping organise the port and training operatives in a match factory. One evening we had a wonderful Chinese meal in a restaurant with the water pouring through the roof. Before returning to our hotel, we were pulled through the streets soaked to the skin, by rickshaw, in the teeming, warm, tropical rain.

Madagascar could be and should be a very good friend to the UK. There are deep links through the church and through education. There is such goodwill. There is so much potential. There are such resources. They did not like being colonised by the French in the late nineteenth century. It is also an incredibly poor country but lacks a dependency mentality. I was astounded therefore to hear last year that the British government had decided to close our embassy in the country.

During my six years with BESO, I learned a lot about Africa as a whole and its potential and about African capability. Those years had given me the opportunity to keep up with life-long friends including many ex-ZTMTT trainees. I had also been able to get my periodic fixes from wild Africa. Sadly, however, by 1999 things were going wrong at BESO. Following the arrival of the new chief executive, the council seems to have got it into its head that we needed a new younger management team. Such a conclusion in my opinion, could not have been more misguided. Amongst our recruiters and promoters – all quasi-volunteers – were some of the most highly motivated, hardworking and effective people I had ever met. Soon there were management consultants interviewing everyone and asking fatuous questions. At the same time, new appointments were being made – new directors of this and that. Clearly we could not afford this. More and more of BESO's scarce financial resources were frittered on expensive appointments, while the number of assignments fell. There was less money available for the essential task of getting the volunteers to the clients, that is, for air fares. All this was perfectly clear. Another factor in my opinion, was our new Chairman Baroness Lynda Chalker's preoccupation with South Africa which was not ready for BESO. The South Africans either did not want us or tended to think that they had a right to help. Our successful assignments were in the countries like Madagascar or Malawi where the expertise we could provide was really needed and the clients took full advantage of the opportunity to acquire new skills, that is to help themselves. We in the BESO community including the volunteers understood what was being achieved. We were quite simply the best and most cost-effective help Britain could provide. Judging by the paltry subsidy we received from DFID, that organisation did not seem to understand what we were achieving and its cost-effectiveness. There was even the impression that it was under pressure from expensive consultants who preferred to see our volunteers as essentially non-professional people. In fact we had some of the best and most committed skills possible. It was just that most happened to be skills which volunteers were prepared to pass them on for nothing. When the inevitable failure came and BESO was absorbed by VSO, it was a tragedy which reflected sad failure rather than the logical coming together which both organisations tried to portray.

I was not around to see the end. In 2000 out of the blue, a piece of good fortune arose which allowed me a way out to a continuing African role. I happened to be on the Council of the Royal African Society and at one of the meetings, the Chairman Sir Michael McWilliam came up with the idea of appointing a part-time non-executive director to represent the society and broaden the membership. A few days later I went to see Michael and put myself forward. I was found to be acceptable, partly it seemed because my PhD would give me greater credibility amongst the academics who made up the bulk of the membership. Soon, equipped with a telephone and a fax machine, I was operating out of our London flat on a three-day-a-week basis for £5000 a year (slightly less than I was getting from BESO). Though I badly missed the camaraderie of BESO, I did not find it too difficult to recruit individual members for £35 annual subscription and businesses for £300. We set up a special diplomatic membership for African Embassies and High Commissions for £100 and most joined.

Things went so well that after a few months Michael suggested that for an additional £3000 a year, I might consider working four days a week instead of three. I thought about this and decided that it was not an attractive proposition as 40 per cent would go on tax. I suggested that instead I should be allowed to go to Africa twice a year to promote the society and claim expenses. This was agreed to.

Over the next two years I arranged trips to individual countries or groups of countries. One of the first was to Zimbabwe where the occupation by so-called war veterans of land owned by whites was in full swing. Sarah came with me. I had somehow imagined that we would find the country on a war footing. In fact we found everything remarkably normal in the towns with the shops full and people as friendly as ever. It was annoying though to be told that although our air tickets provided for a three-week stay, we would be given visas for only two weeks. So we would have to leave the country and then re-enter before flying home. I immediately thought of going up to Binga to see the Van Jaarsvelds and Amos, but that proved impossible to arrange in the time.

Meanwhile, we went down to the farm to stay with Heather, who was having a miserable time. She was still missing Richard dreadfully. She was having to confront, literally, three or four so-called war vets supported by ZANU party activists camped in what had been the workers' crèche and making constant threats and demands. As they seemed to have the tacit support of Mugabe and the government, the police were reluctant to give any help in getting rid of them. The workers too were confused and torn between fear of ZANU party thuggery and loyalty to a good employer. I found the whole thing immensely sad besides being sinister. Perhaps, worst of all was the government's clear disregard for the rule of law. Besides, one thing would lead to another with international confidence lost and a downward economic spiral. It was quite clear that Mugabe, who since independence had put the land issue on the back burner, was using it to try to win back the popular support which the democratic process showed he had lost in the 2000 referendum.

One day I went to Kondozi farm run by the de Klerk family. Over the years I had met Piet de Klerk many times playing tennis at the Odzi Club and had been impressed by his positive attitude to the new Zimbabwe. He told me how proud he was that Zimbabwean Afrikaners were light years ahead of their contemporaries in South Africa. Now I saw his wife in her office on the farm. The de Klerks, keen to do the right thing, had given much of their land away for resettlement and had established the growing of vegetables such as mange tout and baby corn on the rest. They had also organised local so-called outgrowers all black, to produce a range of crops for a UK supermarket chain. The whole operation was highly organised and a pioneering leap forward for Zimbabwean agriculture. Mrs de Klerk told me that a few days before, supposed employees of the government's agricultural arm ARDA had arrived to take over Kondozi. The workers, who knew exactly what was going on, threw out the would-be occupiers. When I got back to the UK, I e-mailed a local friend to ask whether ARDA was now running Kondozi successfully. 'You must be joking', was the reply. 'What they could not steal, they trashed.' So Zimbabwe the great potential African success story, had come to this. It was a tragedy that Zimbabwe which had suffered so much in its dreadful war, but had been given another chance, was now throwing it all away. I could hear the white racists saying that they had said all along that the blacks would ruin the country. Some even seemed to want it that way. The most frightened and bitter people of all were the professional middle-class blacks who had had such high hopes for their country.

Bernard Mutuma would have felt devastated and totally let down. His colleagues including most of my ex-trainees certainly felt so strongly that they were emigrating to South Africa, Botswana and the UK.

On that visit we continued on to cousin Chris's farm which exceptionally remained an island of productivity and happiness with wheat and citrus grown under irrigation. His farm school still flourished with pupils including children of ruling-party officials based in the neighbouring tribal lands.

Finally on that 2004 visit, we drove on to Bulawayo, which never seems to change with its streets wide enough to turn a span of oxen as decreed by Cecil Rhodes, its deep storm drains and its scattered tall buildings dating from the Federal era. From Bulawayo we took the overnight train for the Victoria Falls. We had comfortable berths and slept like tops. We woke in the morning to bird song and the smell of rain. A porter carried our bags from the station to the Victoria Falls Hotel. I asked for a room. 'That will be three hundred and seventy-five American dollars' said the receptionist after he had seen our passports. I think I was pre-programmed to make a fuss. There was also some pent-up frustration waiting to be let out. I exploded into Chitonga, complaining that I had been coming to the hotel for 45 years, had known many people from Zambia who had worked here in the past and did not see why I should pay such a ridiculous price. I looked up to see I was confronting a very tall immaculately dressed black man who told me very politely that the hotel was carrying out government policy on exchange control. 'Nevertheless', he added, 'as a sign of our goodwill we would like to offer you the honeymoon suite for two hundred and fifty dollars.' His offer completely took the wind out of my sails. Lamely I said, 'Yes thank you', and we booked into what was still a marvellous institution with corridors lined with historic pictures of the 1947 royal visit. We had a memorable stay but found it very sad to see how the town, geared up for thousands and thousands of tourists, now had almost none. The manager of the Victoria Falls hotel told me it was still profitable, thanks to most of its earnings being in foreign exchange. He said he was determined to maintain the highest standards whatever was going on in the country. Certainly, in the well-appointed gents changing room at the swimming pool, one still peed onto crushed ice.

17

Stephen's Greeting

We passed through the immigration posts on each side of the Falls Bridge and met our farmer friends the Becketts at the new Royal Livingstone Hotel not more than a few hundred yards upstream of the Eastern Cataract on the Zambian side. It is a fantastic site overlooking the rapids but irresponsibly close in my opinion to this world heritage site. Mike and Gill Beckett were in fine form, and after expensive cokes on the veranda we headed for Livingstone and a snack lunch in a café.

About 20 miles up the familiar road towards Kalomo and Choma you pass the railway siding of Senkobo on the left. As we drove, I remarked to Mike that my old manservant Stephen Mbwainga lived in a village called Masongozi six or seven miles off the main road. Mike's immediate reaction was 'Lets go and see him'. We protested but not too strongly, and Mike was serious. So we were soon driving through the bush on a passable bush track towards the Simango post office as I remembered it. We had not seen Stephen since 1974 when we had called at his village on our way back to Zaire from holiday in Rhodesia. Now I was hugely excited at the prospect of seeing him again. I was pretty sure he was still alive as we had exchanged letters a few months before. I asked Mike to stop beside an old man walking along the track. I asked him in Chitonga if he knew Stephen Mbwainga. 'You must be Bwana Lawley' was his response. He assured us that Stephen was very well. He said that if we continued the way we were going, we would arrive at a clinic where we would be certain to see Stephen. There was to be some gathering of older people. We bundled the old man into the car and soon arrived at the clinic where a number of people had already gathered. As I was asking about Stephen a great shout arose 'Ba Stephen balasika' (Stephen's coming). And here he was emerging from a bush path looking very dapper. I shouted in Tonga, 'How are you old man?' As he approached me his jaw literally dropped and he flung his arms about my neck. I responded likewise.

Author with Stephen

It was one of the most moving moments of my life. Needless to say there was lots to talk about and I wished that my Tonga was less rusty. The atmosphere amongst the onlookers was festive and from amongst them emerged a man of about my age, James Syulukwa who had been a teacher at the Kalomo Township School in my day. We took lots of photos including the Becketts and James and plied Stephen with whatever gifts we could drum up. James told me how much he admired Stephen and how well liked and well respected he was. Then with promises to come again and stay in touch we drove off to the farm at Choma. After a few days the Becketts drove us back to Livingstone where we linked up with a taxi for Victoria Falls Airport and the plane to Harare. We were on board when we saw President Mugabe himself arriving to board our plane with his wife and retinue all dressed up in shirts bearing his portrait. He sat in front of us. I would dearly have loved to talk.

We were back in Choma again within two years this time on a Royal African Society trip to Zambia. I had a twofold objective this time, to get an idea of how the government administration was functioning and to find out how the 30 or so newly arrived white Zimbabwean farmers were settling in. The evening of our arrival there was a party at the Choma Club. Most of the established white farmers from Choma district as well as Kalomo, and the Zimbabweans and their families were there. A good number of black people, mainly civil servants, were present there too and Asian traders who had been instrumental in resuscitating the club. Jo and Seena Brooks were there and the place was full of children of all sizes. I knew some of the Choma farmers, but the Kalomo contingent of a dozen or so were almost without exception sons of people I had known in the early 1960s. It was immensely encouraging to find them still in the country. Some were Afrikaners. Nearly all were a bit worried that the new Zimbabwean arrivals, would by their attitudes and language, upset existing balances and jeopardise race relations. After all the Zambians and their parents had lived with the inevitability and then the reality of black rule all their lives. Actually the Zimbabweans were an impressive bunch: young hardworking and determined to do well. They had received loans to enable them to clear and plant land and to build houses for themselves and their labour, all in a year. They seemed to be rising to the challenge.

I tried without success to get the district administrator in Kalomo on the phone. So I drove 45 miles to the familiar little town past the now very seedy looking hotel where more than 40 years before the girl from Croydon had tickled the farmers' backs at the bar. Then it was over the bridge and up the road to the boma. The building was as I remembered it, but instead of crowds of people seeking permits, petitioning the DC to shoot an elephant which was damaging crops or complaining about an employer there was almost nobody there. Most of the offices seemed to be empty too. I made my way to the secretary's office and sat and talked to her. She told me her boss was out of the office. She was a perceptive and intelligent young woman who seemed anxious to give me her views on what in her opinion was really the matter with the way the government was functioning in the rural areas. She told me that her understanding was that things had started to go wrong when the government politicised the administration about four years after independence. The effect of this in an opposition area like Kolomo was that the district governor as he was called by then, found it very difficult to get things done. There was also a problem with the quality of the incumbents. The close link which had existed in colonial times between the administration and the chiefs through the admirable and uniquely effective district messenger service had long since gone. Now, though the district administrator was supposed to co-ordinate all government activity, the reality was that he had no power because he lacked the funding to do anything. Power lay with the District Council secretary through whom all funding for local projects as well as routine government activity was channelled. I said I was keen to see her boss and she suggested I come back next day. I then drove back to town and called at the council secretary's office. There were a lot of people milling around including several Germans apparently involved in some education project. Though he was obviously very busy, I was able to see him after a brief wait. His interest in my visit waned somewhat when it became clear that I was not dispensing any sort of aid.

The next day when I arrived back at the boma I was shown straight into the administrator's office despite the fact that a large meeting was in progress. He was touchingly welcoming as was everybody else at the meeting. When his visitors had left he told me more or less what his secretary had already said and then gave me someone to show me around. It was a depressing business with the old DC's house built in 1903 and the oldest European-style building in the country and a national monument, in a terrible state. Some repair work had started but it looked to be of very poor quality. The garden had gone and with it most of the trees. The old pioneer cemetery dating from the time when Kalomo was the capital of the then North-Western Rhodesia was an even sadder sight with the gravestones of old administrators, traders, tax collectors and missionaries mostly broken or missing. I wondered if the white farming community had taken any interest in it. The next day Sarah and I set off for the Beckett's cottage at Sinazongwe which had been a sub-boma of my old district, Gwembe. It was now a full district in its own right and I called on the district administrator and council secretary and again received a very warm welcome. The impression I got of what was going on or more to the point, what was not going on, made me even more depressed. I decided to call on Chief Sinazongwe at the chief's village a few miles up the valley road. I had known his father. The present incumbent had been an electrician on the Copperbelt before succeeding to the chieftainship. The chief turned out to be very helpful and gave me some fascinating perspectives. He told me that central government was almost totally ineffective in the district. Government departments he said, employed plenty of people but seemed to exist mainly to pay their wages. Mainly they achieved nothing. He went on to say that the power and influence of chiefs was increasing. They were the authority to which people turned if they wanted anything done. Though he had no official legal roles as chiefs had had in colonial days, he was frequently called on to arbitrate in disputes. Currently he said the chiefs were in negotiation with the government over a new Royal House of Chiefs. Generally he said people in his area were no better off than they had been decades before. Schemes to set up co-operative farming had failed because equipment had broken down and could not be repaired. Furthermore, unemployment was growing due to production cuts at the Mamba colliery in Chief Mwemba's area further up the valley. He said he was in favour of the new enterprise set up near Sinazeze where a young white Zimbabwean was managing an internationally owned enterprise growing vegetables under irrigation for the European market. It provided employment and some food for his people. I was amazed to see this first example of tribal land being used in this way. It would have been unthinkable in pre-independence days when tribal land was sacrosanct under land tenure laws.

When we called on the young white Zimbabwean manager at Sinazeze, he told us he was delighted with what he was being able to achieve and with all the co-operation he was receiving especially from the chief. At around 1700 feet in the Zambezi Valley you could grow anything at any time of the year, he said. He had a huge amount of land under irrigation from 21 centre pivots.

We went on up the tarred road towards Mamba to call on the Chief Mwemba. Sadly he was away but his wives were very welcoming and dressed up on their best clothes to be photographed.

I left the valley that day with the feeling that the local people were no better off than they had been at independence. They were as dependent as ever and had yet to become successful farmers or fishermen. The single bright light seemed to be the prospects for commercial investment particularly in agriculture and fishing.

Back with the Becketts, Mike had been asked by the headmaster of the well-known Mapanza secondary school for boys run by the Anglican Church to give the prizes. In best bib and tucker we set off up the main road to Namwala which was in a dreadful state. The 30 miles took us two and a half hours and Mike reminded me that in the late 1950s the then DC at Namwala the famous one armed Micky Chittenden used to try to drive the 100 miles from Namwala to Choma in his Ford Fairlane in less than an hour. At the school which held memories for me from the days when I was campaigning in 1962 to persuade the population that their vote was secret, the headmaster was very welcoming and put Sarah and me in the VIP line-up. Mike made an excellent speech and then came the prize giving and more speeches. There was a highly suggestive dance with some of the boys dressed as girls. Everyone enjoyed themselves. There was a prize for the most improved teacher whom the headmaster described in his speech as a clear case of beer to bible. I had gained the impression of a body of young men who I was certain, were as intelligent, lively and motivated as it is possible to find anywhere in the world. They were Zambia's future and the future was safe in their hands. When I talked afterwards to some, they mostly told me they wanted to join this or that international charity or NGO. It struck me more forcibly than ever that we in the West do a great deal of harm by giving Africans the impression that their future lies in our hands rather than their own. We really need to remind ourselves and remind Africans that they can do anything. Most of our aid is woefully misplaced.

The next day Mike lent me one of his ancient Volvos to go and call on Stephen 100 miles down the road towards Livingstone. I drove on my own and got to the clinic where we had all met two years before. At the local school lessons were over for the day; I was able to get a boy to show me the way through the bush to Masongozi village. Stephen was away at a nearby beer drink. I asked somebody whether by now he would be drunk? 'Not yet' was the reply. So off I set and found the gathering and a fairly sober Stephen surprised but apparently very pleased to see me. He said immediately that he wanted to leave the beer drink and drive back with me to the village. As we left there was his old wife very much an old crone and asking for some sort of handout. I told her I would leave something for her with Stephen. Back at his hut which stood slightly apart from the rest of the village, we sat on stools under a tree and he brought out the photos of our previous visit I had sent him. I handed over the things I had brought for him including torches and plenty of batteries and disposable razors. I gave him some money too and I remember how he was never ever greedy or grasping and was always totally trustworthy. Despite my rather rusty Tonga we talked for a long time and then he went over to the village to fetch his elder sister to introduce to me. She was a fine old woman, as tall as Stephen was small. When I asked him how old she was he told me that even in his earliest memories she had been an adult and as he was nearly eighty she must have been in her mid-nineties at least. The headman came over as well. I was touched that he and others in the village seemed genuinely pleased to see me and grateful that they had not been forgotten by the outside world.

On this trip it came home to me very strongly how well the British are viewed in modern Zambia. In the immediate post-independence years we were blamed for everything that went wrong. Now I remembered on a recent trip to Zambia we were with our friends the Deans at Mongu en route to camp with them in the wilds of what used to be Barotseland. It is Lozi country so I was surprised to hear Tonga being spoken at the petrol station. I greeted the speakers in their own language. One of them asked me if I was a missionary. I said no but that I had worked many years ago in the PA (the buboma). Why did you leave the country was the response? I replied that Kaunda had sacked us. By now there were a dozen or so people in on the conversation. 'That bloody Kaunda' said someone. 'Hang on', I said. 'Kaunda went when the people no longer wanted him and he never allowed tribalism to take hold in Zambia.' There was a nodding of heads. 'The bwana speaks the truth' was the response.

Stephen was dismissive about what the central government did for village people. He said they never saw an administrator and the district messengers were long gone but much missed. As we said goodbye, I promised to come again but was worried by what he told me about his health. He replied to my next letter and after that there was silence. Subsequently I had an e-mail from the Becketts to say that they had been asked to tell me that Stephen had died. Only a few days later I received two letters giving me the same news, one from the retired teacher James Syulukwa and the other in Tonga from Stephen's daughter Rosemary who was six when we left Zambia in 1969. When Sarah and I visited Rosemary in early 2007 she presented us with a large bag of *ndongwe* (groundnuts) and delicious local beans called *nyemu*. We were much moved by this act of great generosity.

My job as the first director of the Royal African Society was pretty well ideal for me as I approached my three score years and ten and I was able to continue my physical involvement with Africa. In November 2002, I decided it was time to look at the new South Africa starting at Cape Town and then carry on to Kenya via Grahamstown and Johannesburg.

In Cape Town, I went to the Department of African Studies at the Cape Town University. I was not expecting a lot. I found even less. It came home to me how little involvement there had been with the rest of Africa during the apartheid era. At the Cape Town University Business School I was keen to exchange ideas on my specialist subject of culture and its impact on leadership and management. Perhaps inevitably I found myself in an argument with the head of the school over the dangers of giving accelerated and unearned promotion to blacks. There was no desire for a discussion much less to accept the points I wanted to make over how blacks could be helped to see themselves as and to be the genuine article. Even in this institution, window dressing still seemed to be the name of the game in South Africa.

In Grahamstown I stayed with my very dear friend ex-St Andrews and Rhodes University, Chris Stone. Chris a lawyer had never allowed me to get carried away by my strong feelings over race in mid-1950s South Africa. I gave a talk at my alma mater and Chris came. I kicked off by acknowledging the traditional sensitivity in South Africa about anything suggesting advice to the country from the outside. I said I hoped to be forgiven for my frankness as an Old Rhodian who had spent most of his life in Africa. I went on to talk about the importance of South Africa becoming fully aware of how she could contribute to the continent and also what she stood to learn and gain. I suggested that languages spoken in Africa were important and said I was proud to say when asked where I had learned French, that it was in South Africa. I also mentioned my recently acquired Portuguese. Later that day I was to discover that the Portuguese department no longer existed and the French department had been substantially scaled down.

In Johannesburg, I stayed at the Country Club and met up with a number of old school and university friends. It was disappointing to find that with only a few exceptions their views on the new South Africa were negative. Few had seen anything of the rest of Africa. I was not encouraged either by a series of breakfast meetings with three young supposed high-flying blacks. At least one was an ex-Rhodes scholar. All took the view that they were being discriminated against and not being given the promotion they deserved. For me all the signs were that they were being mollycoddled. I gave my views on them to one of my ex-trainees a Zimbabwean Alec Gumbie who also came to breakfast. He was scathing about Black Economic Empowerment (BEE). He was certainly the genuine article with his thriving engineering consultancy business. He and his family were currently moving into a large house in one of Johannesburg's most expensive suburbs.

Back in London two council members of the Royal African Society told me they wanted to meet and talk. They were David Campbell the retired founder of Farm Africa and Father Shanahan of Street Child Africa. The upshot was a meeting with Michael McWilliam when they voiced their opinion that the Society was not as influential as it should be and that the journal *African Affairs* and the meetings programme could be improved. As the Society's first director I was part-time and non-executive with a job linked to recruiting and to raising the society's profile and in these areas the general opinion was that I had succeeded very well. I had no responsibility for the meetings programme or the journal. The logical conclusion was that the society needed a full-time executive director. Richard Dowden was subsequently appointed to the new post. I stopped being director when my contract ran out at the end of 2003.

Shortly after I stopped working for the RAS, Hamish McGregor, director general of the West Africa Business Association (WABA), very kindly asked me if I would like to come and help him recruit members. I gladly accepted and not long after joining WABA on a part-time basis, the Southern Africa Business Association (SABA) went out of business. Hamish and I discussed setting up a new association the Southern Africa Business Forum (SABF) to represent business interests in southern Africa as a whole under WABA's umbrella. I was asked to run it on an expenses-only basis at first. In mid-2004 I started my third retirement job. As consultant, apart from building up the membership and setting up meetings for members, I have been keen to push for ever closer relations between SABF and WABA as part of bringing Africa together through trade and investment. The next step is to bring the East Africa Association into a single business association for Africa and we are making good progress in that direction. It has been a challenging and fulfilling job and I feel at one with our small team under Hamish and fully involved with Africa. The slow pace of our progress in persuading some South African companies to identify with our objectives and join us is sometimes frustrating but should get easier when we can project ourselves as a single association. Of course it is early days, but it seems to me that South Africa has yet to appreciate just how much she has to learn from the rest of Africa as well contribute to it.

SABF-WABA, now Business Council for Africa (West and southern), maintains my African contact and I readily identify with its role of promoting trade and investment in Africa as opposed to dependency perpetuating handouts and debt forgiveness.

In April 2005, I visited Botswana, Namibia, Mozambique and South Africa for SABF. In Gaborone, Sarah and I were entertained to dinner by ex-ZTMTT trainee Leonard Makwinja and his wife. Leonard was technical director of De Beers Botswana, one of the top jobs in world mining. His colleague Charles Siwawa was deputy general manager at Orapa and a third Mutswana Monty Mpathi is general manager at the important Selibe Phikwe Mine. The products of a unique scheme to produce the leaders and managers that Africa needs more than anything else are reaching their zenith.

18

The Unhappy Country

This chapter has two parts. The first describes a trip to Zimbabwe in early 2006 and the way I found it. It reflects on the reasons for the country's downward slide and on the parts played by black and white Zimbabweans over the years, by the British government and by President Robert Mugabe himself. The second part describes a different scenario in early 2008 when despite further deterioration I found more positive attitudes and more hope for a successful future.

Having not been to see friends and relations in Zimbabwe for two years, Sarah and I decided on a holiday there in April 2006. Sadly, there was no question of getting off into the wilds of the Zambezi Valley. We mainly wanted to show support for our friends still running farms and others still in Harare. I also wanted to get a feel for things like the state of race relations, the way the land problem is now viewed and the state of the economy. We were met in Johannesburg by cousin Chris and after two nights at the Country Club, we drove north. At Beitbridge on Easter Saturday, there were large crowds of people at the Zimbabwean border post with bundles of all manner of goods apparently for sale in South Africa. Some of them would have undoubtedly been movable and saleable things stripped from erstwhile European-owned farms occupied by war vets and others. Our small party got speedy, efficient and friendly service from immigration and customs officials and we were through in 20 minutes. I gathered there had been a recent clear out of officials who had been looking for bribes.

On Chris's farm the big news was that the government was coming up with extra fuel, fertiliser and seed to enable more wheat to be grown. It had been senior army officers who had come down from Harare to make the request to the handful of local white farmers in the district. On the farm the atmosphere was subdued with labour very difficult to get. The reason for this was the 1000 per cent inflation which was nearly halving the value of money every month and the fact that for neighbouring villages, food provided by international charities was available. Nevertheless, the farm school was still going strong, and Chris and his son-in-law Brian retained a fantastic reputation as employers. Because the land on the farm is cultivatable only under irrigation owing to the low rainfall, there were no so-called settlers and so none of the constant requests which amount to demands, for help and handouts. A big problem on the farm remained the loss of valuable, experienced farm workers through AIDS. The disease had recently claimed three top employees.

As we drove around Zimbabwe between hosts, we found ordinary people as friendly as ever. There were a few police roadblocks, but we were invariably waved through. At Odzi Farm, where Heather gave us the warmest of welcomes, the atmosphere was again subdued and sad. She and her son Phil were keeping going despite continuing uncertainty. They were the last white farmers in the area and they felt it was only a question of time before they were taken over. This was despite being highly productive and contributing significantly to the country's coffers. It was also despite the fact that hundreds of people, directly or indirectly, were dependent on them for a livelihood. Added to this, they continued to give help and advice to dozens of new local tobacco growers, but were still being robbed regularly of such vital equipment as irrigation pipes on which the farm was completely dependent. Periodic prolonged electricity cuts had the same effect on their ability to keep going. There were several dozen so-called settlers on the farm, many of them demanding all kinds of help to which they felt they were entitled. They and hundreds of thousands like them all over the country personified a massive failure. Instead of representing a new productive future and a triumph over the dependency culture, they had come to represent the very opposite; the idea that somehow the white man was withholding what was their rightful due. If ever there was a step backwards after Zimbabwe's enormous progress after independence, this was it. Actually the settlers were being badly let down by the government, as having been encouraged to occupy farms, they had been left high and dry without the means to carry out successful agriculture.

Whatever the farm had become, Heather and Phil remained there partly out of sheer determination not to give in to the forces of envy, prejudice and destruction and partly out of loyalty to Richard and his father before him. The other thing keeping them there was concern for their employees and their hundreds of dependents. If Heather and Phil were forced out, these people whose families had been on the farm since 1930 would be destitute.

On this visit there was no question of going to the Odzi Club which had been the centre of a highly productive and successful community. I had enjoyed hospitality there during the country's ups and downs over more than half a century. I had been there to hear Richard take issue with Ian Smith's minister of agriculture in 1977. I had particularly enjoyed the tennis there on Saturday afternoons when I was visiting. I knew most of the farmers who in the main, were courageous people who loved their country and had contributed to it mightily. After Saturday tennis there was always drinks and supper at the club and you talked to everyone. Now that whole life had gone and from the main road I could see the weeds growing all over the tennis courts. Down the road from the club, the little Anglican Church where Richard and his parents are buried still stood, but for how long?

I was keen to pursue the Kondozi story two years after the ARDA takeover. I was told that the national Vice President Joyce Majuru had visited recently. Apparently, when she asked about the whereabouts of some piece of equipment, she was told it had been stolen by one of her cabinet colleagues. The story went on that the question had been prompted by her husband, a retired military man with big political ambitions, who was keen to score points in the current infighting over Mugabe's succession. Doing the rounds was the story that she had recently decreed that all car number plates in the country had to be changed. It was said that she owned the factory that made them.

As this visit went on, I was almost overcome with sadness at what Zimbabwe had become in the six years since the land invasions sparked the country's headlong plunge. It was the ordinary people for whom I felt most sorry, particularly the hundreds of unemployed in the cities in their day-to-day struggle to survive. The electoral process still reflected the will of the people, and Mugabe's ZANU party had no seats in any of the four cities. Everyone I talked to told me they wanted him out. They could see quite clearly where his policies were leading. Now the dire and entirely predictable consequences were there for all to see. Even if people were lucky enough to have a job, their money soon became virtually worthless. If they had no job and nothing to sell, they might find food in their home area in the communal lands. Otherwise if they and their families were to survive, they had to leave the country to get hard currency. For the common man this usually meant entering South Africa illegally by swimming the Limpopo. Everyone in the country was looking for hard currency. Erstwhile profitable commercial farms were being stripped of anything that could be sold by the people to whom they were given, usually party or government officials. On this trip we drove past numerous formerly productive and profitable properties which now lay abandoned. A few years before, they had fed half of Africa. One of the saddest aspects of what was happening was that instead of continuing to move away from the issue of race, Mugabe seemed to be trying to return to it. I had seen Zimbabwe as a society which would genuinely fulfil itself without the cloying attentions of the purveyors of international aid. It had been a society that was showing that it valued all its strengths and talents and that making progress did not involve taking from the so-called advantaged (in South African terminology) to give to the 'formerly disadvantaged'.

Now it seemed that perforce everyone was on the make. Even for the erstwhile well-to-do, if for instance school fees needed to be paid, people would often leave the country temporarily to go and earn the money in Britain or South Africa. Amazingly, few people were giving up on their country. Usually they could not afford to. They were finding the means to survive by hook or by crook. Many though were failing, and the vast piles of hundreds of funeral wreathes we saw beside the road at the turnoff to Chitungwiza cemetery south of Harare told the sad story.

On this trip I was particularly keen to talk to educated black people including old friends. Over the years it had been they who had expressed the strongest views and had the greatest fears. They knew what was at stake. As an interested outsider I had always found it relatively easy to find ordinary black people who were prepared to tell me what they really thought. Again this time I found plenty of people ready to talk. From them I detected not one iota of feeling that what Mugabe was doing was anything to do with principle, honour or the good of the country. In Mutare I saw the estate agents letting my house as well as the management of a building society. All the people I met, all black, gave me excellent professional service. All were scathing about Mugabe and what he was doing to the country. Even stronger views in the same vein were expressed to me about the destruction of peoples' homes in the poor townships in Harare and other cities under the government's cruel operation *murambatsvina* (clean out the filth). The government seemed to be trying to force people to return to their original homes in the communal areas. A good friend in Harare, being in a position to know what goes on in the very highest echelons of decision-making, told me that it was now generally agreed amongst educated blacks that the government's policy-making had been totally confused and shown no attempt at all to link cause with effect. He told me that he and other black professionals were united in their detestation of what Mugabe was doing to the country and, by implication, their fear of him. All were desperate to see him go. I was grateful that my friend had paid me the compliment of giving me his real unadulterated views.

I found in the small and beautiful city of Mutare, ringed by mountains, that despite everything, life went on with everyone trying to maintain some sort of normality. There were noticeably fewer whites around than when I was last in the city. I was told that many who do still live there cross the border every day to work in neighbouring Mozambique. In Harare there were still thousands of whites, many of them displaced farmers now occupying suburban houses. While we were in town staying with friends, there was an open-air opera in the main city park featuring international musicians and attended by both whites and blacks. There was a sort of normality too at the delightful Borrowdale Brook Golf Course near where Mugabe has built his retirement palace. There the fairways which wend their way beside or over the babbling brook are lined with high-quality architect-designed houses paid for I was told, by Zimbabweans working in the UK or South Africa.

Reflecting at the time on what had gone wrong in Zimbabwe, the parts played by the whites and by the British had both been important. Returning to the earliest days of independence, there was genuine goodwill particularly amongst blacks towards the British for our part in bringing about peace. Amongst whites there was initial astonishment at the Patriotic Front victory in the election, followed by equal astonishment that Mugabe should be so conciliatory. There were no calls for revenge or for retribution against the former oppressors. All the gaolers, the SAS soldiers and the Selous Scouts were untouched as were the military commanders and the politicians. Mr Ian Smith remained untouched on his farm. He even became a senator. From what I saw on our visit in 1981, a year after independence, the whites were involved in a sort of complacent self-delusion, some even sporting Rhodesian flags and 'Rhodesia is Super' stickers. At the same time the government encouraged not just reconciliation but also recognition of the bravery and patriotism of white farmers who had kept going on their farms for years while they had been in constant danger of being attacked and killed.

From Mugabe's point of view, not only had he shown extraordinary forgiveness and pragmatism but had also given whites and particularly the farmers a new chance to participate in the building of their country. He was perhaps mindful of the lost chance of a multiracial future shown by white failure to grasp partnership with blacks through the failed federation of the 1950s and early 1960s with Northern Rhodesia and Nyasaland. Now Mugabe was backing up reconciliation by holding back on land reform and appointing a white farmer as minister of agriculture.

So how did things start going wrong? It seemed to me that part of the answer lay in the white response to reconciliation as it came over to Mugabe. Far too many whites that I spoke to had been negative right from the start about what was happening in their country. In these pages are accounts of people telling me how the country was rapidly going to the dogs. Yet many such people were not just lucky to be alive, but now had a redeemed opportunity for a new prosperous future. To make matters worse, many whites persisted with racist language and behaviour all the while as if they thought it was so much part of established behaviour that it could continue even after the blacks had gained power. It was a phenomenon which made Zimbabwe very different from other African countries which had soon adapted to new realities. I suspect that Mugabe soon began to think that he had been too slow to show whites how their country had changed forever in 1980. All this bore on Mugabe's actions over land. He saw himself as having been spurned, and his reaction, sometimes irrational, indicated anger and hurt. He felt he had done everything that could be expected of him to accommodate white fears as well as their aspirations and over a long 20 years, they had let him down. When he saw whites actually engaging in politics to oppose him, his anger knew no bounds. Sadly there was nobody to cool him down. He remained very much on his own, feared and revered in equal measure.

Now Mugabe could be seen very clearly to have miscalculated badly over land and not to have balanced the need to maintain prosperity and stability with the need to keep remembering that it was the land issue more than any other that brought him to power. It seemed to me that he had become hopelessly remote and out of touch with all sides. The net result was an unplanned and illegal land reform programme which he gambled would re-establish his popularity. Its failure and the damage to confidence because of the implications behind it led to the catastrophic plunge.

His sensitivities could not excuse policies which, if not pure evil, were so clearly leading to widespread and unnecessary suffering. Now he was loathed and feared as well as despised for his massive failures. I think by now he was probably unaware of how his own citizens felt about him, but perhaps he did not care. If not, he continued to receive the confidence boost he needed every time he was applauded by fellow African leaders as the arch fighter against colonial oppression. The reality was that in his country, where for the moment fear outweighed everything else in peoples' minds, he and his cronies could persuade themselves of virtually anything they wanted. Apart from what he had done to his own country, he had done great harm to Africa as a whole. Yet despite all that had gone wrong, there remained vestiges of loyalty from his citizens for a lifetime fight against white racism and oppression. He deserved credit too for preserving various bits of his colonial cultural inheritance particularly in the field of education. Educated black Zimbabweans understood better than whites that Mugabe had a vision of ZANU party rule coexisting with white know-how and even patriotism. This was conditional on their not taking part in politics. He felt that having won the war, he was entitled to acquiescence from whites. After all, they had had their time to dominate; now it was the people's turn to taste power through him. Of course, never having lived in the UK, he never understood the British from Britain whom he now misguidedly seemed unable to distinguish from his own white citizens.

I could not help reflecting on the British role which had always been of key importance. Broadly, over 50 years, British governments had been trying to get away from their historical involvement in the region only to find that they were locked in as firmly as ever. The way the present British government had handled the land issue made it easier for Mugabe to blame the British for a situation which was of his own making. He calculated that playing the land card would gain him popularity. Yet it was he who for 20 years had failed to tackle the land issue and failed to fulfil his promises to the war vets because agriculture as a revenue earner and a provider of employment was doing so well. Going back to the Thatcher/Carrington initiative and the independence elections and the return to legality, we had given Zimbabwe a marvellous new peaceful and democratic start. Generally speaking, the country had taken advantage of this in the first 20 years of independence. Under the Lancaster House agreement, the land issue, though it was basic to the whole black nationalist struggle, was put on one side pro tem in the interests of maintaining the priority of peace. The British were part of the problem and the solution and needed to continue to be fully aware of this and to show a full understanding of the background to the Zimbabwe government's position. As it was, British politicians such as Peter Hain and Clare Short made a difficult situation worse by their overbearing lecturing attitudes and outbursts. This actually helped Mugabe to project Britain as the unreconstructed colonialist villain of the peace. It was surely not beyond our wit to use all our cards, keep talking and come up with a solution. Even just putting pressure on the Zimbabwean Commercial Farmers Union (CFU) to come up with a realistic plan would have helped. As it was, white farmers were allowed to continue to convince themselves that the land issue was not really important. The fact that the issue of land was fundamental to the whole freedom struggle should have been well understood by everybody. Chris Andersen saw the problem coming because he was aware of how his cabinet colleagues saw it, and he told me so at the time. He tried to warn the CFU and get it to come up with proposals, but was not listened to. To compound the difficulties between Britain and Zimbabwe, which were not being helped by British media reports, came the Peter Tatchell incident when he jumped into Mugabe's car outside Harrods. Understandably, Mugabe was badly shaken and furious. It did not help either that the apology from a media-conscious British government was muted. Even now it seemed Zimbabwe could be rescued from its headlong plunge by a well-considered British diplomatic initiative. Perhaps Lord Carrington could have been persuaded to come out of retirement to take charge.

My golf four ball at Borrowdale Brook Golf Club included a man who had been the biggest producer of tobacco in the world. The company of these prominent white Zimbabweans was good and the hospitality as warm as ever. As elsewhere in the country, this time there was no attempt to rationalise everything in the white man's favour. There was now a universal recognition amongst the whites that they had been complacent about the strength of their position in the country and should have viewed the land issue differently. Race relations remained good; though perhaps the very term was no longer appropriate with the white population now less than 20,000. It seemed a pity that in 2006 so few whites sought common cause with their black professional-class neighbours. I saw this failure born of a terrible negativity, of which I kept on seeing evidence over the years. When it kept on coming up, I had dismissed it as growing pains. I could not believe that white short-sightedness could allow it to become a factor which threatened the country's future. The man who drove me home from golf said he thought that the cultures were so different that there could be no meaningful coming together. I disagreed with him very strongly and cited Zambia, Kenya and specially Mauritius. I was also mindful of friends in Zimbabwe who exceptionally had genuine friends across the colour line like the Van Jaarsvelds at Binga and another farmer friend whose delightful property near Harare looked to be a prime target for takeover but had remained untouched. If only there had been more such people who could combine the essentials of foresight and racial tolerance with the hardworking, entrepreneurial and brave heritage and huge achievements of the Southern Rhodesian whites!

I had been specially looking forward to staying with and talking to Chris Andersen on this trip and hearing how he viewed the future of his beloved country. I was sure that he would give us some hopeful and positive insights. Sadly, just as we were due to stay, Chris was seriously ill in hospital.

Even now after so much damage had been done by the disastrous policies of the last six years, there were few Zimbabweans who were not hopeful about the future. Perhaps there were more people than might be imagined who knew how close the country had come to escaping from sterile considerations of race and the damaging habit of blaming ad nauseam everyone else but yourself for your failings, and all the while claiming a right to be helped. Tragically the country had slipped backwards into this state of mind. Here again Mugabe did not appreciate or did not want to appreciate what had been achieved. Despite the enormity of the country's problems including huge suffering, particularly in the towns, society still functioned with surprising normality. A resilience had developed from deprivation and war and was complemented by fundamental goodwill, tolerance and good sense and the best educated population in Africa. Perhaps Zimbabwe could still be the African success story for which it was destined. I remember feeling that Britain should bear in mind that Zimbabwe was and is the most British and pro-British country in Africa.

Meanwhile, millions sought to escape despite the layers of razor wire and electrified fence that we saw stretching along the banks of the Limpopo as we drove south across the border.

***

Now nearly two years later in February 2008, we were back in Zimbabwe only a few weeks before the combined local government, national and presidential elections. I was nervous. The accumulation of media reports had led me to expect hostility, corruption and bureaucracy at least. I had written and spoken frankly about Zimbabwe, so felt that I could be regarded as unfriendly. In case I was searched, I left at home Judith Todd's book revealing amongst all sorts of other things how within a few months of gaining power in April 1980, Robert Mugabe, fired by half-concealed communist ideology was plotting the downfall of Joshua Nkomo and everyone else who he saw as standing in his way. The book has brought this and much more to light, including his technique of subjugation through humiliation. I felt vulnerable with my bundles of low-denomination American dollars to change more easily and our suitcases bulging with anything we imagined might be hard for our hosts to get. Besides lamps, torches and batteries, we had anything from toothpaste and dental floss to olives and anchovies.

The queues at immigration in the pristine new terminal building at Harare International Airport were short. To my amazement, we went straight through to pick up our bags and clear customs within 15 minutes of landing. Surely, now there would be problems with our hired car. I need not have worried. The car was brand new, full of petrol, and we were given a spare jerry can full, as well as coupons by the friendly and efficient staff. So again, Zimbabweans were showing that Zimbabwe was still different. Was this a reflection of Mugabe's leadership? Why was Zimbabwe different?

Besides seeing friends and relations, Sarah and I wanted to get up to date on how the country was coping under what from the outside looked like a brutal regime which behaved as if at war with its citizens. How did the ordinary people really feel about the party and the leadership and what hope was there that the impending combined presidential, national and local elections would reflect their views? How was the country coping and what future was there for friends and relations? What about our friends amongst the black professional classes? Could Zimbabwe recover and in particular retain the strengths of its cross-cultural heritage? Could it possibly go forward to be a genuine African success story after the land invasions had poisoned or destroyed so much? What about the aftermath of the brutal operation *murambatsvina* (clean out the filth) in the townships?

Amongst first impressions was seeing that though many traffic lights were out of order, traffic regulated itself well and there was not the mad rush to gain temporary advantage as one would find in some countries. We drove past the David Livingstone Primary School where hundreds of small black children were at play in their simple smart blue uniforms. I could see that many Zimbabweans clearly still gave priority to education.

Our old friends Chris and Anne Andersen still lived in the same suburban house, with no Johannesburg-style great wall to keep out intruders. Chris was seriously ill when we were last in Harare and we had not seen him. Now he was fully recovered and back practicing law. Zimbabwe owes Chris a great debt of gratitude for his loyalty and patriotism and for always trying to be positive about his country. He had shown great courage in accepting the invitation to join the government in 1982 in the face of wide misinterpretation of his motives from die-hard whites. In the event, he did marvellous work from his positions as minister for the civil service and minister for mines in upholding and even improving standards. From there he worked tirelessly to explain the government viewpoint to whites and the white viewpoint to the government. Now I could only guess at the depth of his disappointment that he and so many others have been let down by Mugabe. Now for him and Anne, life was not easy with shortages and an astronomical inflation rate which meant that the local money had to be spent immediately if it was to buy anything at all. Most immediate problems concerned electric power and water supplies. The power came on and off intermittently and could never be relied on. Recently it had been off for ten days. However, if they could be afforded, lamps and candles provided the substitute, and for some, though not yet the Andersens, generators. Water was a very serious problem. Though some richer people had boreholes, there were now so many that the water table was seriously low. Mains water simply did not reach the Andersens. They were forced to rely on the swimming pool for their needs, including for washing and flushing the toilets. Perhaps this was just as well, as the city's water supply was dangerously contaminated with raw sewage flowing into the erstwhile Lake MacIlwaine, Harare's water source, through the vast and desperately poor Chitungwiza township where there are no mains drains. Problems with power and water were mainly the result of breakdowns at power stations. Even the mighty Kariba dam hydroelectric plant was working at only 20 per cent capacity due to lack of maintenance and spare parts. It was in the townships that suffering of a totally different order prevailed. The question there was how long and how far the general deterioration could continue. There were those who argued that such was the level of poverty resulting in widespread starvation, that a breaking point was fast approaching. Others said that Zimbabweans' capacity to endure suffering and deprivation was virtually infinite. But how important was the injection of hope that the coming elections would bring longed for change? For many thousands, if they were to stay alive, the only option was still escape across the Limpopo to South Africa.

Our four days in Harare were not all doom and gloom. We went for long walks down suburban avenues and invariably received friendly greetings from passers-by. Everyone appeared to be cheerful. It was the same in suburban shopping areas where some shops had nothing for sale. Others were full of imported goods. I played golf with Chris at the immaculate Royal Harare Club with its resident flock of guinea fowl and numerous dainty duiker. We had lunch with an ex-chairman of the Zimbabwean Wildlife Society.

His preoccupation concerned Indian entrepreneurs who had recently arrived unannounced, with heavy machinery to mine for coal in the Gonarezhou National Park in the far south-east of the country. This is a unique wildlife habitat and it has recently been combined with the famous and contiguous Kruger National Park in South Africa and a park in Mozambique, to form a massive trans-national area of world importance for wildlife. It would appear that Mugabe gave the go-ahead to the Indians without consulting anyone. Serious repercussions were expected.

It was a busy few days and I called on the British Ambassador Andrew Pocock whose grasp of the complexities of modern Zimbabwe was most impressive. I was pleased to hear his views about a very positive future British role. I was disappointed not to see my colleague from early ZTMTT days, Mishek Sibanda, now elevated to secretary of the cabinet, with whom I sought a meeting. There were friendly phone calls with his office, but he was away at the vital time. I only spoke on the phone to another ZTMTT friend Robson Muringi but had a long and fascinating meeting with David Murangari who had moved on from being secretary for mines to running the Chamber of Mines and is now managing a large mining company, Bindura Nickel. He complained about the high proportion of the company's profits which went straight into the government coffers. He gave me news of a number of ex-ZTMTT trainees now in very senior positions all over southern Africa. We agreed that our programme had made a very big impact at a vital time for Zimbabwe and the region including South Africa. We went on to discuss education in Zimbabwe which retained its high standards and inherited culture at many leading schools. There were other schools though, where he said the children had to teach each other. I also saw the two top men at Standard Bank. All these highly impressive black Zimbabweans continued to maintain standards in a country which despite its difficulties still had a multiracial professional class head and shoulders above anywhere else in southern Africa. No need for the artificiality of the South African BEE here. Did Mugabe have any idea of the value of what he seemed intent on throwing away? Be that as it may, just about everybody seemed optimistic about the future and felt that the country would recover quickly under new leadership. Several people mentioned the deep anger in the townships which could well be turned against the perceived fat cats or chefs. The latter were the people kept sweet and in a life of luxury with allocations of hard currency. They were allowed to acquire this at the official rate of exchange, which at the time of our visit was only Zim$ 30,000 to the American dollar when the real market or parallel rate of exchange was Zim$ 10,000,000.

From virtually everybody I met on this trip I got the impression of a country which was longing for change. Virtually all the working people I spoke to at every opportunity were sure that Mugabe would be defeated in the forthcoming elections. One or two white cynics felt that fear would prevail over anger and that the people would continue to suffer in silence. It is so difficult to tell, but I could not help feeling from all I heard and saw that the country was at a pivotal point and that radical change had to come soon. From my conversations, I gathered that the main opposition leader Morgan Tsvangari had every reason to expect that the majority of Zimbabweans would vote for him. I just hoped he and Simba Makoni, the other candidate and the defector from ZANU and a new hope for the country whom everyone was talking about, were taking great care of themselves. Despite his long association with ZANU, Makoni was considered to be honest. He has done what few before have dared to do; he has spoken out and set a new opposition ball rolling. He has gained instant hero status. The rest of the politbureau I was told, would follow if they dared. But will they ever? Mugabe seemed to have an extraordinary ability to exercise power over people. But this relationship only generated ever-growing hate and fear. It was also suggested to me that if the political bully boys tried to continue to intimidate an electorate which is at the end of its tether, there had to be the risk of serious violence. I wondered whether the army and police would support the government or the people. I was told they were getting fed up. Perhaps this was just peoples' wishful thinking. Was there even the slightest chance that Mugabe himself might decide that his time was up? The nation would be hugely grateful.

We left Harare and drove east to Heather still on her farm with son Phil now an established farmer in his own right and doing very well. Both remained respected by everyone. The farm was not without its problems including shortages, particularly of labour. No wonder, as the monthly agricultural wage set by the government at $40 million was worth about £2 per month. In common with most Zimbabwean workers, what kept them at work were the food rations from employers. Otherwise they would starve.

The first evening on the farm I went for a walk by myself down the straight road through the bush towards the river. From a distance I saw an old man approaching, carrying the traditional spear. I recognised him and we greeted each other warmly. He said he remembered me coming to the farm as Richard's friend from the 1950s. As we walked back to the farm speaking Portuguese (he came originally from Mozambique), he told me how much he admired Phil and Heather staying on the farm and looking after their employees.

The farm continued to grow the tobacco and wheat that Zimbabwe needs so desperately to earn foreign exchange and to feed itself. Phil had taken on a new manager, a Zimbabwean Afrikaner who had emigrated to South Africa and had now returned with a wife, an ex-police woman. The couple had feared for their safety in the Limpopo Province (ex-Northern Transvaal) where literally hundreds of white farmers have been murdered in the last few years. The lack of publicity for this scandal is a disgrace, and it contrasts sharply with Zimbabwe, where despite the thuggery of the politically inspired farm invasions since 2000, by comparison, violence has been minimal. Now a sort of stability prevails so that though the so-called war vets or 'settlers' remained on the farm, mostly they kept to themselves. Most of the cattle had been stolen or sold and the beautiful kudu had been poached, but the farm somehow carried on. One morning I motored over with the new manager to talk to the black owner of a neighbouring farm which Phil had leased mainly, I gathered, as an insurance against being obliged to leave his own. All was well with the tobacco crop and land was being prepared for winter wheat under irrigation. However, the continuing theft of precious diesel was a worry. That afternoon Sarah and I were having tea with Heather and Phil when two visitors arrived. They were the son of a new neighbour, the Zimbabwean minister of energy who now owns a farm, and a friend. Now their preoccupation concerned the people whom they saw as invading them. The young men were starting to farm regularly and sought Phil's help and advice on growing tobacco. The relationship was certainly friendly and with Phil having his father Richard's sense of humour, there was some hilarious banter across the tea cups. A joking relationship is the best one you can have in southern Africa.

A trip into the city of Mutare was another eye-opener. En route we went to visit our house we bought on a hill farm 12 years ago. The garden is the bush with the *masasa* and kuduberry trees and lots of birds and the view was fabulous. It has been let over the years. In 2006 there had been enough rent money in the building society for a tank of petrol, but this time the 24 million rent money accumulated over two years was barely enough for a couple of beers. Despite the dire state of the national economy, Mutare was full of activity and enterprise. We called on the estate agents letting our house and found them as professional as ever. I also went to see a white businessman who deals in fuel and changes money. My £80 was worth getting on for two billion Zim dollars at the parallel rate, certainly enough to pay for lunch in the garden at the Green Coucal restaurant. This establishment in the avenues opposite the still-thriving Mutare Club which dates from the 1890s is white owned and serves superb locally grown food and good local beer and wine. Its shop which sells artefacts and simple local jewellery, is another example not only of enterprise but also of Zimbabwean determination at all levels to keep going.

It was the same story at Troutbeck Inn 7000 feet up in the Nyanga Mountains were Sarah and I had spent our honeymoon after our marriage in Lusaka in 1966. To get there we took the main road towards Mutare and turned left on the road built in the mid-1950s in the early days of the federation. I remember the Northern Rhodesians used to complain that their money from copper mining profits was being used by the Federal government to fund Southern Rhodesian tourist roads leading nowhere. Now we were driving first through the erstwhile commercial farming area, and then up through crowded and eroded communal land. We were reminded it was Sunday by all the church-goers along the road, all in their Sunday best, many waving a friendly greeting. There were separate groups of little girls immaculately turned out and as always in southern Africa, perfectly safe. On and up we went. Now we were in plantation country with swathes of pine and wattle coming down to the road as we crossed and recrossed the Odzi River in spate. In just over an hour, we were up at Juliasdale in country very different from the savannah bush of Odzi and Mutare. Now it was bare hills or plantation alternating with a sort of mountain scrub and cris-crossed with fast-flowing rivers. On we went through the estate bequeathed to Rhodesia by Cecil Rhodes and past the turning to the little hotel which still bears his name. Another turning, and we were climbing steeply for several miles until we were looking down into a valley with a lake and beside the lake the Troutbeck Inn. The scene could almost have been somewhere in the highlands of Scotland. At the hotel gates we were welcomed with a shuddering and crunching salute from an immaculately turned out guard. We found the hotel almost unchanged with the portrait of the founder Major MacIlwaine who played rugby for Scotland before and after the First World War and taught Rhodesia how to fish for trout, sitting with rod in hand, glaring down from above the fireplace. The fire, welcome at that altitude even in summer, is kept going constantly and makes the reception area a cheerful place. Sarah and I sat in the lounge and took in the view which includes the Lindi Falls on the other side of the lake with the Rio Tinto cottage perched beside it on a cliff. There I had stayed many times in ZTMTT days, sometimes with Donald and Barbara Tebbit and John Donaldson and Sue Grimes. It was there that I drove with Richard to pick up some binoculars brought for him from England and promised not to abandon Heather after his death. How could we, especially after discovering that Sarah's and Heather's great uncles, both Rhodesian pioneers, had been brothers? So they were newly discovered second cousins. Now we were all family and only sorry that Richard and Sarah's mother, Mary Anne, never knew.

We waited in the hotel lounge where after dinner on the first night of our honeymoon we had been joined beside another roaring log fire by a friendly Ian Smith and his wife. Right on time, cousin Chris and his partner Bubbles arrived for lunch, which was beers and snacks looking out over the lake. They love Nyanga and were staying at Chris's rustic cottage with its magnificent 40-mile views down over the hills and mountains to Mozambique. They gave us the latest news about the farm near Beitbridge with its thousands of citrus trees, many acres of wheat and high-achieving farm school. Fortunes have changed since 2006 with a local entrepreneur who happens to be well known to the Valentines putting up a modern juicing plant bought second hand from America, on the communal land just across the Umzingwane River. The juice goes straight to South Africa and earns all important hard currency. Sadly there was not enough time to make the 500-mile journey to the farm this time. We would, however, go on to stay with Chris and Bubbles at the cottage next day.

We were immensely impressed by the way the local all-black management keeps Troutbeck going as a first-class hotel in the face of all sorts of difficulties. Keeping up standards is the name of the game, and they succeed. Here again was an example of Zimbabwean determination to keep going. We had an excellent dinner for about a billion dollars and an even better traditional English breakfast. Then having met up with a white man from Harare who imports generators from China, we played golf with him on the still-magnificent Troutbeck course. The late great Henry Longhurst in his book described the sixth as one of the best short holes in the world. We had a wonderful game and revelled in the mountain scenery. Over drinks afterwards with the family, we were impressed to witness the small son being reminded of his manners when he failed to thank the waiter.

After the golf it was a short drive to Chris's cottage where we had two days of walking and much talk. We particularly enjoyed the thousands of St Joseph's lilies and yellow arums growing everywhere. One afternoon we drove up the road to get some milk from a farm that has a herd of

120 jersey cows. The owners have a beautiful garden and sell cream teas with home-made strawberry jam. On another day a neighbour came to visit. She was complaining bitterly about being refused a visa to visit Libya to see her daughter who has just had a baby. According to her, the Libyans at their Harare Embassy, who had originally been supporters of Mugabe, were now telling her that Zimbabwe was a rogue state.

En route back to Harare we stayed with old friends in their beautiful house on a small farm which amongst other things produces gum poles for fencing and for the building trade. The long views over the bush are stunning. The couple has always been positive about Zimbabwe and remains so even after numerous attempts by local politicians to intimidate them into leaving the farm. For many years they have been exceptional in the way they have developed friendships across the colour line. Their daughter-in-law who also lives on the farm, is a leading artist and also produces fruit and various herbs for the market. She lives in a fascinating house full of objets d'art and within short shouting distance of her retainers' and tenants' compound where they stand ready to come to her assistance if needed. Some are in partnership with her on various agricultural projects. Besides being highly talented, she is a tough lady who has faced up to several attempts to oust her from her property. She and her in-laws are typical of the Zimbabweans, many of them white, whose energy and enterprise is keeping the country going. Many are finding ways of producing some of the basic necessities such as meat, dairy products and fruit and vegetables. Some work individually and others in informal co-operatives such as the Old Georgian milk producers we were told about. Were such people to leave, the country would be very much poorer in very many ways. Luckily their love for it is matched by a determination to contribute to it in every way they can. I think too there is a gritty determination not to give way to the forces of destructive prejudice, greed and blatant theft, which are so wholly unworthy of Africa. Ordinary Zimbabweans recognise these things and more than ever are conscious that their multi-cultural heritage gives the country special strengths. Wise men like Julius Nyerere and Samora Machel recognised this at independence and earnestly urged Mugabe to value it. Now our hostess spends much of her time running and raising money for a charitable home at nearby Melfort for old, crippled and displaced people. Such actions and attitudes on the part of whites, who as a whole have been abused and disgracefully treated since the start of the land invasions in 2000, are heroic. Often they are motivated by the desire to look after their employees, otherwise by sheer love and concern for their fellow human beings. Luckily for the country, few are now thinking of leaving. A friend at Rio Tinto told me she had been all packed up and ready to leave for the Cape. Now she is thankful she changed her mind. She is amongst the many whites as well as blacks who feel that the country's troubles have at last truly brought the races together. Looking to the future it does not seem to me that Zimbabwe is about to collapse. The economy and Mugabe notwithstanding, Zimbabwe is a country of high standards. Since I was last in the country in 2006, it seemed to me that many people were now more positive and more hopeful about the future. I think this was partly a reflection of the prospect of Mugabe's departure. Certainly they seemed to have lost their fear of expressing their opinions of him. I think too that deprivation has brought them together at last. Whites and blacks are working closely together and on no occasion during our two weeks in the country did we encounter the slightest feeling of antipathy from anyone. In their own way the people are resisting their president and preventing the collapse of their country, which he seems intent on bringing about. A leading lawyer told me that despite the government's flouting of the rule of law in its actions over land and in suppressing political opposition, by and large the legal system still works surprisingly well. Its main problem, he considered, was that the judges lacked experience. During our visit, we had no problem with a police force which was existing on almost no pay and was still well turned out and seemed on reasonable terms with the population. It was not like Mobutu's Zaire where the police and the army thought only of the bribes they could extract. That is simply not the way they do things in Zimbabwe. With all its natural resources, the rump of industry and its mines, its agriculture, its cross-cultural heritage and above all its educated population, the country is still a going concern, and it is in the interests of the world that it remains so. A strong public opinion and the determination to keep going and not to give way to the forces of evil are complimentary strengths. I think they will prevail and that after so much suffering, Zimbabwe will emerge from its trauma stronger and with an increased awareness of its inherent strengths and a renewed determination to rebuild itself. In this it will look principally to Britain hopefully, not for handouts but for investment, trade and training and technical help of all sorts. I wonder how ready they will be to forgive those countries particularly African which have succumbed to sterile and wholly misguided anti-colonial rhetoric which sustained Mugabe. Even neighbouring countries have failed to give support to the people of Zimbabwe when they most needed it. Through their trauma, the latter have come to see what they really value. The same cannot be said for their neighbours.

19

The New Africans

I hope the reader will forgive me for seeking to relate the twists and turns of my career to the way the Africa I know has progressed and evolved over the past 60 years or so. Increasingly my work and experience has been concerned with a new generation of both high-achieving and high-potential Africans. All the while I have become more and more aware of the crucial importance of these people for the future and what needs to happen if there are to be more of them. I relate this to the way the outside world understands and responds to this need which is related to the continent's self-fulfillment and ability to punch its weight in the world. This chapter details my own Rake's Progress.

In Northern Rhodesia and Zambia, where I came to live after Southern Rhodesia and South Africa, I found a peaceful country where there was a high level of trust in the British colonial administration. This, despite the free rein enjoyed by the two African nationalist political parties. Under the admirable system of indirect rule developed in Nigeria and Uganda by Lord Lugard, there was respect for local culture and institutions. The big point of contention in Northern Rhodesia was that in 1953 the country, while still a colony and protectorate, had been pushed into a federation with white-ruled Southern Rhodesia, mainly, it subsequently transpired, because Britain wanted to divest itself of its responsibilities. With the federation gone, we hurried to give independence to Northern Rhodesia in October 1964. I was deeply unhappy because Britain clearly did not see or did not want to see a continuing role for herself in a part of the world which desperately needed a moderate and non-racial example to steer it away from extremes, particularly in southern Africa. I had invested my future in a positive British role in the region and I saw her withdrawal as short-sighted and irresponsible. The other worry was that we were handing independence to a country which we had not adequately prepared for it, with a lack of concern for the inevitable consequences for the ordinary people that was unworthy of us.

It seemed to me a distortion bordering on dishonesty that the whole process was being dressed up as a noble act. I had seen the inter-party violence misinterpreted by the UK press as a struggle for freedom. In the civil service too I had seen the promotion of people who were nowhere near up to the jobs they had been given. I understood and sympathised with the fears of so many loyal African civil servants like the district messengers whom we were letting down and who were deeply saddened and disappointed by our behaviour. I had seen at close hand how we had given way to the violence and thuggery on the Copperbelt as well as the consequences of nationalist power at local government level, leading to the terrible loss of life in the Lumpa troubles for instance. What I had seen at Nchelenge of the nationalists reaction to anybody who stood in their way, made me worry about the minorities and fear that tribalism would take hold. I was worried too that many nationalist politicians regarded Soviet block countries and China as their friends. There was the fact that democracy itself, which had been clamoured for, was a totally new concept for the nationalists. Kenneth Kaunda himself had told me that he thought it would be a very long time before the principle of tolerance of the other man's viewpoint would be understood.

Yet when the flag came down that midnight at Chikuni mission, at least half of me was excited at what this represented. Here in a context of a new goodwill, we were watching the birth of a new nation, a nation which would assuage the sort of humiliation and denigration which had made me cringe over the years in Southern Rhodesia and South Africa and even Northern Rhodesia. There had been the brief hope of a multiracial future for the region represented by the establishment of the Federation of Rhodesia and Nyasaland, but this had been thrown away by white short-sightedness and black distrust of white motives. At the crucial moment, the British government had showed it did not care enough to put real pressure on either side to make partnership work.

What chance was there that the Zambians whom we had left in charge could take the country forward? After all, the country had only a handful of black graduates, no experienced senior black civil servants, a political party in power on the back of all sorts of promises which it clearly would be unable to keep, a mining industry in which all the skills were white and an economy in which indigenous enterprise barely existed. Bear in mind too that there were next to no Zambians who had been educated in the UK or elsewhere in the West and consequently they had no real understanding of our culture or values, even if rural people might understand and trust the British administrators. The new rulers did not understand enterprise and tended to think that it was all a matter of taking from the whites to give to the blacks. Soon after independence Kaunda castigated female vegetable sellers at the Lusaka market for extortion, calling them capitalist exploiters. His understanding of the real needs of his country was very seriously limited by his lack of education or experience. On top of all this was a party in power which had been encouraged by its friends in the British Labour party to expect everything to fall into the people's laps after all the years of so-called 'exploitation' under colonial rule. Meanwhile Kaunda was being lauded as a great leader. I recorded my opinion in my diary that we should wait for real achievement before giving him plaudits. My worries intensified when I saw the attitude of my successor when he took over my beloved Gwembe district and when I witnessed moves towards the nationalisation of the mines and the politicisation of the civil service. The UNIP party to which so much had been entrusted, seemed to be quite happy to go back to square one and throw away all the achievements and the accumulated experience of running a country.

The main problems at that stage centred not so much on the qualifications and experience of our new leaders in Zambia. Those of us who were familiar with the country knew that there was the legacy of colonialism to cope with. This was the association of role with race and the stereotyping and self-stereotyping that this produced. This factor could produce seemingly insuperable barriers within an individual's psyche. These barriers within oneself had to be cleared if one was going to be able to go on and do the job. It was emphatically not a matter of individuals being nominally responsible. It was a matter of being genuinely effective. In the Zambia of the mid and late 1960s, one certainly knew the difference between 'window dressing' and the genuine article.

Such were the realities of the unpromising starts given to the newly independent African countries in the 1960s. We can fast forward through the post-independence years in Zambia when my misgivings notwithstanding, thanks to high copper prices, levels of prosperity were high. Though perhaps limited and misguided in certain respects, Kaunda's policies ensured that tribalism never came to rear its ugly head and that in the civil service some remarkable young men came to take on huge responsibilities and succeed. They were supported by second-level British members of HMOCS like me (most senior men left at independence). We gave our total support and loyalty to the new Zambia. For most of us this often meant avoiding telling the new powers-that-be what they wanted to hear.

It was not just the mistakes of the new government such as the national-isation of the mines which caused problems. Those of us staying on could see clearly that most Western aid too was misconceived and betrayed ignorance of the situation on the ground. Much of it was wasted on projects designed to kick-start rural development which had no chance of success. In rural agri-culture for instance, instead of heeding the advice of Rene Dumont in his book *False Start in Africa* about modernising agriculture in stages, inappro-priate aid in the form of tractors and farm machinery given to subsistence cultivators ended up unused, rusting or wasted. The vast spending brought little or no progress. Co-operatives, mostly funded from abroad, sprang up all over the place. I can't remember a single success story mainly because the need for effective local indigenous management and decision-making was not taken into consideration. It was certainly not loads of money that was going to solve our problems. Nearly 50 years on, this fundamental fact is still not really understood by Western politicians or international donors.

Yet despite all this, when the economic turndown came, thanks to a fall in the price of copper in the early 1970s, there was by then a good number of high achievers all over the country. Perhaps most importantly, Zambia was no longer blaming everyone but itself for its problems. It was learning its own lessons. I found it depressing, however, on my return to the country prior to going to work in the Congo about that time, to find on the Copperbelt that a mindset conditioned by former white authority still persisted. This came home to me when an experienced and senior black personnel officer told me that when Zambia Airways took on a black pilot he would never fly with them again. Such a mindset was symptomatic and an obvious block to progress.

The legacy of colonialism as it affected attitudes to race was different in the Congo (Zaire when we were there) where under the Belgians there had been a totally different attitude to the appointment of black artisans on the mines than that prevailing in Northern Rhodesia. There until inde-pendence white trade unions had blocked African advancement into artisan grades. Consequently in the early 1970s the Congo's national mining com-pany Gecamines had policies which were far in advance of those brought in from Zambia by my company Charter Consolidated which was effectively the international arm of Harry Oppenheimer's Anglo American/De Beers group. For Charter's managers the idea of black technical management was virtually unthinkable and actually worked against. Contrastingly, Gecamines already had an important programme to develop such people. Gecamines helped us in the training of young drivers of 100 and 200-ton haul-trucks and I remember being astounded at how quickly they learned. I can't imagine any group of young people anywhere in the world learning faster. For me this was a significant indicator of African ability and potential.

By now, however, I was beginning to wonder whether there was any hope of lessons learned in African countries whether positive or negative, being passed on to each other as they stumbled along after independence. In the Congo, Charter with Anglo American in the driving seat, genuinely thought it was applying the lessons of Zambia, but looking back it certainly was not. Now fast forward to 1980 and newly independent Zimbabwe where Anglo as well as my new employers Rio Tinto both had significant interests. There, thanks to the relatively high standard of education for all races, there had been some progress though this did not extend to the technical management grades. Now a remarkable initiative by Ronnie Walker, Metals Director of Rio Tinto and formally head of Rio Tinto in Rhodesia/Zimbabwe, changed the whole outlook for the indigenisation of management in the mining industries of the region. I was taken on by the company to set up and run the Zimbabwe Technical Management Training Trust (ZTMTT), a scheme to be based in London to help the region's mining industry as a whole. My task was to find suitable Zimbabweans and Namibians to train to become technical managers in the countries' mines. In Zimbabwe, due to the departure of many skilled whites after independence, there was a very big problem becoming apparent over the future management of the industry. In Namibia where Rio Tinto also had interests, prospects were even worse with independence coming very soon. Thanks to apartheid there was a total lack of educated black people with the potential to be future managers in the country's mines. In Zimbabwe, at least there were a lot of high-potential people with technical degrees most obtained in the UK, who might fit the bill for the future if they could overcome the psychological legacy of white supremacy and relate the function of management to themselves. In Namibia there was a mere handful of people who had had the courage and foresight to flee the country, join the SWAPO independence movement and perhaps get themselves an education. Such people were studying in Moscow, Eastern Europe, Cuba and Angola.

The Zimbabweans we were looking for were not difficult to get hold of. They had mostly returned home and were occupying low-level technical jobs all over the country. Into the picture steps Bernard Mutuma, at that stage deputy secretary of the Ministry of Mines in Harare. I soon realised that here was a man of a sort I had never come across before. He must have had strong feelings about the old Rhodesian regime when he left the country to escape the regime and seek his fortune. Now, however, he was without rancour or consciousness of race. He had somehow got himself to Egypt during the war years, had got a degree in chemical engineering and had risen fast in a technical career. Now he was back in Zimbabwe, fiercely proud of his Shona culture, certain of the big future of a new Zimbabwe and was an example of a modern man shaped by struggle and by the chance to gain the benefit of the strengths of another culture and new perspectives to complement his own culture. From my perspective Bernard was an outstanding new African. He saw reason not to press for over-hasty indigenisation of technical management in the mining industry, which would have been very damaging for the industry as a whole. This gave us in Rio Tinto and ZTMTT time to make something of the first intake of six Zimbabweans and two Namibians and develop an approach which worked.

I have told of our anxiety to do the right thing by a bunch of highly intelligent, very well-qualified young men with unlimited potential. Principally we wanted to take a short cut by helping young, energetic, intelligent people to turn themselves into big people, confident people, people who understood the importance of leadership and management and related it to themselves; people who could become the genuine article. We hoped they could escape most effectively from the self-stereotyping which was a product of their past. The barriers faced by such people are far greater than is generally appreciated, and if they are not overcome the individual will not make progress. The blocks are within oneself or come from historic white attitudes to blacks as well as from fellow blacks not used to associating their own race with management. The idea was to help the individual overcome these barriers and gain vital self-confidence through training and work experience outside their own country. At the same time we hoped it would make it as easy as possible for them to learn and gain inspiration from a variety of experiences in different disciplines and from general 'rub off' situations.

I have described how at first we failed for very ordinary reasons which would apply to any group of people in any cross-cultural situation who were over-indulged. In most respects our thinking was right, but we had not foreseen attitudinal blocks which we had inadvertently encouraged. We had not disabused trainees of the idea that they had a right to be helped and that somehow we were giving them an automatic qualification to manage. Returning home with such ideas got trainees nowhere. Most failed initially because of their attitude, and this gave the old conservative hands in the mining industry the excuse to say 'I told you so'.

We had to start again and for me, despite the many years of work and training in many African situations, the basic lesson was simple. Achievement never comes automatically; and you have to struggle for it. A change of policy to reflect this reality brought almost instant results. It was not difficult to point out to trainees that if they did not put themselves forward, and show keenness and willingness to learn and to make friends, they would be wasting everybody's time and so should be sent home. Of importance were seemingly little things like requiring all trainees to go on their own on work attachments and making it clear that they must do as they were told and that some work experience would be at the lowest level. This new tough approach and the deliberate avoidance of soft options moved us away from the implication of special treatment due to perceived previous disadvantage. In the event as one might have expected, most accepted and thrived on the tough approach and made ever more rapid progress. I think our initial mistake reflected the common misconception that people can be helped by making the normal challenges of life easy and by trying to bypass the hard school of experience and reality. In fact we had provided the means for fulfillment and self-discovery, escape from self-stereotyping and the means to become the genuine article.

For me there was stunning discovery and fulfillment at our successes. It was as if I had made some massive new discovery which would transform Africa's prospects. Actually it was just a matter of treating ordinary intelligent people as just that. For them though, their experiences were far from ordinary. Over the years I kept in very close touch with trainees while in the UK and after they returned home, and so I could see at close quarters how they were changing and how they reacted to what was happening.

The pattern of change and what caused it was very much the same for most people: hard work, self-fulfillment, acceptance, self-discovery, recognition, new perspectives and a great blast of self-confidence. What we hoped for was that trainees should return home not only with technical knowledge and practical management experience, but also with a totally new and well-based confidence in themselves in relation to the management function. They felt managerial and they were managerial and for them there was no turning back. For me these people were the new Africans; almost to a man and a woman. Several realised that on getting back to their careers, it might be in their interest to take a step or two backward in order to make more rapid progress in the future. They were now not merely technically qualified to hold down management jobs, but dedicated to the sustained hard work necessary for success in them. Hearing people talk in almost ecstatic terms of how it felt to be empowered was music to my ears. It was a culmination of hopes and a justification for all the arguments with racists or just doubters about African capabilities. It was nearly as fulfilling to hear senior white managers in Zimbabwe, Botswana or Namibia say how indeed ex-trainees were new men. Most would go on to say how their view of black people in management had been transformed. All this happened in a very few years in Zimbabwe and the mining industry was transformed.

In southern African terms, the ZTMTT achievement was monumental because it showed what could be done by people for themselves, rather than by others for them, in a very short time span. It was an emphatic message to those who doubted African capabilities. It provided a proven and tested model for future help of the sort Africa still needs more than anything else. The men and woman who passed through the programme went on to spearhead a new breed of indigenous technical manager throughout southern Africa. They fill many top positions in its mining industry and are role models for others to follow. Perhaps the top spot for achievement goes to the technical director of the Debswana (De Beers Botswana) mining company in Botswana. Also in Botswana is the general manager of the huge Selibe Phikwe mine. There are several ex-trainees managing some of Zimbabwe's biggest mines and also very significantly several in South Africa occupying senior technical management roles denied to local black people by the legacy of the education policies of apartheid South Africa. One ex-trainee Alec Gumbie, now a top engineering consultant in Johannesburg, told me how he is the only black man on a regular annual tour with a bunch of Afrikaner golfers. He is pioneering both work and social scenes. He and his wife Florence, also a golfer and a fellow pioneer, had been the leading lights at their golf club at Zvishavane in what should have remained the successful new Zimbabwe.

It is sad to reflect that the methodology of the programme which was offered to the South African industry as early as 1993 was not taken up at that time. Then, the likes of Anglo American and De Beers seemed to think they had nothing to learn from it. The white mindset at that time was illustrated by the Union Carbide manager in Johannesburg who was seeking advice and told me an almost comical story of trying to solve the problem of black management by the appointment of an inexperienced individual to a senior position with salary, conditions and perks to match, only to find that the new appointee was robbing the company. I don't find this way of thinking very far removed from the Black Economic Empowerment (BEE) policies of today. It looks to me like a degree of pandering to the old view which ZTMTT so clearly disproved, that black advancement and window dressing are synonymous. I wonder how many genuine articles have come out of the policy. I don't have the evidence but my experience backed up by what I have been told, suggests that there is now a large number of high-potential black people who are in positions in which they are unproductive. Of course the incumbents know this deep down and their self-confidence is likely to be permanently damaged. It is surely very damaging to South Africa for current political correctness to suggest that the priority of recompense for the so-called 'formally disadvantaged' has to override everything. I fear for a perpetuation of the mindset in 1993 when in his own interests I should have thrown out the highly promising South African we had on the ZTMTT programme. He thought he had nothing to learn and that for him success in his career was already assured. The really sad thing was that this man, it seemed to me, had a higher potential than anyone else on the programme. I fear that insofar as such attitudes are widespread, the wherewithal for fundamental change to high-achieving black technical management in South Africa is seriously wanting.

Of course there has been constant change affecting personal growth, leadership and individual responsibility in Africa over the past 50 years. However, ZTMTT was the only systematic approach that I know of and it provides a model. The experience underlined the importance of the culture factor and showed how profound and fundamental change can come so very quickly. It was in those years when I spent so much time in Zimbabwe and made so many friends there that I came to appreciate fully the reality of a whole new category of modern high-achieving black Africans. The wherewithal for change was all there in all parts of the economy, in society as a whole and in the education system for the new generation, until Mugabe's policies put Zimbabwe into a tailspin from 2000. Certainly until then progress seemed to be an accelerating process and my job brought me into contact with a number of new, competent and confident Zimbabweans working in the civil service, the banks and the financial sector and in industry as a whole.

Circumstances were different in Zambia to which I started to return regularly in the early 1990s. My contacts there were mostly older people who had gained much experience in the civil service, the mines and in business in very difficult circumstances. Amongst these people there was a lack of self-delusion and a good measure of what might be termed objective introspection. It was fascinating too to meet so many African women in positions of authority and as forerunners in the new entrepreneurial society. The cultural reality of the predominant role of women when it comes to really hard work in traditional society had resulted in their playing leading roles in the new modern Zambia. Most significantly though, Zambia had learned many lessons from its difficult years and had come out the other side more mature and more aware of what is important and what it needs to do to deal with its own problems. Meeting so many young people at one of Zambia's leading schools who told me their main ambition was to join some NGO or another was depressing. Hopefully such sentiments arising from the dependency mentality that western policies have engendered, will disappear as the country becomes more prosperous and more aware of the need to set its own priorities as more opportunities open up throughout the economy.

Another pattern emerged in Namibia where I was heavily involved for ZTMTT and Rio Tinto and later with BESO. There was a desperate shortage of educated and qualified people, but I became increasingly aware of a very widespread desire to gain maximum self-sufficiency and make the best of the country's human resources. Such sentiments were personified by people such as the highly impressive chairman of Rossing Uranium, the female high commissioner in London and of course my ex-trainee who went on to become the country's director of mines and then manage a major mining company. Close to my heart too are the black Namibian environmentalist who is carrying on the work of my dear friend the late Blythe Loutit and a new generation of indigenous environmentalists and tour guides. Amongst the latter were several members of the supposedly 'backward' Himba tribe whom circumstances and geography kept away from the influence of missionaries and their tendency to sap local pride in culture. These people have a clear idea of where they are going. All are immensely proud of their country and their culture. They are most significantly assuming ownership of their country's problems and priorities, surely a prerequisite for African achievement.

On the environmental front so vital to Africa's future, I am reminded of the mangrove development officer who rescued us in the middle of the night as we limped into Kilwa Masoko on the coast of southern Tanzania and showed us a clean little hotel which cost us all of £1 each per night. The next day he showed us where to camp on the beach. We saw him castigate fishermen who were simultaneously destroying the environment and their own livelihood and prospects by short-sightedly blowing up the coral to make cement. He came to dine with us on the beach and talked passionately about the environment of the Tanzanian coast. He and the other Tanzanians we met on our camping trip with two families of white Zambian farmers, personified the priorities of pride in country and self-sufficiency engendered by the late President Julius Nyerere. More recently I have met more committed and professional Tanzanian environmentalists working on the problems of Lake Victoria. In the remote parts of the country where we went, the children who gathered round our cars were there to practise their English, not to beg. More new Africans abound in Mozambique where again maturity and new awareness of priorities have arisen from the crucible of conflict, suffering and deprivation. I met several highly impressive government ministers, mostly educated in Portugal but proud new Africans. Once again in Mozambique it was the contacts made through BESO which awakened my awareness of the abundance of the vital ingredient of the desire of people to help themselves. This I found sadly lacking amongst people apparently qualifying for BESO help in South Africa despite BESO Chairman Lynda Chalker's wish to increase our involvement there and the pushing she gave us. Such a desire amongst people to help themselves is certainly not lacking in two other countries I saw a lot of, Malawi and Madagascar. In the latter in the late 1990s BESO provided the only British help there was to the country with its 30 million people. I found it to be intensely pro-British, following our association with it in the nineteenth century when we brought in education and Christianity and built the royal palace. This was before Madagascar was colonised by the French in the 1890s. The people I met there wanted to strengthen their British ties as they found French attitudes towards the country patronising and overbearing with their presumption of French cultural superiority. Yet in 2005, unbelievably, Britain withdrew its diplomatic mission for want of a miserable £250,000 per annum.

There are of course impressive new Africans all over Africa. I was deeply impressed during a visit to Kenya to witness Kenyan heart surgeons working and sharing skills with a top FRCS from Guys Hospital in London. I don't know West Africa nearly so well as southern parts, but I have seen a fair amount of Ghana, Senegal and Cameroon in the last few years. I was most impressed by the former with its democracy, energy and stability. It seems to me that countries in the south, particularly South Africa, have a very great deal to learn from Ghana, and vice versa. In the hotel and tourist industry for instance, there is much scope for South African experience and expertise.

In fact all African countries have things to learn from each other if only they would realise it. The new trans-African entrepreneurs are pioneers and standard bearers. The Cameroonian entrepreneur and expert in electronic communication whom I met in Douala, was talking of investing in a flat in Johannesburg because he does so much business in South Africa. His father, who used to be West Africa head of a major international accounting firm, has had me to stay several times at his impressive villa at Buea on the slopes of Mount Cameroon. When I first met him at the BESO office in London he invited me to Cameroon and asked me if I wanted to come and 'stay with the natives'. Through him I went to the Buea club, more British than in Britain, and met an array of new Africans from police chiefs to poets. Through him too I met two most impressive women, the vice chancellor of Buea University and the chief environmentalist for the national park taking in the slopes of Mount Cameroon. The latter and my other friends were deeply worried about the large-scale destruction of their country's rainforest. In Senegal I met intellectuals who despite the strong French economic and cultural influence, had a high-level knowledge of the English language and culture and at the same time put a priority on their indigenous culture. One writer I met had been to Rwanda shortly after the genocide and had written a book about it. He was so incensed by what he had learned of the French role in what led to the massacre that he decided from then on to write only in his own native Wolof language.

Thanks to a lifetime's close involvement with Zimbabwe, it is from that country that I gain most optimism about African capability and the emergence of the new Africans. This despite the country's current travails. The background is not typical of the rest of Africa. Here is a country where there was real struggle and real suffering, and perhaps this has something to do with the phenomenal progress in barely 100 years since the time of the first white settlers and the first contacts with modernity. During that time even though the two sides may have been unaware of it, there were strengths involving work and education as well as patience and manners for instance, that passed between the black and white cultures. Though unacknowledged, they helped to make the country special. Out of this pot pourri came some very special achievements and some very special people of all races. I can think of dozens of new Africans, modern, educated, broad-minded people who could hold their own with anyone in the world. Closest involvement for me was with my ZTMTT trainees, most of whom were sons of labourers or ordinary rural people who lived in grass and mud huts in the African bush.

That there should be such ambition, determination, vision and strength to go on and better themselves is extraordinary. Such achievements put Western attitudes in the shade. Compare them with our attitudes to education. It was such people who turned the whole mining industry in Zimbabwe round in a mere 20 years so that between 1980, when it was managed entirely by whites, and 2000 management was almost entirely black and without any drop in standards. Part of the achievement was thanks to the Mugabe government's sticking to the policy of not pushing for the promotion of people just because they were black; in the background too were whites. Though they recognised the need for rapid black advancement, they were determined that this should not be at the expense of maintaining standards. I wish I could name all these impressive people, but they and their counterparts in industry as a whole and in the civil service made Zimbabwe a very special place. All the while the country was attaining cricketing test status and producing the likes of Henry Olonga and Pommie Mbanga. I really don't think Mugabe could have had a real idea of the importance of what he had preserved and built on through his initial patience and pragmatism. In a way he is a tragic figure and I hope history will give him some credit.

Despite the current gloom all is certainly not lost in Zimbabwe, and such are its strengths and commitment that when change comes there will be thousands of black and white Zimbabweans who will return home strengthened by other cultures and by what they have learned from work experience in other parts of the world. I find it immensely encouraging that despite hyper-inflation, and all its other problems, standards in Zimbabwe remain amongst the highest in Africa. Is this because people are determined to resist Mugabe? It is wonderful too that so many Zimbabwean exiles remain so committed to their country and culture. This is illustrated by the case of a good friend of mine, a senior civil servant in the UK and a highly educated modern man who takes his teenage children back home regularly to Zimbabwe to reinforce the contact with their home culture and teach them manners. Rather than be confused in the global environment, black Africans seem to be as sure of their culture-based values as anyone; perhaps more certain than the British who seem to need reminding by outstanding new Africans like the Archbishop of York of what we stand for.

I think that a real leap forward is just beginning. The wherewithal is there with a new self-confidence based on strengths of which Africans are increasingly becoming aware. There is the growing realisation too that they have everything to learn and to gain from contact with each other and with the outside world. Yet some are still finding it difficult to cast off the idea that they need to erect barriers of red tape and bureaucracy to keep out people they imagine would exploit them or somehow do them harm. They should welcome virtually all contacts. Experience has shown how quickly they gain from outside contact of all sorts, both continentally and globally. This certainly includes the great, growing Asian superpowers India and China who are destined to strike up mutually beneficial partnerships with Africa as all parties come to appreciate more about what they stand to gain from each other.

In the BCA (Business Council for Africa) where I now work, I meet numerous high-flying and high-achieving African businessmen and professionals. What gives me most pleasure and confidence for the future is the emergence of growing numbers of young African entrepreneurs, both male and female, with cross-continental ambitions and perspectives. This coming together across the continent is what the Council is about and more than anything else attracts me to the work.

Some readers may wonder why South Africa does not feature more positively in this chapter given its power and influence and despite the hugely important roles played by two African giants Nelson Mandela and Desmond Tutu. If only, now that Africa is free, and leaders like Nyerere, Kenyatta and Samora Machel are gone, more people of such calibre would appear in South Africa, particularly when they are urgently needed at home and in Zimbabwe. Perhaps it is unfair to hope for too much given the legacy of apartheid, subjugation, humiliation and inadequate education. But surely the world should be able to expect South African leadership in situations which are doing real harm to Africa as a whole. Surely the incredibly brave Archbishop Pius Ncube of Bulawayo, who seems to me to be the real voice of the Zimbabwean people, deserves more support. One is left wondering when South Africa will take up the leadership role for which it is surely destined. It is certainly needed in the region and in other parts of Africa. Mbeki has let himself, his country and Africa down very badly over Zimbabwe. One is left wondering what South Africa really stands for and whether she really cares. Both government and commerce should surely be engaging with the rest of Africa in all fields, but instead of jumping in, South Africa seems to be either indifferent or paralysed by uncertainty and self-doubt.

What about the attitude towards Africa in the UK and the West, and how this is affecting progress on the continent? There is a store of goodwill and the desire to help which is admirable. There is, however, minimal real understanding, particularly amongst politicians. Gone are the days when a

substantial number of them had had real African experience and the understanding that went with it. The only ones I have come across are Sir Malcolm
Rifkind who spent a few years at the University of Rhodesia about 40 years
ago, Lord Luce who was in the colonial service and Lord David Steel who
was in Kenya as a child. This situation does not prevent several politicians
acting as if a commitment to Africa somehow equated to an understanding
of the continent's needs. There is a great deal of confusion with much gener-
alisation mixed with wishful thinking and unjustified pessimism and gloom.
Overall, I fear we are still in thrall to attitudes which assume past exploitation and colonial suppression for which we are supposed to continue to feel
guilty. Together with generous doses of sentiment, this has led us to assume
that with our efforts to atone for the past we are occupying the high ground
of moral rectitude. Such attitudes are reflected by leaders of our main political parties and they don't do Africa any good at all. They produce a sort of
reverse colonial mentality and the assumption of a right to help and to special
treatment which becomes a major block to progress. We must surely stop
moralising and move away from the idea that Africa depends on our generosity and that we need to put our hands ever deeper into our pockets and follow
policies which umpteen times over many years have been shown to fail. It is
or should be elementary psychology. If you give someone the idea that his future is in your hands rather than his own, he is unlikely to be motivated to help
himself. The certainty that you are doing good may even cause you to ignore
an African leader pleading for the West to understand that what Africa really
needs is involvement, investment and trade; or a high commissioner who
points out yet again that Africans are neither helpless nor hopeless. Surely it
is time to learn the lessons of the past 50 years which are there for all to see,
put aside the guilt and sentiment and start being positive and realistic.

At present we are making it more difficult for Africa to take charge of its
own destiny and catch up with the modern world by trying to make it easier with handouts, concessions and watered-down principles. They smack
of patronisation and condescension and send all the wrong messages. There
are of course African politicians (frequently not truly representative) who
will milk this attitude till the cows come home. The only realistic option is
for Africa to join the hard school of normality as quickly as possible through
normal interaction. If Africa is to get the loans it needs to build up its infras-
tructure for instance, the West is doing it a disservice by giving everyone the
impression that loans to Africa need not be repaid. I went to a conference
recently on China's growing role in Africa. The implication seemed to be
that Africa needed to be saved from Chinese exploitation. Surely Africa is

capable of making up its own mind on such issues. Surely, hard experience is the only way.

So what can we actually do to help? Surely anything we can provide by way of education, training and experience, which helps train leaders and decision makers and prepares them to decide their own priorities, has to be top of the list if there is to be a real impact. This includes experience of other cultures which enhances perspectives on one's own culture and thus boosts self-confidence. It does not in my opinion necessarily include building schools or colleges which need to be staffed and maintained. Their importance and priority must surely be decided by Africans themselves when set against all the other claims on limited finances.

What I have seen suggests that help in the way of work experience and training can be given by commercial companies large and small, or by governments central or local. Africa still has a lot of catching up to do. The experience and training must involve real work. If it does not, the individuals will not be accepted by their hosts' employees, learning will not take place and the particular programme will not be sustainable. Of course all experience of this sort cannot take place outside the individual's home country, but it could take place in another African country from which cultural strengths could be gained. Multinational companies have done a lot to develop high-potential people in this way and with encouragement would no doubt do more. Another way to help Africa, which is well proven but could be massively expanded, is the hands-on BESO approach which would make use of the multiplicity of skills in all disciplines and at all levels which exist amongst retired people in the UK and other developed countries. This is a very different matter from the young enthusiast who goes to Africa to do things for the locals which they are quite capable of doing themselves. I remember numerous wonderful assignments from my BESO days which concentrated on helping small local business people who could not possibly afford a professional consultant. The one-to-one help is exactly what the individual businessman and his organisation needed and valued, and the help given over a month or two could be transformational. I remember so many good news stories including the baker in Lusaka who needed help to teach him how to operate his new machinery. After the assignment the volunteer left him with a motto in Gaelic on the shop front. In Mozambique a volunteer whose assignment was supposed to be confined to accounting help, repaired all the broken-down machinery at a cashew nut processing factory and trained someone in how to maintain it. I am not sure whether the immense value of such help was ever really understood by DFID. I felt at the time that there was pressure on them from paid consultants to keep out the volunteers. Despite being the most effective and the most cost-effective help that Britain could give the developing world, BESO only received one million pounds per annum from the government in contrast to VSO's £25 million. In any event a revived BESO could transform prospects for thousands of new African entrepreneurs and keep a lot of retired Britons happy and fulfilled at the same time.

It is most encouraging to see evidence that even if they do not learn from each other, individual countries are now learning from their own mistakes rather than blaming all and sundry. This applies particularly in Zambia which seemed at various stages in its short history to be destined for disaster. I still think we the colonisers were irresponsible not to prepare the country for several more years with a lot more education and on-the-job training before granting independence. This would have spared the country many years of poverty and decline. It would also have provided a good example in sound non-racial administration to the Rhodesians. Nevertheless I must acknowledge that though it was certainly not the intention, being cast adrift is one way of learning the essentials of navigation. It is a tribute to the country and underlines the fact of basic African strengths and capabilities that it is now forging ahead. There has been a total restructuring of the mining industry and investment has poured in. The same goes for tourism with the country taking advantage of Zimbabwe's own goal. Where the ability to learn from mistakes is combined with such things as genuine encouragement of foreign investment, fantastic national parks and the friendliest people in Africa, success is guaranteed. The present government does not give the priority we colonial administrators gave to keeping in touch with local people through village-to-village touring for instance. But this is its choice. Meanwhile it is strengthening democracy and the free-enterprise system. It is also gradually reassessing policy and practice on the delicate issue of rural land tenure. It has taken the Zambians a few years since my day to reach their conclusions, but it is they who are making the decisions. Of course I am delighted that in getting to this point they have reached new positive perspectives on their British colonial legacy which reflect very well on us.

There are of course no limits at all to African capabilities and increasingly its people are discovering this. They are becoming more aware of their many significant strengths, including those arising from their culture, which help them to achieve. These include communication and community strengths, the ability to learn quickly and to change and the ability to cope with uncertainty. To complement all this are the strongly ingrained traditions of courtesy amongst young and old and an almost uncanny ability to judge character. In combination these strengths guarantee African success in the future. The rest of the world must wake up quickly to what the new Africans can do for themselves, for Africa and for the world and the remarkable progress they have made in a mere 50 years since the independence era. It is obviously in the world's interest that Africa should overcome poverty and instability and start fulfilling its potential, and that all possible doors to trade, tourism, investment and involvement should be opened. All this needs to be matched by altogether higher expectations of Africa. It really does it no good to continually be treated as a special case. At the same time I don't think it is a contradiction to expect the new Africans and the African diaspora to assert themselves, come up with more ideas about their role in the world and put an end to the idea that it is the West's preserve to set the agenda for their continent. If some continue to act as if they have a right to every sort of help the world can give, then this is only a reflection of what we have led them to expect and should be recognised as such.

We in the West must stop treating Africa as if it is a sort of international cripple which warrants different rules and standards from the rest of the world. Niall Ferguson in his book *Empire* even floats the possibility of a new sort of consensual colonialism funded and run by the Americans. He does, however, recognise American failures in recent times as having been largely due to their seemingly sole preoccupation with imposing democracy. Therefore, as part of this new approach he calls for emphasis on the historic British preoccupation with understanding the culture, aspirations and needs of local people.

On the whole I agree with Ferguson's analysis of the historic differences between the British and the American approaches. However, he does not seem to appreciate fully either how much and how quickly Africa has progressed or the alarming speed with which Britain has forgotten what running an empire was really all about. Now instead of giving a lead which arises from our experience, we slavishly go along with the distorted and utterly misguided American analysis arising from the view that what is good for them must be good for everyone else. My conclusion suggested in these pages is that whatever the achievements of the British colonial record, the days of empire are well and truly passed. Furthermore and most importantly, Africans are perfectly capable of drawing their own conclusions and rising to the challenges that confront them in the real world. Our interaction with them must reinforce this reality and not undermine it.

Index